P9-CDM-042

The Author

WOLE SOYINKA, winner of the Nobel Prize for Literature in 1986, is the author of more than thirty works, including his most recent, *The Burden of Memory, The Muse of Forgiveness*, and the play *King Baabu*. He is active in various international artistic and human rights organizations, among them the United Nations Commission on Human Rights and the International Parliament of Writers. Soyinka recently ended his exile from his native Nigeria.

The Editor

SIMON GIKANDI is Robert Hayden Professor of English Language and Literature at the University of Michigan, Ann Arbor. He is the recipient of numerous awards from organizations such as the American Council of Learned Societies, the Mellon Foundation, and the Guggenheim Fellowship. His many books include *Reading the African Novel, Reading Chinua Achebe, Writing in Limbo: Modernism and Caribbean Literature, Maps of Englishness: Writing Identity in the Culture of Colonialism*, and *Ngugi wa Thiong'o*. He is the general editor of *The Encyclopedia of African Literature*.

W. W. NORTON & COMPANY, INC.
Also Publishes

ENGLISH RENAISSANCE DRAMA: A NORTON ANTHOLOGY
edited by David Bevington et al.

THE NORTON ANTHOLOGY OF AFRICAN AMERICAN LITERATURE
edited by Henry Louis Gates Jr. and Nellie Y. McKay et al.

THE NORTON ANTHOLOGY OF AMERICAN LITERATURE
edited by Nina Baym et al.

THE NORTON ANTHOLOGY OF CHILDREN'S LITERATURE
edited by Jack Zipes et al.

THE NORTON ANTHOLOGY OF DRAMA
edited by J. Ellen Gainor, Stanton B. Garner Jr., and Martin Puchner

THE NORTON ANTHOLOGY OF ENGLISH LITERATURE
edited by M. H. Abrams and Stephen Greenblatt et al.

THE NORTON ANTHOLOGY OF LITERATURE BY WOMEN
edited by Sandra M. Gilbert and Susan Gubar

THE NORTON ANTHOLOGY OF MODERN AND CONTEMPORARY POETRY
edited by Jahan Ramazani, Richard Ellmann, and Robert O'Clair

THE NORTON ANTHOLOGY OF POETRY
edited by Margaret Ferguson, Mary Jo Salter, and Jon Stallworthy

THE NORTON ANTHOLOGY OF SHORT FICTION
edited by R. V. Cassill and Richard Bausch

THE NORTON ANTHOLOGY OF THEORY AND CRITICISM
edited by Vincent B. Leitch et al.

THE NORTON ANTHOLOGY OF WORLD LITERATURE
edited by Sarah Lawall et al.

THE NORTON FACSIMILE OF THE FIRST FOLIO OF SHAKESPEARE
prepared by Charlton Hinman

THE NORTON INTRODUCTION TO LITERATURE
edited by Alison Booth and Kelly J. Mays

THE NORTON READER
edited by Linda H. Peterson and John C. Brereton

THE NORTON SAMPLER
edited by Thomas Cooley

THE NORTON SHAKESPEARE, BASED ON THE OXFORD EDITION
edited by Stephen Greenblatt et al.

For a complete list of Norton Critical Editions, visit
www.wwnorton.com/college/English/nce_home.htm

A NORTON CRITICAL EDITION

Wole Soyinka
DEATH AND THE
KING'S HORSEMAN

AUTHORITATIVE TEXT
BACKGROUNDS AND CONTEXTS
CRITICISM

Edited by

SIMON GIKANDI

UNIVERSITY OF MICHIGAN, ANN ARBOR

W • W • NORTON & COMPANY • *New York* • *London*

Copyright © 2003 by W. W. Norton & Company, Inc.

DEATH AND THE KING'S HORSEMAN copyright © 1975 by Wole Soyinka. This play may not be reprinted in the US in whole or in part in any
form without the written permission of the publisher, W. W. Norton & Company, 500 Fifth Avenue, New York, NY 10110. All rights whatsoever in this
play are strictly reserved, and application for performance should be made to
Wole Soyinka, c/o Melanie Jackson Agency, LLC, 250 West 57th Street,
Suite 1119, New York, NY 10107. No performance may be given unless a
license has been obtained.
Every effort has been made to contact the copyright holders of each of the
selections. Rights holders of any selections not credited should contact
W. W. Norton & Company, Inc., 500 Fifth Avenue, New York, NY 10110,
for a correction to be made in the next printing of our work.

All rights reserved.
Printed in the United States of America.
First Edition.

The text of this book is composed in Fairfield Medium
with the display set in Bernhard Modern.
Composition by PennSet, Inc.
Manufacturing by Maple-Vail, Binghamton.
Book design by Antonina Krass.
Production manager: Benjamin Reynolds.

Library of Congress Cataloging-in-Publication Data

Soyinka, Wole.
    Death and the king's horseman : backgrounds and sources, criticism / Wole
      Soyinka ; edited by Simon Gikandi.
      p. cm.— (A Norton critical edition)
    Includes bibliographical references.

ISBN 0-393-97761-7 (pbk.)

    1. Yoruba (African people)—Drama. 2. Suicide—Prevention—Drama.
    3. British—Nigeria—Drama. 4. Fathers and sons—Drama. 5. Nigeria—
    Drama. 6. Soyinka, Wole. Death and the king's horseman. I. Gikandi,
    Simon. II. Title.

PR9387.9.S6 D4 2002
822'.914—dc21   2002026539
W. W. Norton & Company, Inc., 500 Fifth Avenue, New York, N.Y. 10110
www.wwnorton.com

W. W. Norton & Company Ltd., Castle House, 75/76 Wells Street,
London W1T 3QT

0

Contents

Introduction

In 1986, Wole Soyinka became the first African writer to win the Nobel Prize for literature. In its citation for the award, the Swedish Academy for Literature, which selects the winner of the Nobel award, called attention to Soyinka's broad cultural perspective, the poetic overtones of his work, and his concern with the drama of existence. In reflecting on the work of the playwright over a period of twenty years, the Swedish Academy recognized *Death and the King's Horseman* as the synthesis of Soyinka's primary concerns as a writer. In this play, the Swedish Academy noted, "the relationship between the unborn, the living, and the dead, to which Soyinka reverts several times in his works, is fashioned here with strong effect."

The awarding of the Nobel Prize was, however, just the culmination of a long journey that began when Soyinka started writing plays as an undergraduate at the University of Leeds in the north of England and as a play reader at the famous Royal Court Theatre in London in the late 1950s. Soyinka became a writer in an important period in the history and literary culture of Africa. He began writing in the very last years of colonial rule in Nigeria, and his major plays were published during crucial moments in the politics of decolonization in Africa. At this time, his works came to be recognized as powerful reactions to the complicated drama of African politics, especially in the painful period of transition from colonialism to national independence and, quite often, his pronouncements on culture and politics became the moral barometers by which the claims and limits of the postcolonial political order were judged. By the time he won the Nobel Prize, Soyinka had published almost thirty books of drama, poetry, fiction, memoir, and autobiography. During this time, he came to be recognized as a towering giant of African letters, the continent's leading playwright, and one of its most influential cultural voices.

But as a playwright and cultural commentator, Soyinka has been as controversial as he has been distinguished, as complex as he has been influential. He is controversial because, as readers of *Death and the King's Horseman* will recognize, his major works have been written both within and against the dominant traditions of modern and African drama. For this reason, Soyinka has built his literary career on a remarkable mastery of Western and African cultures and his willingness to challenge these traditions. Although he is proud of his African heritage and has been one of the staunchest defenders of African cultural interests, Soyinka has resisted identification with one singular tradition; in both their content and form, his works reflect the multiplicity of sources and references that are very much part of his background and education. In spite of this, Soyinka's works are solidly located in the cosmic systems of the Yoruba people of western Nigeria and the Republic of Benin. Of all modern African writers, Soyinka is the one whose works derive their power from the essential forces of an African culture; it is impossible to conceive of his work outside Yoruba religious beliefs and systems of thought. At the same time, however, Soyinka is the most cosmopolitan and avant-garde of African playwrights. Some of the major literary influences in his plays have derived from the works of such experimental modern playwrights as Samuel Beckett, Bertolt Brecht, and Eugene O'Neill. The philosophy that undergirds his writings is derived as much from the legends of Ogun, the Yoruba god of war and creativity, as from the works of Friedrich Nietzsche, the modern philosopher of antitradition and rebellion. It is this confluence of forces, influences, and traditions that has made Soyinka a major and controversial figure in African and modern literature.

Soyinka's literary works are considered difficult due to the complex range of references in which esoteric Yoruba rituals are merged with the idiom of modern drama, the politics of everyday life in Nigeria, Shakespeare, and Greek tragedy. It is a difficulty that is sometimes explained in terms of Soyinka's preference for opaque metaphysical systems and an abstract, poetic language. But perhaps one of the reasons why Soyinka is considered to be difficult, not to mention elitist, has to do with his refusal to concede to two of the doctrines central to African literature of the 1950s and 1960s. The first is the belief that the writer needs to be committed to the rehabilitation of the cultural image of the African—that is, the liberation of the collective portrait of black peoples from negative and disfiguring colonial images and representations. Second, Soyinka was an early and vocal critic of the dominant belief that the function of the new literature emerging in Africa during the last years of colonial rule was to educate its readers about their cultures and societies. Soyinka has no patience for those who argue that works of art are most effective when they are clear, direct and didactic. His major plays have been concerned with what he calls the self-apprehension of African subjects. He has insisted that he is committed to eliciting an African sense of self from history, mythology, and literature. But he has been equally adamant in his belief that true self-apprehension can be acquired neither through the language of cultural liberation and the assertion of pride in one's identity nor through contrast to the cultural system of others. Soyinka would prefer the question of African realities and identities to be apprehended and represented outside the orbit of external factors, including the colonial experience itself. It is precisely because of his quest for modes of representation that are inherent in African cultures and worlds that Soyinka has developed a reputation as the most vocal critic of established ideologies of identity such as the African image and *négritude*.

Indeed, Soyinka came to prominence as a cultural critic in the early 1960s by positioning himself against what was emerging, especially in the last two decades of independence, as collective notions of African culture and African identity. In his early essays, renowned for their aggressive and polemic edge, his primary concern was a reassessment and critique of the African image as it had emerged in the canonical texts of nationalism. Soyinka was unhappy with the romanticism, naïveté, and idealization of the African image in classic African novels such as Camara Laye's *The Dark Child*. He understood the political imperative behind such works— namely, the desire by a whole generation of African writers to counter the European image of Africa—but was categorical in his belief that idealization was not a substitute for what he considered to be literary truth. However, in explaining why he had disavowed and attacked movements that celebrated African or black identity, Soyinka was keen to insist that he was not against the idea of the African world as such—indeed, he was unhappy with critics who had used his pronouncements against *négritude* to deny the existence of an African world. It would appear that he was wholly committed to the idea of an African world but against its celebration. He wanted the African world—and this has important implications for the history of *Death and the King's Horseman* and the debates that have come to surround the play—to be taken for granted as a self-evident historical and cultural experience. As far as Soyinka was concerned, the artist's commitment was not to a particular idea of Africa, a set of political or ideological commitments, but the self-apprehension of the African world: "I have long been preoccupied with the process of apprehending my own world in full complexity, also through its contemporary progression and distortions—evidence of this is present both in my creative work and in one of my earliest essays," he asserted in his preface to *Myth, Literature, and the African World* (p. ix).

Despite his attempts to distance himself from the cultural claims of many African intellectuals of his generation, most prominentl·

the assertion of a collective identity and literary mission, Soyinka's works cannot be understood outside the parameters established by other writers. He is, after all, part of a remarkable generation of African writers, many of them born in the 1930s, who came of age in the last years of colonial rule in Africa and almost single-handedly created the institution of African literature in English. Like other writers in this tradition, Soyinka's literary career was defined by the tension between the desire to account for African worlds and experiences at the end of colonial rule, using the language and literary models borrowed from the departing colonizer. Soyinka's early plays were not concerned with celebrating a mythical African past, but they were connected to the literary projects of his generation through their concern for the meaning of the African past both before and after colonialism. Soyinka's attitude toward history and the past was much more critical than that of other African writers, and early in his career he worried about the transformation of history or memory into an instrument of power and domination by the postcolonial elite; at the same time, however, he was conscious of how the legacy of the past continued to haunt the political order ushered in by independence.

In any case, Soyinka's skepticism toward the myth and romance of the African past did not preclude a serious attempt on his part to discover forms of drama that had developed in precolonial African societies and to incorporate them into his plays. In his early essays, Soyinka often insisted on the distinction between two types of reality: one that reflects the surface experience of societies and nations going through a period of transition, and one that reflects a deeper experience that goes beyond the politics of everyday life and reaches down to the essence of culture itself. He lamented the fact that in their dealings with the aspirations of nationalism, a fascination with the past, and a concern with the contingencies of everyday life, African writers had negated another kind of reality, one informed by depth and vision. It is this second kind of reality that he came to associate with art and literature. As he has argued in *Myth, Literature, and the African World* and *Art, Dialogue, and Outrage*, the truth of literature emerges out of a deeper realm of meaning and experience, a metaphysics rather than an engagement with an ever-changing world. Ironically, the distinction Soyinka continued to make between a deeper and an ephemeral reality did 't mean that his works were concerned solely with larger meta- ʻal questions. While works such as *Death and the King's Horse-* long to Soyinka's explicitly metaphysical plays, his larger with questions of being and experience are continuously ed by an equally important engagement with the every- –the world of taxi drivers, market women, and the unemployed—which he positions at the center of the cosmic universe of his plays. In this regard, Soyinka's literary career was very much concerned with the contradictions of modern life and their connection to larger realms of experience. What perhaps distinguishes Soyinka from other African writers of his generation, many of whom are focused on the problems of contemporary life, is his attempt to use language to go beyond the visible, everyday world.

Soyinka was born in 1934, in Abeokuta, in what was then western Nigeria. As he has shown in his lyrical and compelling autobiography *Aké: The Years of Childhood*, he grew up and came of age in a family and in a social context dominated by the equally powerful forces of colonial and Yoruba cultures. His parents, major figures in the modern culture of Abeokuta, were involved in the promotion of education and trade. Soyinka's father was a schoolteacher; his mother came from one of the most distinguished Anglican families in western Nigeria; his maternal grandfather was a minister in the local Anglican church; and his uncle was the principal of Abeokuta Grammar School. Christianity and its belief systems may not be a marked feature of Soyinka's drama except perhaps as a subject of satire in his comical plays or the source of aberration and alienation in his metaphysical plays, but it was a central element in his early life and education. It is not an exaggeration to say that Soyinka came from one of the most religious and Westernized families in colonial Nigeria. On the other hand, Soyinka's paternal grandfather led a life that was guided by ancient Yoruba beliefs and practices, and it was through extended visits to this side of his family that Soyinka was exposed to the rituals and cosmologies of his people. At a time when members of the African elite were ashamed of their African traditions, Soyinka was keen to learn more about Yoruba religious rituals and systems of thought and to incorporate them into his plays.

After starting his secondary education in the local Abeokuta Grammar School, which was sponsored by the Anglican church, Soyinka was admitted to Government College, Ibadan, one of the most selective schools in the country. Like most such schools in colonial Africa, Government College was fashioned after British public schools—in America, prep schools—such as Eton and Harrow. These schools, one in each region of Nigeria, were primarily intended to develop an elite corps of Africans highly educated in English culture, history, and literature. Even though these schools were located in the heart of African communities (the Yoruba, in the case of Government College, Ibadan), there was no place for African cultural studies. The schools were seen as islands of European culture in the midst of a sea of barbarism. They produced students who were proficient in almost all aspects of European history and culture, well read in the canon of English literature, but often ignorant of the institutions of local society. With perhaps the exception of the police and the military, the products of these schools were to dominate almost all aspects of Nigerian society after independence.

After completing his high-school education at Government College, Soyinka proceeded to another, equally prestigious, institution —University College, Ibadan—which was then an affiliate of the University of London. Although he spent only two years at Ibadan, the college was crucial to Soyinka's budding career as a writer. Literature was at the center of the arts and humanities curriculum and covered an impressive range of writers, from Shakespeare to Yeats and Joyce. Beyond literary studies, students at Ibadan were active in writing clubs and dramatic societies. It was here that Soyinka began to write plays, short stories, and poems, and act in student productions. Most important, in the early 1950s Ibadan had brought together a group of students who were to change the face of African writing in the age of decolonization, including many who were to play a major role in the making of modern literary culture and criticism: Chinua Achebe, J. P. Clark, Christopher Okigbo, Elechi Amadi, Flora Nwapa, V. C. Ike, John Munonye, Michael Echeruo, and Abiola Irele. All of these students had arrived at Ibadan after graduating from elite regional high schools.

When Soyinka arrived at the institution in 1952, curriculum and general culture at University College, Ibadan, was designed to continue the high-school English education that the elite had received. But times were changing. In the 1950s, it had become apparent that Nigeria was, like other African countries, on its way to becoming independent from Britain, and the future of its educated classes would not be in the Anglophone culture promoted or promised by the government schools. Soyinka and other members of his generation were being forced to rethink their relationship to both the African histories and institutions that their education had virtually eliminated and the colonial culture that they had assimilated. Although Soyinka left Ibadan in 1954 to study at the University of Leeds in northern England, his literary works from this period proved to be a continuation of a generational project started at Ibadan. Like his contemporaries at Ibadan, he conceived creative writing as one way of questioning his colonial inheritance and rethinking his Africa context. As he would insist in many of his early writings, literature—especially drama—was the medium through which he would apprehend the complexity of his culture outside the institutions of colonialism. In Britain, then, apart from studying for his B.A. honors degree in English, Soyinka began what was to become a lifetime relationship with drama and the stage, writing his first two plays and serving as a play reader at the influential and experimental Royal Court Theatre in London before returning to Nigeria in 1960, the year of that country's independence.

Not unexpectedly, Nigerian independence was to change the context in which Soyinka's work was produced and, by extension, its mission. As we have already seen, Soyinka consistently argued, especially early in his career, that his plays were not intended to educate his readers or audiences. He also insisted that he was not interested in producing plays that responded to specific episodes either in Africa's colonial past or present. In retrospect, however, Soyinka's major texts came to be read, sometimes against his own wishes and intentions, as specific interventions into the drama of politics and social life in postcolonial Africa in general and Nigeria in particular. For example, his first major play, *A Dance of the Forest*, which won the first prize in an independence-day literary contest, raised fundamental questions about the idea of an African future haunted by a past that had not yet been adequately accounted for; it was seen as providing lessons about the official postcolonial romantic view of the African past. *Kongi's Harvest* was one of the first literary works in Africa to dramatize the emergence of political dictatorship, a theme that Soyinka was to develop further in *A Play of Giants*, a work in which the major players are some of the infamous African dictators of the period. His first novel, *The Interpreters*, used the techniques and language of modernism to probe the pitfalls of national consciousness and the forms of realism that had dominated the African novel in the 1950s and early 1960s. Soyinka may have wanted his works to transcend their time, but they were often both topical and prophetic.

But perhaps more than the topical element in his works, a remarkable aspect of Soyinka's literary career so far has been the diversity of his output. Not only has he produced works in a variety of genres, including poems and memoirs, but his plays have been diverse in their thematic concerns, methodologies, and ideas. In a career spanning over forty years, Soyinka has written and produced memorable comedies (*The Trials of Brother Jero, Jero's Metamorphosis*, and *Opera Wonyosi*), powerful political dramas (*Kongi's Harvest* and *A Play of Giants*), and influential metaphysical plays (*The Strong Breed, The Road, Madmen and Specialists*, and *Death and the King's Horseman*). Each of his major works has generated controversy in literary and theatrical circles. While many of these controversies have been a reaction to the message of the plays or to some of their technical features or to Soyinka's own commentaries on how his works should be read or perceived, there is no doubt that the major source of contention has been the politics of the dramas or, rather, what some radical critics have considered to be the absence of political commitment in Soyinka's work.

And yet to raise the question of political commitment in regard to Soyinka's literary works is to call attention to one of the most enigmatic sides to this complex writer—the fact that while he has stubbornly refused to write plays that serve an explicit political function or that are read as direct commentaries on social problems, he is, in his nonliterary life, one of the most politically active writers in the world today; there is no single moment of political crisis in Nigeria, Africa, and the world that has escaped his interest. In 1959, as a young student at Leeds, Soyinka was one of the first African writers to call attention to the death of political prisoners in colonial Kenya. In the early 1960s, he was actively involved in movements against the corrupt government of western Nigeria. He was one of a very few Nigerian intellectuals who intervened to try and stop the country's slide into civil war in the mid-1960s, seeking to develop a third force between the federal government and the secessionist forces in eastern Nigeria. For these efforts, Soyinka was arrested by the Nigerian federal government and imprisoned for two years, without trial, at the notorious Kaduna prison in northern Nigeria. After his release in 1970, Soyinka was forced into exile. But he returned to Nigeria in 1975 to teach, write, and continue his involvement with a variety of political and civic organizations. In the 1990s, he was the leader of the movement against the military dictatorship in Nigeria. During this period, he was subjected to harassment by the government, his life was threatened, and he was eventually forced into exile in 1996. In 1997, he was tried for treason in absentia. As we can see, Soyinka's acts of bravery on behalf of the persecuted in Africa and elsewhere are legendary. He has often put his own life in danger to rescue other writers and citizens from violent political institutions. His political acts are always matched by the stinging words of his political and cultural essays. Clearly, Soyinka is not apolitical. Still, he has sought to separate his political activities from his art, and this separation of the aesthetic from the politics of everyday life has only added to the complexity, some might say the enigmatic character, of his literary works, including *Death and the King's Horseman*.

Upon its publication in 1975, *Death and the King's Horseman* was immediately recognized as one of Soyinka's major dramatic works. From its initial publication in London and New York, and subsequent productions at the University of Ife and in major theaters in Chicago and Washington, D.C., the reception of the play has been characterized by a certain kind of duality. On the one hand, *Death and the King's Horseman* has been recognized as a major modern play; Soyinka's production of the play at the Goodman Theater in Chicago was described as a unique stage experience, one that changed the rules of performance on the Western stage. On the other hand, the meaning of the play and its intelligibility has been the subject of debate, controversy, and misunderstanding; while the play was greeted with acclaim in Nigeria, reviews of the play in Chicago and Washington, D.C., were not only mixed, but often the source of verbal duels between theater critics for major American newspapers and Soyinka and his supporters.

These controversies seem to have been triggered by three factors. First, some reviewers found the play difficult to understand within the established conventions of the modern theater. *Death and the King's Horseman* relies heavily on a cluster of metaphysical ideas drawn from the Yoruba cosmology, including a concern with the space of transition between life and death, and readers or viewers without a proper sense of this background or context are bound to miss or misunderstand what Soyinka considers to be the major dramatic movement in the play.

Second, in its structure, language, and form, the play is founded on a set of conventions and idioms derived from Yoruba traditional and popular drama. Music, masking rituals, and proverbial language are important sources of meaning in Soyinka's play. It is in these formal features, rather than in direct dialogue and dramatic conflict, that Soyinka locates the meaning of his play. And yet, these are also the elements that are hardest to translate on stage.

As a student of African and modern drama and as a director, Soyinka is keenly aware of the potential problems of interpretation that his plays raise. He has been particularly concerned that the central conflict in *Death and the King's Horseman*—that is, the confrontation between colonial authority and the custodians of African ritual—might be reduced to a cultural cliché—namely, the conflict between Western and African values. For this reason, Soyinka has included an "Author's Note" (reproduced in this edition) in the program of the play's American productions. Here, he provides some minimal context for the play and, most important, tries to direct his audience away from the transparent cultural conflict that they might witness on stage and toward what he considers to be the deeper metaphysical confrontation in the play. And here, Soyinka adamantly insists that his play is not about the conflict between colonialism and its African subjects. For him, the colonial factor was "an incident, a catalytic incident merely." This claim is the third source of the controversies surrounding *Death and the King's Horseman*. Reviewers of the play—and, one might suspect, most members of the American audience—tended to see the play in the very terms that Soyinka had tried to minimize: it was a memorable clash of culture between English colonialism and African traditionalism. Soyinka was irritated at the failure of critics of his production to go beyond this clichéd view of the African encounter with the colonial culture. It is our hope that this Norton Critical Edition will provide students and readers with the tools to grasp both the surface and the deep structure of the play.

Along with the 1975 text of *Death and the King's Horseman*, this edition contains four additional sections. The first section, "Backgrounds and Contexts," contextualizes the play both within the Yoruba world that constitutes its central point of reference and in terms of Soyinka's own relation to the African world and its forms of cultural representation. This section also contains essays dealing with the problems that this play presents to readers and students who may not be familiar with the context that its author takes for granted. The first entry here is a map and an excerpt from *Yoruba: Nine Centuries of African Art and Thought*. This book, written by John Drewal, John Pemberton III, and Rowland Abiodun, three distinguished historians of Yoruba art, was initially published as the catalogue for an exhibition on Yoruba art and culture presented at major American museums, including the Museum of African Art at the Smithsonian and the Art Institute of Chicago, in 1989. The brief excerpt included here is from the first chapter of the book, appropriately entitled "The Yoruba World." In this section, the authors outline the geography of the Yoruba world and its complex cosmological system. As the authors of this essay note, the Yoruba-speaking peoples of western Nigeria and the Republic of Benin are the builders and custodians of one of the most influential civilizations in the world. In addition to being associated with urban cultures dating to the ninth century, the Yoruba spread their civilization from their west African homeland to the Americas during the Atlantic slave trade. And because the Yoruba were some of the last Africans to be sent to the New World as slaves in the nineteenth century, their cultural influence continued to be felt in black communities in both North and South America well into the twentieth century.

There has never been one unified Yoruba culture in either historical or geographical terms. Indeed, as the authors of the "The Yoruba World" show, the Yoruba have historically been divided into distinct regional groups and kingdoms. While they would build a civilization that was distinguished by common characteristics, most prominently an ancient urban culture, the Yoruba kingdoms were also bitter rivals and fought major wars among themselves, especially in the sixteenth and nineteenth centuries. Many of the Yoruba who ended up in the Americas were victims of both the civil wars and the activities of European colonizers and slave traders on the west African coast. At the same time, however, Yoruba kingdoms shared a uniform body of religious beliefs and cosmological views that often transcended political and social divisions. In "The Yoruba World," the authors present a succinct description of the impact of the slave trade and colonialism on Yoruba kingdoms, while underscoring one of the unintended consequences of these extraneous factors—namely, the spread of Yoruba artistic and religious ideas to the Americas. As art historians, the authors of "The Yoruba World" have an acute sense of the fundamental concepts that are distinctive to the Yoruba worldview and how these have shaped Yoruba art and culture. The brief discussion of the Yoruba cosmos presented here is particularly important to our understanding of the metaphysical ideas that Soyinka drew upon in structuring the dramatic conflict in *Death and the King's Horseman*. These ideas include the Yoruba view of the cosmos as the bringing together of the realms of the living and the unborn. Also important in the Yoruba cosmology is the powerful presence of deities and ancestors in everyday life (usually through artistic representations), the nature of life and death in the structuring of aesthetic forms, and, most pertinently, the space of transition that both divides and conjoins the realms of the living and the dead.

Within the context of Soyinka's literary career, neither the central themes of *Death and the King's Horseman* nor its dramatic techniques are new. Indeed, for most scholars and critics, this play is a continuation of themes and techniques that the playwright had first taken up in *The Strong Breed*, one of his earliest metaphysical plays. But *Death and the King's Horseman* represents a significant departure for Soyinka in its concern with a specific historical episode, an event that took place in Oyo, western Nigeria, in 1946. Soyinka's choice of event is intriguing because until the publication of *Death and the King's Horseman* he had expressed strong reservation about the invocation of history in creative works. In fact, in an early essay, "The Writer in the Modern African State" (collected in *Art, Dialogue, and Outrage*), Soyinka had asserted that one of the limitations of African writing after decolonization was its obsession with the past. Did *Death and the King's Horseman* represent a reversal of Soyinka's earlier doubts about the writer's obsession with history? Can *Death and the King's Horseman* be considered a historical play? For many critics, Soyinka's use of a historical account as the basis for the dramatic conflict in *Death and the King's Horseman* was deceptive: while the central episode dramatized in his play had actually taken place in colonial Nigeria, it was apparent that Soyinka was not interested in an accurate account of this episode, nor did he seem particularly interested in representing the aborted ritual suicide of the king's horseman exactly the way it had taken place.

and idiom, foregrounds the problem of cultural differences in the modern world. Far from being a hindrance to our reading of the play, then, an understanding and discussion of the cultural differences inherent in the theme and form of the play should enrich our comprehension of the deeper meanings of Soyinka's text. In his essay, the Nigerian poet and scholar Tanure Ojaide draws on his experiences of teaching the play both in Africa and in the United States to present a lucid discussion of the problems the play presents to those who might consider it outside the familiar traditions of modern drama. In the final essay in this section, Martin Rohmer presents a case study of the challenges and opportunities of producing Soyinka's play on stage. In a detailed study of the 1990 production of *Death and the King's Horseman* at the Royal Exchange Theatre (RET) in Manchester, England, Rohmer examines the thematic and dramaturgical problems that the play presents to Western directors, who are asked to translate a multiplicity of stylistic devices and to make them intelligible to cultural outsiders without negating the complexity of Soyinka's script. Rohmer's essay focuses on the ideas and approaches of one British director of this particular production as she sets out to realize Soyinka's dramatic vision. In the process, a commentary on the staging of the play becomes a serious engagement with some of the theoretical issues it raises, including the nature of tragic action on stage, the range of actors deployed in the RET production, and the relation between the playwright's ideas and one specific kind of theatrical space.

As we have already noted, *Death and the King's Horseman* became the subject of widespread criticism soon after its publication. The essays contained in the "Criticism" section of this edition represent the range of critical response to the play at three crucial stages in its history: its initial incorporation into the critical literature on Soyinka; its reevaluation after it was cited as one of the major works that justified awarding the Nobel Prize for literature to its author; and in the aftermath of the emergence of what has come to be known as postcolonial theory. The first two essays in this section are by two of the leading figures of literary criticism in Africa. In "Mediation in Soyinka: The Case of the King's Horseman," D. S. Izevbaye considers the role of mediation in Soyinka's understanding and treatment of tragedy in his critical essays and early plays and in the shaping of the tragic event in *Death and the King's Horseman*. Tracing the development of the theme of mediation in the playwright's early works, Izevbaye considers how the tragic event occurs when movements of transition are interrupted or paralyzed. He argues that *Death and the King's Horseman* is an extended representation of the tragedy that arises when the psychic and cultural harmony of Oyo traditional culture is interrupted. The act of interruption as the source of tragic action is not, however, limited to Soyinka and his Yoruba cosmology; rather, Izevbaye argues, it can be found in other African cultures in which festivals and rituals are considered central to performance. In the next essay, Eldred Durosimi Jones shifts the debate on the meaning of tragedy in the play from Yoruba cosmology to the actions of individual subjects. In "*Death and the King's Horseman,*" taken from a chapter in the second edition of *The Writing of Wole Soyinka,* Jones locates the sources of tragic action not so much in Soyinka's understanding of the Yoruba cosmology, but in the consciousness of Elesin Oba and the tenuousness of his attitude toward the larger demands of his community. Jones's focus in this essay is the opposition between Elesin's individual desires, especially his love of material life, and the cosmic demands of his community, implied by his role as the custodian of the king's body to the other world. Through a close reading of certain crucial scenes in the play, Jones concludes that Elesin's real tragedy is ultimately individual, not cosmic—the loss of his personal honor and the death of his son.

Like other critics of their generation, Izevbaye and Jones are keen to establish the meaning and architecture of tragic action in *Death and the King's Horseman* in the continuum of the themes and forms developed in Soyinka's early plays and the author's own claims on the nature of tragedy and ritual. In a slight shift in emphasis, another generation of critics, many of them Soyinka's former students or younger colleagues, emerged in the 1980s to elaborate and question the foundations of the playwright's understanding of tragedy and the cultural or linguistic logic driving his play. Armed with the new techniques of literary analysis that had emerged in the 1970s and 1980s, these critics were in essence deconstructing or demythologizing the authorial intentions and ideologies that had hitherto determined the criticism of Soyinka's work. In "Being, the Will, and the Semantics of Death," Henry Louis Gates, Jr., who had been a student of Soyinka at Cambridge and had witnessed the writing of *Death and the King's Horseman,* considers the play a classical tragedy, one in which the structure and metaphysics of the drama are intertwined. While Izevbaye and Jones think of tragedy in terms of the Yoruba cosmology, Gates's essay calls attention to the influence of Greek tragedy in Soyinka's work in general and this play in particular. But perhaps the most significant aspect of Gates's essay is the attention it gives to the formal features of Soyinka's language, especially Yoruba speech acts, in the elaboration of tragic action. Working within the framework of structuralist and post-structuralist theory, Gates argues that Soyinka's major achievement is "the creation of a compelling world through language, in language, and of language." In Gates's view, however, language in Soyinka's work is not singular; on the contrary, the notion of language as speech exists in a reciprocal and opposed relation with the language of music and dance. Gates's major claim is that the mastery of spoken language in the play is constantly reinforced and challenged by the language of music and dance; in this respect, he reads tragic action in *Death and the King's Horseman* as a consequence of the relation among these linguistic registers rather than as a representation of a world that exists outside the play.

In contrast, Biodun Jeyifo's concern in "Ideology and Tragedy," excerpted from an influential book on the sociology of African drama, is with Soyinka's ambiguity toward the historical events that are the fulcrum around which his play revolves. Focusing on what he calls "ideological connotations," Jeyifo uses Marxist theory to probe the status of the historical event in Soyinka's imagination. Contrary to the playwright's claim that his play is not about cultural conflict or the colonial encounter, Jeyifo analyzes key scenes in which *Death and the King's Horseman* polarizes an alien world against an indigenous African world. This polarization, he argues, is at the heart of tragic action in the play. The excerpt represented here ends with Jeyifo's controversial claim that Soyinka's work is predicated on a metaphysics that "idealizes and effaces the conflicts and contradictions in African societies" and rationalizes the rule of the powerful and privileged.

The Marxist critique of Soyinka's that is evident in Jeyifo's essay was constantly echoed in many discussions of *Death and the King's Horseman* in Nigeria in the 1980s. Soyinka responded to these criticisms in "Who's Afraid of Elesin Oba?" In the excerpt from this essay, reprinted here, Soyinka resists attempts to stretch the horizon of his play beyond its author's intentions. He rejects the idea that the writer should be committed to a fixed notion of history or to the accurate representation of a historical event. For Soyinka, history functions primarily as a source for what he calls "mythopoeic resourcefulness." The excerpt ends with Soyinka's reflections on the theme of death in his drama and his use of poetic license in regard to the historical events that triggered his play.

Surprisingly, few of the essays concerned with the material world of Soyinka's play have considered the role of women in the unfolding of the tragic moment. An exception is Joan Hepburn's essay, parts of which are reproduced here as "Ritual Closure in *Death and the King's Horseman*," which first appeared in a special issue of *Black American Literature Forum* published to celebrate Soyinka's winning of the Nobel Prize for literature. In this essay, Hepburn argues that ritual closure is central to the meaning of Soyinka's play. She also makes the important claim that Iyaloja, the leader of the market women, is a key figure in the elaboration, mediation, and closure of the ritual process in the play. Hepburn's essay provides a detailed explication of the scenes in which Iyaloja functions as the overseer of Elesin's struggle with the ritual process. In Hepburn's view, Iyaloja goads Elesin into the passage between life and death in a bid to set aright the cosmological order he has disrupted; in this sense, she is the true mediator of the metaphysical conflict in the play and the custodian of ritual.

The final three critical essays are responses to Soyinka's play from the vantage point of a variety of poststructuralist theories. Adebayo Williams's "Ritual and the Political Unconscious" attempts to bring together three strands of criticism of the play that had remained separated until the 1990s—namely, the formalist, mythological, and materialist modes of criticism. Drawing on Frederic Jameson's theory of the political unconscious, Williams seeks a middle point between Gates's reading of the world of the play as a function of its language and Jeyifo's search for a material referent for the tragic moment. While he agrees with Jeyifo's conclusion that the play provides a metaphysical rationalization for a patriarchal and feudal code, Williams insists that there is an important utopian dimension to *Death and the King's Horseman*, one that emerges when the hegemony of the kingdom of Oyo is compared and contrasted to the power and authority of the colonizers. If we consider the old order represented by the dead king of Oyo as an institution of power intended to maintain privilege and inequality in the same way as the colonial system does, then we have to see Elesin's actions as the belated and desperate struggle to maintain and defend a defeated culture. And if colonialism and the traditional order both wind up being irrelevant at the end of the play, then Soyinka's brilliance, argues Williams, is to be found in his unconscious criticism of the very cultural system that he appears to have set out to defend in his play.

David Richards's essay is a detailed anthropological exploration of ritual masks and their relation to the language of Soyinka's play. Unlike previous discussions in which Soyinka's use of ritual was often judged in relation to anthropological accounts of Yoruba traditions, Richards shows that the playwright's deployment of masking and related traditions goes beyond their social function as rites of passage. Rituals surrounding the *egungun*, argues Richards, are not merely assertions of a social order; more than this, liminal rituals "both make and unmake the world." The last section of Richards's essay contains a discussion of proverbial speech in key instances in the play. Here, Richard shows that Soyinka's borrowing from traditional Yoruba proverbs is extensive and that these figures of speech are at the core of the language of *Death and the King's Horseman*.

In the final essay in this section, "Tragedy, Mimicry, and 'The African World,'" Olakunle George focuses the reader's attention on the role of Amusa and Joseph, two characters that are considered minor figures in the elaboration of the tragic moment in the play. Contrary to what may appear to be their marginality, George shows that these figures are crucial in stirring up the contradictions in the colonial enterprise. Using Homi Bhabha's postcolonial theories on mimicry, George examines the nature and the meaning of the colonized subjects' collaboration with the colonizer; and instead of positing this as a betrayal of African values, he sees the representation of these characters as the medium through which the play forces us to reflect on modes of social identity and transformation that are predicated on the colonial event. George concludes his essay by discussing the cultural paradoxes presented by Olunde, who is caught between his Western education and the desire to defend local traditions and thus provide compensation for his father's failure. George makes a powerful case for Olunde's alienation and deformation within the very institutions that have shaped his hybrid identity.

The selections in each section have been arranged chronologically. Some selections have been included in their entirety while others have been edited for reasons of space and the overall coherence of each section. Where necessary, footnotes have been edited, renumbered, or adjusted to conform to the style of this edition.

The chronology contains information about the key events in Soyinka's life and education as well as important details about his works, including their dates of performance and publication.

The last section of the book is a bibliography of some of the key critical writings on Wole Soyinka's work in general and on *Death and the King's Horseman* in particular.

Acknowledgments

In preparing this edition, I have relied on the works of many scholars of Wole Soyinka's work, African drama and theater, and Yoruba art and thought. Some of the works of these scholars are referred to in the bibliography, but I want to acknowledge others whose works, though not directly cited in this edition, constitute an important context for Soyinka's play. I would like to thank Wole Soyinka for agreeing to the publication of this edition and for his many essays on African drama and politics. In order to understand key Yoruba words and phrases, I have relied heavily on R. C. Abraham's classic *Dictionary of Modern Yoruba.* My understanding of the intricate cultural and social systems of the Yoruba has been helped by listening to Abiola Irele and Biodun Jeyifo over the years. I would like to thank Olakunle George for responding to my queries at a crucial moment in the editing of this text. The preparation of this edition would have been impossible without the research skills and intelligence of Meredith Martin, a dream research assistant if ever there was one. Finally, I would like to thank Carol Bemis, my editor at W. W. Norton & Company, for her patience, care, and professionalism.

The Text of
DEATH AND THE KING'S
HORSEMAN

Dedicated
In Affectionate Greeting
to
My Father, Ayodele
who lately danced, and joined the Ancestors.

Author's Note

This play is based on events which took place in Oyo,[1] ancient Yoruba city of Nigeria, in 1946. That year, the lives of Elesin (Olori Elesin),[2] his son, and the Colonial District Officer[3] intertwined with the disastrous results set out in the play. The changes I have made are in matters of detail, sequence and of course characterisation. The action has also been set back two or three years to while the war was still on, for minor reasons of dramaturgy.

The factual account still exists in the archives of the British Colonial Administration. It has already inspired a fine play in Yoruba (Oba Wàjà) by Duro Ladipo. It has also misbegotten a film by some German television company.

The bane of themes of this genre is that they are no sooner employed creatively than they acquire the facile tag of 'clash of cultures', a prejudicial label which, quite apart from its frequent misapplication, presupposes a potential equality *in every given situation* of the alien culture and the indigenous, on the actual soil of the latter. (In the area of misapplication, the overseas prize for illiteracy and mental conditioning undoubtedly goes to the blurb-writer for the American edition of my novel *Season of Anomy* who unblushingly declares that this work portrays the 'clash between old values and new ways, between western methods and African traditions'!) It is thanks to this kind of perverse mentality that I find it necessary to caution the would-be producer of this play against a sadly familiar reductionist tendency, and to direct his vision instead to the far more difficult and risky task of eliciting the play's threnodic[4] essence.

One of the more obvious alternative structures of the play would be to make the District Officer the victim of a cruel dilemma. This is not to my taste and it is not by chance that I have avoided dialogue or situation which would encourage this. No attempt should be made in production to suggest it. The Colonial Factor is an incident, a catalytic incident merely. The confrontation in the play is largely metaphysical, contained in the human vehicle which is Elesin and the universe of the Yoruba mind—the world of the living, the dead and the unborn, and the numinous passage which links all: transition. *Death and the King's Horseman* can be fully realised only through an evocation of music from the abyss of transition.[5]

W.S.

1. Yoruba cities are some of the most ancient in Africa, dating to A.D. 800–1000.
2. Literally, the owner of the horse.
3. Also known as D.O., a junior colonial administrator but one with enormous political and police power at the local level.
4. Having the quality of death and lamentation.
5. In Yoruba cosmology, the space between life and death.

Characters

PRAISE-SINGER	
ELESIN	*Horseman of the King*
IYALOJA	*'Mother'[1] of the market*
SIMON PILKINGS	*District Officer*
JANE PILKINGS	*his wife*
SERGEANT AMUSA	
JOSEPH	*houseboy to the Pilkingses*
BRIDE	
H.R.H. THE PRINCE	
THE RESIDENT	
AIDE-DE-CAMP	
OLUNDE	*eldest son of Elesin*

DRUMMERS, WOMEN, YOUNG GIRLS, DANCERS AT THE BALL

The play should run without an interval. For rapid scene changes, one adjustable outline set is very appropriate.

Note * * *
Certain Yoruba words which appear in italics in the text are explained in a brief glossary at the [end of the play].

---

1. Leader of the market women.

1

A passage through a market in its closing stages. The stalls are being emptied, mats folded. A few WOMEN *pass through on their way home, loaded with baskets. On a cloth-stand, bolts of cloth are taken down, display pieces folded and piled on a tray.* ELESIN OBA *enters along a passage before the market, pursued by his* DRUMMERS *and* PRAISE-SINGERS. *He is a man of enormous vitality, speaks, dances and sings with that infectious enjoyment of life which accompanies all his actions.*

PRAISE-SINGER   Elesin o! Elesin Oba! Howu![2] What tryst[3] is this the cockerel[4] goes to keep with such haste that he must leave his tail behind?

ELESIN [*slows down a bit, laughing*]   A tryst where the cockerel needs no adornment.

PRAISE-SINGER   O-oh, you hear that my companions? That's the way the world goes. Because the man approaches a brand-new bride he forgets the long faithful mother of his children.

ELESIN   When the horse sniffs the stable does he not strain at the bridle? The market is the long-suffering home of my spirit and the women are packing up to go. That Esu[5]-harassed day slipped into the stewpot while we feasted. We ate it up with the rest of the meat. I have neglected my women.

PRAISE-SINGER   We know all that. Still it's no reason for shedding your tail on this day of all days. I know the women will cover you in damask[6] and *alari*[7] but when the wind blows cold from behind, that's when the fowl[8] knows his true friends.

ELESIN   Olohun-iyo![9]

PRAISE-SINGER   Are you sure there will be one like me on the other side?

ELESIN   Olohun-iyo!

PRAISE-SINGER   Far be it for me to belittle the dwellers of that place but, a man is either born to his art or he isn't. And I don't know for certain that you'll meet my father, so who is going to sing these deeds in accents that will pierce the deafness of the ancient ones. I have prepared my going—just tell me: Olohun-iyo, I need you on this journey and I shall be behind you.

ELESIN   You're like a jealous wife. Stay close to me, but only on

2. "Why have you come?"
3. The appointed time and place of a meeting.
4. A young domestic rooster.
5. The Yoruba trickster god often associated with doubleness, ambivalence, and duplicity.
6. Expensive embroidered or patterned cloth.
7. A rich, woven cloth, brightly coloured [Soyinka's glossary].
8. Domestic or barnyard hen or rooster.
9. Praise-singer.

this side. My fame, my honour are legacies to the living; stay behind and let the world sip its honey from your lips.

PRAISE-SINGER   Your name will be like the sweet berry a child places under his tongue to sweeten the passage of food. The world will never spit it out.

ELESIN   Come then. This market is my roost. When I come among the women I am a chicken with a hundred mothers. I become a monarch whose palace is built with tenderness and beauty.

PRAISE-SINGER   They love to spoil you but beware. The hands of women also weaken the unwary.

ELESIN   This night I'll lay my head upon their lap and go to sleep. This night I'll touch feet with their feet in a dance that is no longer of this earth. But the smell of their flesh, their sweat, the smell of indigo[1] on their cloth, this is the last air I wish to breathe as I go to meet my great forebears.

PRAISE-SINGER   In their time the world was never tilted from its groove, it shall not be in yours.

ELESIN   The gods have said No.

PRAISE-SINGER   In their time the great wars came and went, the little wars came and went; the white slavers came and went, they took away the heart of our race, they bore away the mind and muscle of our race.[2] The city fell and was rebuilt; the city fell and our people trudged through mountain and forest to found a new home[3] but—Elesin Oba do you hear me?

ELESIN   I hear your voice Olohun-iyo.

PRAISE-SINGER   Our world was never wrenched from its true course.

ELESIN   The gods have said No.

PRAISE-SINGER   There is only one home to the life of a river-mussel; there is only one home to the life of a tortoise; there is only one shell to the soul of man; there is only one world to the spirit of our race. If that world leaves its course and smashes on boulders of the great void,[4] whose world will give us shelter?

ELESIN   It did not in the time of my forebears, it shall not in mine.

PRAISE-SINGER   The cockerel must not be seen without his feathers.

ELESIN   Nor will the Not-I bird[5] be much longer without his nest.

PRAISE-SINGER   [stopped in his lyric stride]   The Not-I bird, Elesin?

ELESIN   I said, the Not-I bird.

---

1. A blue dye obtained from plants; it is associated with royalty and power.
2. A reference to the numerous wars between Yoruba kingdoms in the eighteenth and nineteenth centuries and to the transatlantic slave trade and its consequences.
3. As it sought to consolidate its authority in the sixteenth century, the Yoruba kingdom of Oyo had to build and rebuild its capital several times.
4. Another reference to the space of transition between life and death (see note 5, p. 3.).
5. A bird whose chirping sounds like it is saying "Not I" in Yoruba.

PRAISE-SINGER   All respect to our elders but, is there really such a bird?

ELESIN   What! Could it be that he failed to knock on your door?

PRAISE-SINGER [*smiling*]   Elesin's riddles are not merely the nut in the kernel[6] that breaks human teeth; he also buries the kernel in hot embers and dares a man's fingers to draw it out.

ELESIN   I am sure he called on you, Olohun-iyo. Did you hide in the loft and push out the servant to tell him you were out?

> [ELESIN *executes a brief, half-taunting dance. The* DRUMMER *moves in and draws a rhythm out of his steps.* ELESIN *dances towards the market-place as he chants the story of the Not-I bird, his voice changing dexterously to mimic his characters. He performs like a born raconteur, infecting his retinue with his humour and energy. More* WOMEN *arrive during his recital, including* IYALOJA.]

Death came calling.
Who does not know his rasp of reeds?
A twilight whisper in the leaves before
The great araba[7] falls? Did you hear it?
Not I! swears the farmer. He snaps
His fingers round his head, abandons
A hard-worn harvest and begins
A rapid dialogue with his legs.

'Not I,' shouts the fearless hunter, 'but—
It's getting dark, and this night-lamp
Has leaked out all its oil. I think
It's best to go home and resume my hunt
Another day.' But now he pauses, suddenly
Lets out a wail: 'Oh foolish mouth, calling
Down a curse on your own head! Your lamp
Has leaked out all its oil, has it?'
Forwards or backwards now he dare not move.
To search for leaves and make *etutu*[8]
On that spot? Or race home to the safety
Of his hearth? Ten market-days[9] have passed
My friends, and still he's rooted there
Rigid as the plinth of Orayan.[1]

---

6. The soft, edible part of a palm nut.
7. Silk cotton tree or kapok.
8. Placatory rites or medicine [Soyinka's glossary].
9. Considered to be the equivalent of one week.
1. A tall plinth or landmark in Ile-Ife, considered to be the ancestral home of the Yoruba. Orayan was one of the children of Oduduwa, the founding father of the Yoruba people.

The mouth of the courtesan barely
Opened wide enough to take a ha'penny *robo*[2]
When she wailed: 'Not I.' All dressed she was
To call upon my friend the Chief Tax Officer.
But now she sends her go-between instead:
'Tell him I'm ill: my period has come suddenly
But not—I hope—my time.'

Why is the pupil crying?
His hapless head was made to taste
The knuckles of my friend the Mallam:[3]
'If you were then reciting the Koran
Would you have ears for idle noises
Darkening the trees, you child of ill omen?'
He shuts down school before its time
Runs home and rings himself with amulets.

And take my good kinsman Ifawomi.
His hands were like a carver's, strong
And true. I saw them
Tremble like wet wings of a fowl
One day he cast his time-smoothed *opele*[4]
Across the divination board.[5] And all because
The suppliant looked him in the eye and asked,
'Did you hear that whisper in the leaves?'
'Not I,' was his reply; 'perhaps I'm growing deaf—
Good-day.' And Ifa spoke no more that day
The priest locked fast his doors,
Sealed up his leaking roof—but wait!
This sudden care was not for Fawomi[6]
But for Osanyin,[7] courier-bird of Ifa's
Heart of wisdom. I did not know a kite
Was hovering in the sky
And Ifa now a twittering chicken in
The brood of Fawomi the Mother Hen.

Ah, but I must not forget my evening
Courier from the abundant palm, whose groan
Became Not I, as he constipated down
A wayside bush. He wonders if Elegbara[8]
Has tricked his buttocks to discharge

2. A delicacy made from crushed melon seeds, fried in tiny balls [Soyinka's glossary].
3. Muslim teacher.
4. String of beads used in Ifa divination [Soyinka's glossary]. Divination is the art of trying
   to foretell the future or to discover hidden knowledge through supernatural means.
5. The carved board on which divination beads are thrown and then interpreted.
6. Contraction of "Ifawomi," meaning "Ifa watches over me." Ifa is the Yoruba god of
   divination.
7. Patron deity of diviners and medicine men in Yoruba culture.
8. Another name for Esu, the trickster god.

Against a sacred grove. Hear him
Mutter spells to ward off penalties
For an abomination he did not intend.
If any here
Stumbles on a gourd of wine, fermenting
Near the road, and nearby hears a stream
Of spells issuing from a crouching form,
Brother to a *sigidi*,[9] bring home my wine,
Tell my tapper[1] I have ejected
Fear from home and farm. Assure him,
All is well.

PRAISE-SINGER   In your time we do not doubt the peace of farm-
stead and home, the peace of road and hearth, we do not doubt
the peace of the forest.

ELESIN   There was fear in the forest too.
Not-I was lately heard even in the lair
Of beasts. The hyena cackled loud Not I,
The civet[2] twitched his fiery tail and glared:
Not I. Not-I became the answering-name
Of the restless bird, that little one
Whom Death found nesting in the leaves
When whisper of his coming ran
Before him on the wind. Not-I
Has long abandoned home. This same dawn
I heard him twitter in the gods' abode.
Ah, companions of this living world
What a thing this is, that even those
We call immortal
Should fear to die.

IYALOJA   But you, husband of multitudes?

ELESIN   I, when that Not-I bird perched
Upon my roof, bade him seek his nest again,
Safe, without care or fear. I unrolled
My welcome mat for him to see. Not-I
Flew happily away, you'll hear his voice
No more in this lifetime—You all know
What I am.

PRAISE-SINGER   That rock which turns its open lodes
Into the path of lightning. A gay
Thoroughbred whose stride disdains

---

9. A squat, carved figure, endowed with the powers of an incubus [Soyinka's glossary]. An incubus is an imaginary evil spirit that descends on people when asleep.
1. A person whose profession is to tap palm trees for their sap, which is fermented into a wine.
2. Catlike carnivorous mammal with coarse hair, rounded ears, and narrow muzzle.

    To falter though an adder reared
    Suddenly in his path.
ELESIN   My rein is loosened.
    I am master of my Fate. When the hour comes
    Watch me dance along the narrowing path
    Glazed by the soles of my great precursors.
    My soul is eager. I shall not turn aside.
WOMEN   You will not delay?
ELESIN   Where the storm pleases, and when, it directs
    The giants of the forest. When friendship summons
    Is when the true comrade goes.
WOMEN   Nothing will hold you back?
ELESIN   Nothing. What! Has no one told you yet?
    I go to keep my friend and master company.
    Who says the mouth does not believe in
    'No, I have chewed all that before?' I say I have.
    The world is not a constant honey-pot.
    Where I found little I made do with little.
    Where there was plenty I gorged myself.
    My master's hands and mine have always
    Dipped together and, home or sacred feast,
    The bowl was beaten bronze, the meats
    So succulent our teeth accused us of neglect.
    We shared the choicest of the season's
    Harvest of yams. How my friend would read
    Desire in my eyes before I knew the cause—
    However rare, however precious, it was mine.
WOMEN   The town, the very land was yours.
ELESIN   The world was mine. Our joint hands
    Raised houseposts of trust that withstood
    The siege of envy and the termites of time.
    But the twilight hour brings bats and rodents—
    Shall I yield them cause to foul the rafters?
PRAISE-SINGER   Elesin Oba! Are you not that man who
    Looked out of doors that stormy day
    The god of luck[3] limped by, drenched
    To the very lice that held
    His rags together? You took pity upon
    His sores and wished him fortune.
    Fortune was footloose this dawn, he replied,
    Till you trapped him in a heartfelt wish
    That now returns to you. Elesin Oba!

---

3. Possibly a reference to Esu Elegba, the trickster god, who, especially in New World versions, limps because one foot is shorter than the other.

I say you are that man who
Chanced upon the calabash[4] of honour
You thought it was palm wine and
Drained its contents to the final drop.

ELESIN Life has an end. A life that will outlive
Fame and friendship begs another name.
What elder takes his tongue to his plate,
Licks it clean of every crumb? He will encounter
Silence when he calls on children to fulfill
The smallest errand! Life is honour.
It ends when honour ends.

WOMEN We know you for a man of honour.

ELESIN Stop! Enough of that!

WOMEN [puzzled, they whisper among themselves, turning mostly to IYALOJA] What is it? Did we say something to give offence? Have we slighted him in some way?

ELESIN Enough of that sound I say. Let me hear no more in that vein. I've heard enough.

IYALOJA We must have said something wrong. [Comes forward a little.] Elesin Oba, we ask forgiveness before you speak.

ELESIN I am bitterly offended.

IYALOJA Our unworthiness has betrayed us. All we can do is ask your forgiveness. Correct us like a kind father.

ELESIN This day of all days . . .

IYALOJA It does not bear thinking. If we offend you now we have mortified the gods. We offend heaven itself. Father of us all, tell us where we went astray. [She kneels, the other women follow.]

ELESIN Are you not ashamed? Even a tear-veiled
Eye preserves its function of sight.
Because my mind was raised to horizons
Even the boldest man lowers his gaze
In thinking of, must my body here
Be taken for a vagrant's?

IYALOJA Horseman of the King, I am more baffled than ever.

PRAISE-SINGER The strictest father unbends his brow when the child is penitent, Elesin. When time is short, we do not spend it prolonging the riddle. Their shoulders are bowed with the weight of fear lest they have marred your day beyond repair. Speak now in plain words and let us pursue the ailment to the home of remedies.

ELESIN Words are cheap. 'We know you for
A man of honour.' Well tell me, is this how
A man of honour should be seen?

---

4. Half of a gourd usually used to serve food or water.

Are these not the same clothes in which
I came among you a full half-hour ago?

[*He roars with laughter and the* WOMEN, *relieved, rise and rush into stalls to fetch rich cloths.*]

WOMEN   The gods are kind. A fault soon remedied is soon forgiven.
Elesin Oba, even as we match our words with deed, let your heart
forgive us completely.

ELESIN   You who are breath and giver of my being
How shall I dare refuse you forgiveness
Even if the offence were real.

IYALOJA [*dancing round him. Sings*]
He forgives us. He forgives us.
What a fearful thing it is when
The voyager sets forth
But a curse remains behind.

WOMEN   For a while we truly feared
Our hands had wrenched the world adrift
In emptiness.

IYALOJA   Richly, richly, robe him richly
The cloth of honour is *alari*
Sanyan[5] is the band of friendship
Boa-skin[6] makes slippers of esteem

WOMEN   For a while we truly feared
Our hands had wrenched the world adrift
In emptiness.

PRAISE-SINGER   He who must, must voyage forth
The world will not roll backwards
It is he who must, with one
Great gesture overtake the world.

WOMEN   For a while we truly feared
Our hands had wrenched the world
In emptiness.

PRAISE-SINGER   The gourd you bear is not for shirking.
The gourd is not for setting down
At the first crossroad or wayside grove.
Only one river may know its contents

WOMEN   We shall all meet at the great market[7]
We shall all meet at the great market
He who goes early takes the best bargains
But we shall meet, and resume our banter.

5. A richly valued woven cloth [Soyinka's glossary].
6. Skin from a large nonvenomous snake that usually kills its victim by constriction and suffocation.
7. In the afterlife.

[ELESIN *stands resplendent in rich clothes, cap, shawl, etc. His sash is of a bright red* alari *cloth. The* WOMEN *dance round him. Suddenly, his attention is caught by an object off-stage.*]

ELESIN   The world I know is good.

WOMEN   We know you'll leave it so.

ELESIN   The world I know is the bounty
Of hives after bees have swarmed.
No goodness teems with such open hands
Even in the dreams of deities.

WOMEN   And we know you'll leave it so.

ELESIN   I was born to keep it so. A hive
Is never known to wander. An anthill[8]
Does not desert its roots. We cannot see
The still great womb of the world—
No man beholds his mother's womb—
Yet who denies it's there? Coiled
To the navel of the world is that
Endless cord that links us all
To the great origin. If I lose my way
The trailing cord will bring me to the roots.

WOMEN   The world is in your hands.

[*The earlier distraction, a beautiful* YOUNG GIRL, *comes along the passage through which* ELESIN *first made his entry.*]

ELESIN   I embrace it. And let me tell you, women—
I like this farewell that the world designed,
Unless my eyes deceive me, unless
We are already parted, the world and I,
And all that breeds desire is lodged
Among our tireless ancestors. Tell me friends,
Am I still earthed in that beloved market
Of my youth? Or could it be my will
Has outleapt the conscious act and I have come
Among the great departed?

PRAISE-SINGER   Elesin-Oba why do your eyes roll like a bush-rat who sees his fate like his father's spirit, mirrored in the eye of a snake? And all these questions! You're standing on the same earth you've always stood upon. This voice you hear is mine, Oluhun-iyo, not that of an acolyte[9] in heaven.

ELESIN   How can that be? In all my life
As Horseman of the King, the juiciest

---

8. A mound of earth formed by a colony of ants in the construction of their underground nests.
9. A student or attendant.

Fruit on every tree was mine. I saw,
I touched, I wooed, rarely was the answer No.
The honour of my place, the veneration I
Received in the eye of man or woman
Prospered my suit and
Played havoc with my sleeping hours.
And they tell me my eyes were a hawk
In perpetual hunger. Split an iroko[1] tree
In two, hide a woman's beauty in its heartwood[2]
And seal it up again—Elesin, journeying by,
Would make his camp beside that tree
Of all the shades in the forest.

PRAISE-SINGER Who would deny your reputation, snake-on-the-loose in dark passages of the market! Bed-bug who wages war on the mat and receives the thanks of the vanquished! When caught with his bride's own sister he protested—but I was only prostrating myself to her as becomes a grateful in-law. Hunter who carries his powder-horn[3] on the hips and fires crouching or standing! Warrior who never makes that excuse of the whining coward —but how can I go to battle without my trousers?—trouserless or shirtless it's all one to him. Oka[4]-rearing-from-a-camouflage-of-leaves, before he strikes the victim is already prone! Once they told him, Howu, a stallion does not feed on the grass beneath him: he replied, true, but surely he can roll on it!

WOMEN Ba-a-a-ba O!

PRAISE-SINGER Ah, but listen yet. You know there is the leaf-nibbling grub and there is the cola-chewing beetle; the leaf-nibbling grub lives on the leaf, the cola-chewing beetle lives in the colanut.[5] Don't we know what our man feeds on when we find him cocooned in a woman's wrapper?

ELESIN Enough, enough, you all have cause
To know me well. But, if you say this earth
Is still the same as gave birth to those songs,
Tell me who was that goddess through whose lips
I saw the ivory pebbles of Oya's[6] river-bed.
Iyaloja, who is she? I saw her enter
Your stall; all your daughters I know well.

---

1. An African teak, a large tree believed, in Yoruba folklore, to be inhabited by a roguish fairy or spirit.
2. The heartwood, or inside, of the iroko tree is made up of a variety of colors.
3. Yoruba hunters carry their gunpowder in a horn.
4. Python.
5. The seed of the cola (kola) nut tree valued by long-distance drivers for its caffeine, but also used as a ritual symbol of welcome.
6. Oya is the goddess of the Niger River and patron of fishermen and sailors.

No, not even Ogun[7]-of-the-farm toiling
Dawn till dusk on his tuber patch
Not even Ogun with the finest hoe he ever
Forged at the anvil could have shaped
That rise of buttocks, not though he had
The richest earth between his fingers.
Her wrapper was no disguise
For thighs whose ripples shamed the river's
Coils around the hills of Ilesi.[8] Her eyes
Were new-laid eggs glowing in the dark.
Her skin . . .

IYALOJA   Elesin Oba . . .

ELESIN   What! Where do you all say I am?

IYALOJA   Still among the living.

ELESIN   And that radiance which so suddenly
Lit up this market I could boast
I knew so well?

IYALOJA   Has one step already in her husband's home. She is betrothed.

ELESIN [*irritated*]   Why do you tell me that?

[IYALOJA *falls silent. The* WOMEN *shuffle uneasily.*]

IYALOJA   Not because we dare give you offence Elesin. Today is your day and the whole world is yours. Still, even those who leave town to make a new dwelling elsewhere like to be remembered by what they leave behind.

ELESIN   Who does not seek to be remembered?
Memory is Master of Death, the chink
In his armour of conceit. I shall leave
That which makes my going the sheerest
Dream of an afternoon. Should voyagers
Not travel light? Let the considerate traveller
Shed, of his excessive load, all
That may benefit the living.

WOMEN [*relieved*]   Ah Elesin Oba, we knew you for a man of honour.

ELESIN   Then honour me. I deserve a bed of honour to lie upon.

IYALOJA   The best is yours. We know you for a man of honour. You are not one who eats and leaves nothing on his plate for children.

---

7. The god of iron and war, of hunters, soldiers, and blacksmiths; also considered to be the patron of artists.
8. A district and town in Oyo, western Nigeria.

Did you not say it yourself? Not one who blights the happiness
of others for a moment's pleasure.

ELESIN   Who speaks of pleasure? O women, listen!
     Pleasure palls. Our acts should have meaning.
     The sap of the plantain[9] never dries.
     You have seen the young shoot swelling
     Even as the parent stalk begins to wither.
     Women, let my going be likened to
     The twilight hour of the plantain.

WOMEN   What does he mean Iyaloja? This language is the language
of our elders, we do not fully grasp it.

IYALOJA   I dare not understand you yet Elesin.

ELESIN   All you who stand before the spirit that dares
     The opening of the last door of passage,
     Dare to rid my going of regrets! My wish
     Transcends the blotting out of thought
     In one mere moment's tremor of the senses.
     Do me credit. And do me honour.
     I am girded for the route beyond
     Burdens of waste and longing.
     Then let me travel light. Let
     Seed that will not serve the stomach
     On the way remain behind. Let it take root
     In the earth of my choice, in this earth
     I leave behind.

IYALOJA [*turns to* WOMEN]   The voice I hear is already touched by
the waiting fingers of our departed. I dare not refuse.

WOMAN   But Iyaloja . . .

IYALOJA   The matter is no longer in our hands.

WOMAN   But she is betrothed to your own son. Tell him.

IYALOJA   My son's wish is mine. I did the asking for him, the loss
can be remedied. But who will remedy the blight of closed hands
on the day when all should be openness and light? Tell him, you
say! You wish that I burden him with knowledge that will sour
his wish and lay regrets on the last moments of his mind. You
pray to him who is your intercessor to the world—don't set this
world adrift in your own time; would you rather it was my hand
whose sacrilege wrenched it loose?

WOMAN   Not many men will brave the curse of a dispossessed
husband.

IYALOJA   Only the curses of the departed are to be feared. The
claims of one whose foot is on the threshold of their abode sur-

---

9. A variety of banana, a popular staple of the tropical regions of Africa.

passes even the claims of blood. It is impiety even to place hindrances in their ways.

ELESIN   What do my mothers say? Shall I step
    Burdened into the unknown?

IYALOJA   Not we, but the very earth says No. The sap in the plantain does not dry. Let grain that will not feed the voyager at his passage drop here and take root as he steps beyond this earth and us. Oh you who fill the home from hearth to threshold with the voices of children, you who now bestride the hidden gulf and pause to draw the right foot across and into the resting-home of the great forebears, it is good that your loins be drained into the earth we know, that your last strength be ploughed back into the womb that gave you being.

PRAISE-SINGER   Iyaloja, mother of multitudes in the teeming market of the world, how your wisdom transfigures you!

IYALOJA [*smiling broadly, completely reconciled*]   Elesin, even at the narrow end of the passage I know you will look back and sigh a last regret for the flesh that flashed past your spirit in flight. You always had a restless eye. Your choice has my blessing. [*To the* WOMEN.] Take the good news to our daughter and make her ready. [*Some* WOMEN *go off.*]

ELESIN   Your eyes were clouded at first.

IYALOJA   Not for long. It is those who stand at the gateway of the great change to whose cry we must pay heed. And then, think of this—it makes the mind tremble. The fruit of such a union is rare. It will be neither of this world nor of the next. Nor of the one behind us. As if the timelessness of the ancestor world and the unborn have joined spirits to wring an issue of the elusive being of passage . . . Elesin!

ELESIN   I am here. What is it?

IYALOJA   Did you hear all I said just now?

ELESIN   Yes.

IYALOJA   The living must eat and drink. When the moment comes, don't turn the food to rodents' droppings in their mouth. Don't let them taste the ashes of the world when they step out at dawn to breathe the morning dew.

ELESIN   This doubt is unworthy of you Iyaloja.

IYALOJA   Eating the awusa[1] nut is not so difficult as drinking water afterwards.

ELESIN   The waters of the bitter stream are honey to a man
    Whose tongue has savoured all.

IYALOJA   No one knows when the ants desert their home; they leave

---

1. A climbing plant.

the mound intact. The swallow is never seen to peck holes in its nest when it is time to move with the season. There are always throngs of humanity behind the leave-taker. The rain should not come through the roof for them, the wind must not blow through the walls at night.

ELESIN   I refuse to take offence.

IYALOJA   You wish to travel light. Well, the earth is yours. But be sure the seed you leave in it attracts no curse.

ELESIN   You really mistake my person Iyaloja.

IYALOJA   I said nothing. Now we must go prepare your bridal chamber. Then these same hands will lay your shrouds.

ELESIN   [exasperated]   Must you be so blunt? [Recovers.] Well, weave your shrouds, but let the fingers of my bride seal my eyelids with earth and wash my body.

IYALOJA   Prepare yourself Elesin.

> [She gets up to leave. At that moment the WOMEN return, leading the BRIDE. ELESIN's face glows with pleasure. He flicks the sleeves of his agbada² with renewed confidence and steps forward to meet the group. As the girl kneels before IYALOJA, lights fade out on the scene.]

2

The verandah of the District Officer's bungalow.¹ A tango is playing from an old hand-cranked gramophone and, glimpsed through the wide windows and doors which open onto the forestage verandah are the shapes of SIMON PILKINGS and his wife, JANE, tangoing in and out of shadows in the living-room. They are wearing what is immediately apparent as some form of fancy-dress. The dance goes on for some moments and then the figure of a 'NATIVE ADMINISTRATION' POLICEMAN² emerges and climbs up the steps onto the verandah. He peeps through and observes the dancing couple, reacting with what is obviously a long-standing bewilderment. He stiffens suddenly, his expression changes to one of disbelief and horror. In his excitement he upsets a flowerpot and attracts the attention of the couple. They stop dancing.

PILKINGS   Is there anyone out there?

JANE   I'll turn off the gramophone.

2. Large flowing robe usually worn by men and often embroidered at the neck and chest.
1. A verandah is a roofed and large open porch; a bungalow is a one-story house usually surrounded by a verandah, favored by colonial officials as a protection against the tropical heat. Both words are of Indian (Hindi) origin.
2. A policeman belonging to a unit charged with the policing of Africans and considered inferior to the regular police.

PILKINGS [*approaching the verandah*] I'm sure I heard something fall over. [*The* CONSTABLE *retreats slowly, open-mouthed as* PILKINGS *approaches the verandah.*] Oh it's you Amusa. Why didn't you just knock instead of knocking things over?

AMUSA [*stammers badly and points a shaky finger at his dress*] Mista Pirinkin . . . Mista Pirinkin . . .

PILKINGS What is the matter with you?

JANE [*emerging*] Who is it dear? Oh, Amusa . . .

PILKINGS Yes it's Amusa, and acting most strangely.

AMUSA [*his attention now transferred to* MRS PILKINGS] Mammadam . . . you too!

PILKINGS What the hell is the matter with you man!

JANE Your costume darling. Our fancy dress.

PILKINGS Oh hell, I'd forgotten all about that. [*Lifts the face mask over his head showing his face. His wife follows suit.*]

JANE I think you've shocked his big pagan heart bless him.

PILKINGS Nonsense, he's a Moslem. Come on Amusa, you don't believe in all this nonsense do you? I thought you were a good Moslem.

AMUSA Mista Pirinkin, I beg you sir, what you think you do with that dress? It belong to dead cult, not for human being.

PILKINGS Oh Amusa, what a let down you are. I swear by you at the club you know—thank God for Amusa, he doesn't believe in any mumbo-jumbo. And now look at you!

AMUSA Mista Pirinkin, I beg you, take it off. Is not good for man like you to touch that cloth.

PILKINGS Well, I've got it on. And what's more Jane and I have bet on it we're taking first prize at the ball. Now, if you can just pull yourself together and tell me what you wanted to see me about . . .

AMUSA Sir, I cannot talk this matter to you in that dress. I no fit.

PILKINGS What's that rubbish again?

JANE He is dead earnest too Simon. I think you'll have to handle this delicately.

PILKINGS Delicately my . . . ! Look here Amusa, I think this little joke has gone far enough hm? Let's have some sense. You seem to forget that you are a police officer in the service of His Majesty's Government. I order you to report your business at once or face disciplinary action.

AMUSA Sir, it is a matter of death. How can man talk against death to person in uniform of death? Is like talking against government to person in uniform of police. Please sir, I go and come back.

PILKINGS [*roars*] Now! [AMUSA *switches his gaze to the ceiling suddenly, remains mute.*]

JANE Oh Amusa, what is there to be scared of in the costume?

You saw it confiscated last month from those *egungun*[3] men who were creating trouble in town. You helped arrest the cult leaders yourself—if the juju[4] didn't harm you at the time how could it possibly harm you now? And merely by looking at it?

AMUSA [*without looking down*]   Madam, I arrest the ringleaders who make trouble but me I no touch *egungun*. That *egungun* itself, I no touch. And I no abuse 'am. I arrest ringleader but I treat *egungun* with respect.

PILKINGS   It's hopeless. We'll merely end up missing the best part of the ball. When they get this way there is nothing you can do. It's simply hammering against a brick wall. Write your report or whatever it is on that pad Amusa and take yourself out of here. Come on Jane. We only upset his delicate sensibilities by remaining here.

> [AMUSA *waits for them to leave, then writes in the notebook, somewhat laboriously. Drumming from the direction of the town wells up.* AMUSA *listens, makes a movement as if he wants to recall* PILKINGS *but changes his mind. Completes his note and goes. A few moments later* PILKINGS *emerges, picks up the pad and reads.*]

PILKINGS   Jane!

JANE [*from the bedroom*]   Coming darling. Nearly ready.

PILKINGS   Never mind being ready, just listen to this.

JANE   What is it?

PILKINGS   Amusa's report. Listen. 'I have to report that it come to my information that one prominent chief, namely, the Elesin Oba, is to commit death tonight as a result of native custom. Because this is criminal offence I await further instruction at charge office. Sergeant Amusa.'

> [JANE *comes out onto the verandah while he is reading.*]

JANE   Did I hear you say commit death?

PILKINGS   Obviously he means murder.

JANE   You mean a ritual murder?

PILKINGS   Must be. You think you've stamped it all out but it's always lurking under the surface somewhere.

JANE   Oh. Does it mean we are not getting to the ball at all?

PILKINGS   No-o. I'll have the man arrested. Everyone remotely involved. In any case there may be nothing to it. Just rumours.

---

3. Ancestral masquerade [Soyinka's glossary]. The masked figures in the masquerade are considered to be the reincarnated spirits of ancestors; their dress is often a long grass robe and a wooden mask representing the face or head of an animal.
4. Magic, usually attributed to a fetish.

JANE   Really? I thought you found Amusa's rumours generally reliable.

PILKINGS   That's true enough. But who knows what may have been giving him the scare lately. Look at his conduct tonight.

JANE [*laughing*]   You have to admit he had his own peculiar logic. [*Deepens her voice.*] How can man talk against death to person in uniform of death? [*Laughs.*] Anyway, you can't go into the police station dressed like that.

PILKINGS   I'll send Joseph with instructions. Damn it, what a confounded nuisance!

JANE   But don't you think you should talk first to the man, Simon?

PILKINGS   Do you want to go to the ball or not?

JANE   Darling, why are you getting rattled? I was only trying to be intelligent. It seems hardly fair just to lock up a man—and a chief at that—simply on the er . . . what is the legal word again?—uncorroborated word of a sergeant.

PILKINGS   Well, that's easily decided. Joseph!

JOSEPH [*from within*]   Yes master.

PILKINGS   You're quite right of course, I am getting rattled. Probably the effect of those bloody drums. Do you hear how they go on and on?

JANE   I wondered when you'd notice. Do you suppose it has something to do with this affair?

PILKINGS   Who knows? They always find an excuse for making a noise . . . [*Thoughtfully.*] Even so . . .

JANE   Yes Simon?

PILKINGS   It's different Jane. I don't think I've heard this particular—sound—before. Something unsettling about it.

JANE   I thought all bush drumming sounded the same.

PILKINGS   Don't tease me now Jane. This may be serious.

JANE   I'm sorry. [*Gets up and throws her arms around his neck. Kisses him. The* HOUSEBOY *enters, retreats and knocks.*]

PILKINGS [*wearily*]   Oh, come in Joseph! I don't know where you pick up all these elephantine[5] notions of tact. Come over here.

JOSEPH   Sir?

PILKINGS   Joseph, are you a christian or not?

JOSEPH   Yessir.

PILKINGS   Does seeing me in this outfit bother you?

JOSEPH   No sir, it has no power.

PILKINGS   Thank God for some sanity at last. Now Joseph, answer me on the honour of a christian—what is supposed to be going on in town tonight?

---

5. Huge, ponderous, clumsy.

JOSEPH   Tonight sir? You mean the chief who is going to kill himself?

PILKINGS   What?

JANE   What do you mean, kill himself?

PILKINGS   You do mean he is going to kill somebody don't you?

JOSEPH   No master. He will not kill anybody and no one will kill him. He will simply die.

JANE   But why Joseph?

JOSEPH   It is native law and custom. The King die last month. Tonight is his burial. But before they can bury him, the Elesin must die so as to accompany him to heaven.

PILKINGS   I seem to be fated to clash more often with that man than with any of the other chiefs.

JOSEPH   He is the King's Chief Horseman.

PILKINGS [in a resigned way]   I know.

JANE   Simon, what's the matter?

PILKINGS   It would have to be him!

JANE   Who is he?

PILKINGS   Don't you remember? He's that chief with whom I had a scrap some three or four years ago. I helped his son get to a medical school in England, remember? He fought tooth and nail to prevent it.

JANE   Oh now I remember. He was that very sensitive young man. What was his name again?

PILKINGS   Olunde. Haven't replied to his last letter come to think of it. The old pagan wanted him to stay and carry on some family tradition or the other. Honestly I couldn't understand the fuss he made. I literally had to help the boy escape from close confinement and load him onto the next boat. A most intelligent boy, really bright.

JANE   I rather thought he was much too sensitive you know. The kind of person you feel should be a poet munching rose petals in Bloomsbury.[6]

PILKINGS   Well, he's going to make a first-class doctor. His mind is set on that. And as long as he wants my help he is welcome to it.

JANE [after a pause]   Simon.

PILKINGS   Yes?

JANE   This boy, he was the eldest son wasn't he?

PILKINGS   I'm not sure. Who could tell with that old ram?

JANE   Do you know, Joseph?

---

6. An area of central London next to the British Museum; it is associated with art and high culture.

JOSEPH Oh yes madam. He was the eldest son. That's why Elesin cursed master good and proper. The eldest son is not supposed to travel away from the land.

JANE [*giggling*] Is that true Simon? Did he really curse you good and proper?

PILKINGS By all accounts I should be dead by now.

JOSEPH Oh no, master is white man. And good christian. Black man juju can't touch master.

JANE If he was his eldest, it means that he would be the Elesin to the next king. It's a family thing isn't it Joseph?

JOSEPH Yes madam. And if this Elesin had died before the King, his eldest son must take his place.

JANE That would explain why the old chief was so mad you took the boy away.

PILKINGS Well it makes me all the more happy I did.

JANE I wonder if he knew.

PILKINGS Who? Oh, you mean Olunde?

JANE Yes. Was that why he was so determined to get away? I wouldn't stay if I knew I was trapped in such a horrible custom.

PILKINGS [*thoughtfully*] No, I don't think he knew. At least he gave no indication. But you couldn't really tell with him. He was rather close you know, quite unlike most of them. Didn't give much away, not even to me.

JANE Aren't they all rather close, Simon?

PILKINGS These natives here? Good gracious. They'll open their mouths and yap with you about their family secrets before you can stop them. Only the other day . . .

JANE But Simon, do they really give anything away? I mean, anything that really counts. This affair for instance, we didn't know they still practised that custom did we?

PILKINGS Ye-e-es, I suppose you're right there. Sly, devious bastards.

JOSEPH [*stiffly*] Can I go now master? I have to clean the kitchen.

PILKINGS What? Oh, you can go. Forgot you were still there.

[JOSEPH *goes.*]

JANE Simon, you really must watch your language. Bastard isn't just a simple swear-word in these parts, you know.

PILKINGS Look, just when did you become a social anthropologist, that's what I'd like to know.

JANE I'm not claiming to know anything. I just happen to have overheard quarrels among the servants. That's how I know they consider it a smear.

PILKINGS   I thought the extended family system[7] took care of all that. Elastic family, no bastards.

JANE [*shrugs*]   Have it your own way.

> [*Awkward silence. The drumming increases in volume.* JANE *gets up suddenly, restless.*]

That drumming Simon, do you think it might really be connected with this ritual? It's been going on all evening.

PILKINGS   Let's ask our native guide. Joseph! Just a minute Joseph. [JOSEPH *re-enters.*] What's the drumming about?

JOSEPH   I don't know master.

PILKINGS   What do you mean you don't know? It's only two years since your conversion. Don't tell me all that holy water nonsense also wiped out your tribal memory.

JOSEPH [*visibly shocked*]   Master!

JANE   Now you've done it.

PILKINGS   What have I done now?

JANE   Never mind. Listen Joseph, just tell me this. Is that drumming connected with dying or anything of that nature?

JOSEPH   Madam, this is what I am trying to say: I am not sure. It sounds like the death of a great chief and then, it sounds like the wedding of a great chief. It really mix me up.

PILKINGS   Oh get back to the kitchen. A fat lot of help you are.

JOSEPH   Yes master. [*Goes.*]

JANE   Simon . . .

PILKINGS   Alright, alright. I'm in no mood for preaching.

JANE   It isn't my preaching you have to worry about, it's the preaching of the missionaries who preceded you here. When they make converts they really convert them. Calling holy water nonsense to our Joseph is really like insulting the Virgin Mary before a Roman Catholic. He's going to hand in his notice tomorrow you mark my word.

PILKINGS   Now you're being ridiculous.

JANE   Am I? What are you willing to bet that tomorrow we are going to be without a steward-boy?[8] Did you see his face?

PILKINGS   I am more concerned about whether or not we will be one native chief short by tomorrow. Christ! Just listen to those drums. [*He strides up and down, undecided.*]

JANE [*getting up*]   I'll change and make us some supper.

PILKINGS   What's that?

JANE   Simon, it's obvious we have to miss this ball.

---

7. The domestic system in which the distinction between the immediate family and other relatives is not strictly maintained.
8. Houseboy.

PILKINGS   Nonsense. It's the first bit of real fun the European club[9] has managed to organise for over a year, I'm damned if I'm going to miss it. And it is a rather special occasion. Doesn't happen every day.

JANE   You know this business has to be stopped Simon. And you are the only man who can do it.

PILKINGS   I don't have to stop anything. If they want to throw themselves off the top of a cliff or poison themselves for the sake of some barbaric custom what is that to me? If it were ritual murder or something like that I'd be duty-bound to do something. I can't keep an eye on all the potential suicides in this province. And as for that man—believe me it's good riddance.

JANE   [laughs]   I know you better than that Simon. You are going to have to do something to stop it—after you've finished blustering.

PILKINGS   [shouts after her]   And suppose after all it's only a wedding. I'd look a proper fool if I interrupted a chief on his honeymoon, wouldn't I? [Resumes his angry stride, slows down.] Ah well, who can tell what those chiefs actually do on their honeymoon anyway? [He takes up the pad and scribbles rapidly on it.] Joseph! Joseph! Joseph! [Some moments later JOSEPH puts in a sulky appearance.] Did you hear me call you? Why the hell didn't you answer?

JOSEPH   I didn't hear master.

PILKINGS   You didn't hear me! How come you are here then?

JOSEPH   [stubbornly]   I didn't hear master.

PILKINGS   [controls himself with an effort]   We'll talk about it in the morning. I want you to take this note directly to Sergeant Amusa. You'll find him at the charge office.[1] Get on your bicycle and race there with it. I expect you back in twenty minutes exactly. Twenty minutes, is that clear?

JOSEPH   Yes master. [Going.]

PILKINGS   Oh er . . . Joseph.

JOSEPH   Yes master?

PILKINGS   [between gritted teeth]   Er . . . forget what I said just now. The holy water is not nonsense. I was talking nonsense.

JOSEPH   Yes master. [Goes.]

JANE   [pokes her head round the door]   Have you found him?

PILKINGS   Found who?

JANE   Joseph. Weren't you shouting for him?

PILKINGS   Oh yes, he turned up finally.

JANE   You sounded desperate. What was it all about?

9. A club reserved for Europeans only.
1. The booking office of a police station.

PILKINGS   Oh nothing. I just wanted to apologise to him. Assure him that the holy water isn't really nonsense.

JANE   Oh? And how did he take it?

PILKINGS   Who the hell gives a damn! I had a sudden vision of our Very Reverend Macfarlane drafting another letter of complaint to the Resident about my unchristian language towards his parishioners.

JANE   Oh I think he's given up on you by now.

PILKINGS   Don't be too sure. And anyway, I wanted to make sure Joseph didn't 'lose' my note on the way. He looked sufficiently full of the holy crusade to do some such thing.

JANE   If you've finished exaggerating, come and have something to eat.

PILKINGS   No, put it all away. We can still get to the ball.

JANE   Simon . . .

PILKINGS   Get your costume back on. Nothing to worry about. I've instructed Amusa to arrest the man and lock him up.

JANE   But that station is hardly secure Simon. He'll soon get his friends to help him escape.

PILKINGS   A-ah, that's where I have out-thought you. I'm not having him put in the station cell. Amusa will bring him right here and lock him up in my study. And he'll stay with him till we get back. No one will dare come here to incite him to anything.

JANE   How clever of you darling. I'll get ready.

PILKINGS   Hey.

JANE   Yes darling.

PILKINGS   I have a surprise for you. I was going to keep it until we actually got to the ball.

JANE   What is it?

PILKINGS   You know the Prince is on a tour of the colonies don't you? Well, he docked in the capital only this morning but he is already at the Residency. He is going to grace the ball with his presence later tonight.

JANE   Simon! Not really.

PILKINGS   Yes he is. He's been invited to give away the prizes and he has agreed. You must admit old Engleton is the best Club Secretary we ever had. Quick off the mark that lad.

JANE   But how thrilling.

PILKINGS   The other provincials are going to be damned envious.

JANE   I wonder what he'll come as.

PILKINGS   Oh I don't know. As a coat-of-arms[2] perhaps. Anyway it won't be anything to touch this.

---

2. Crest.

JANE   Well that's lucky. If we are to be presented I won't have to start looking for a pair of gloves. It's all sewn on.

PILKINGS [*laughing*]   Quite right. Trust a woman to think of that. Come on, let's get going.

JANE [*rushing off*]   Won't be a second. [*Stops.*] Now I see why you've been so edgy all evening. I thought you weren't handling this affair with your usual brilliance—to begin with that is.

PILKINGS [*his mood is much improved*]   Shut up woman and get your things on.

JANE   Alright boss, coming.

[PILKINGS *suddenly begins to hum the tango to which they were dancing before. Starts to execute a few practice steps. Lights fade.*]

3

A swelling, agitated hum of women's voices rises immediately in the background. The lights come on and we see the frontage of a converted cloth stall in the market. The floor leading up to the entrance is covered in rich velvets and woven cloth. The WOMEN *come on stage, borne backwards by the determined progress of Sergeant* AMUSA *and his two* CONSTABLES *who already have their batons out and use them as a pressure against the* WOMEN. *At the edge of the cloth-covered floor however the* WOMEN *take a determined stand and block all further progress of the men. They begin to tease them mercilessly.*

AMUSA   I am tell you women for last time to commot my road.[1] I am here on official business.

WOMAN   Official business you white man's eunuch? Official business is taking place where you want to go and it's a business you wouldn't understand.

WOMAN [*makes a quick tug at the* CONSTABLE's *baton*]   That doesn't fool anyone you know. It's the one you carry under your government knickers[2] that counts. [*She bends low as if to peep under the baggy shorts. The embarrassed* CONSTABLE *quickly puts his knees together. The* WOMEN *roar.*]

WOMAN   You mean there is nothing there at all?

WOMAN   Oh there was something. You know that handbell which the whiteman uses to summon his servants . . . ?

AMUSA [*he manages to preserve some dignity throughout*]   I hope you

1. "Get out of my way"; literally translated from pidgin English as "come out of my road."
2. Women's underpants. The reference here is to the khaki shorts worn by colonial policemen.

women know that interfering with officer in execution of his duty is criminal offence.

WOMAN   Interfere? He says we're interfering with him. You foolish man we're telling you there's nothing to interfere with.

AMUSA   I am order you now to clear the road.

WOMAN   What road? The one your father built?

WOMAN   You are a Policeman not so? Then you know what they call trespassing in court. Or—[*Pointing to the cloth-lined steps*] —do you think that kind of road is built for every kind of feet.

WOMAN   Go back and tell the white man who sent you to come himself.

AMUSA   If I go I will come back with reinforcement. And we will all return carrying weapons.

WOMAN   Oh, now I understand. Before they can put on those knickers the white man first cuts off their weapons.

WOMAN   What a cheek! You mean you come here to show power to women and you don't even have a weapon.

AMUSA   [*shouting above the laughter*]   For the last time I warn you women to clear the road.

WOMAN   To where?

AMUSA   To that hut. I know he dey dere.

WOMAN   Who?

AMUSA   The chief who call himself Elesin Oba.

WOMAN   You ignorant man. It is not he who calls himself Elesin Oba, it is his blood that says it. As it called out to his father before him and will to his son after him. And that is in spite of everything your white man can do.

WOMAN   Is it not the same ocean[3] that washes this land and the white man's land? Tell your white man he can hide our son away as long as he likes. When the time comes for him, the same ocean will bring him back.

AMUSA   The government say dat kin' ting[4] must stop.

WOMAN   Who will stop it? You? Tonight our husband and father will prove himself greater than the laws of strangers.

AMUSA   I tell you nobody go prove anyting tonight or anytime. Is ignorant and criminal to prove dat kin' prove.

IYALOJA   [*entering, from the hut. She is accompanied by a group of* YOUNG GIRLS *who have been attending the* BRIDE]   What is it Amusa? Why do you come here to disturb the happiness of others.

AMUSA   Madame Iyaloja, I glad you come. You know me, I no like trouble but duty is duty. I am here to arrest Elesin for criminal

3. The Atlantic Ocean.
4. "That kind of thing" in pidgin English.

intent. Tell these women to stop obstructing me in the performance of my duty.

IYALOJA And you? What gives you the right to obstruct our leader
of men in the performance of his duty?

AMUSA What kin' duty be dat one Iyaloja.

IYALOJA What kin' duty? What kin' duty does a man have to his
new bride?

AMUSA [bewildered, looks at the WOMEN and at the entrance to the
hut] Iyaloja, is it wedding you call dis kin' ting?

IYALOJA You have wives haven't you? Whatever the white man has
done to you he hasn't stopped you having wives. And if he has,
at least he is married. If you don't know what a marriage is, go
and ask him to tell you.

AMUSA This no to wedding.

IYALOJA And ask him at the same time what he would have done
if anyone had come to disturb him on his wedding night.

AMUSA Iyaloja, I say dis no to wedding.

IYALOJA You want to look inside the bridal chamber? You want to
see for yourself how a man cuts the virgin knot?[5]

AMUSA Madam . . .

WOMAN Perhaps his wives are still waiting for him to learn.

AMUSA Iyaloja, make you tell dese women make den no insult me
again. If I hear dat kin' insult once more . . .

GIRL [pushing her way through] You will do what?

GIRL He's out of his mind. It's our mothers you're talking to, do
you know that? Not to any illiterate villager you can bully and
terrorise. How dare you intrude here anyway?

GIRL What a cheek, what impertinence!

GIRL You've treated them too gently. Now let them see what it is
to tamper with the mothers of this market.

GIRL Your betters dare not enter the market when the women say
no!

GIRL Haven't you learnt that yet, you jester in khaki and starch?

IYALOJA Daughters . . .

GIRL No no Iyaloja, leave us to deal with him. He no longer knows
his mother, we'll teach him.

[With a sudden movement they snatch the batons of the two
CONSTABLES. They begin to hem them in.]

GIRL What next? We have your batons? What next? What are you
going to do?

[With equally swift movements they knock off their hats.]

5. The hymen.

GIRL   Move if you dare. We have our hats, what will you do about it? Didn't the white man teach you to take off your hats before women?

IYALOJA   It's a wedding night. It's a night of joy for us. Peace . . .

GIRL   Not for him. Who asked him here?

GIRL   Does he dare go to the Residency without an invitation?

GIRL   Not even where the servants eat the left-overs.

GIRL   [in turn. In an 'English' accent]   Well well it's Mister Amusa. Were you invited? [Play-acting to one another. The older WOMEN encourage them with their titters.]

—Your invitation card please?

—Who are you? Have we been introduced?

—And who did you say you were?

—Sorry, I didn't quite catch your name.

—May I take your hat?

—If you insist. May I take yours? [Exchanging the POLICEMEN's hats.]

—How very kind of you.

—Not at all. Won't you sit down?

—After you.

—Oh no.

—I insist.

—You're most gracious.

—And how do you find the place?

—The natives are alright.

—Friendly?

—Tractable.

—Not a teeny-weeny bit restless?

—Well, a teeny-weeny bit restless.

—One might even say, difficult?

—Indeed one might be tempted to say, difficult.

—But you do manage to cope?

—Yes indeed I do. I have a rather faithful ox called Amusa.

—He's loyal?

—Absolutely.

—Lay down his life for you what?

—Without a moment's thought.

—Had one like that once. Trust him with my life.

—Mostly of course they are liars.

—Never known a native to tell the truth.

—Does it get rather close around here?

—It's mild for this time of the year.

—But the rains may still come.

—They are late this year aren't they?

—They are keeping African time.

—Ha ha ha ha

—Ha ha ha ha

—The humidity is what gets me.

—It used to be whisky.

—Ha ha ha ha

—Ha ha ha ha

—What's your handicap old chap?

—Is there racing by golly?

—Splendid golf course, you'll like it.

—I'm beginning to like it already.

—And a European club, exclusive.

—You've kept the flag flying.

—We do our best for the old country.

—It's a pleasure to serve.

—Another whisky old chap?

—You are indeed too too kind.

—Not at all sir. Where is that boy? [*With a sudden bellow.*] Sergeant!

AMUSA [*snaps to attention*]   Yessir!

[*The* WOMEN *collapse with laughter.*]

GIRL   Take your men out of here.

AMUSA [*realising the trick, he rages from loss of face*]   I'm give you warning . . .

GIRL   Alright then. Off with his knickers! [*They surge slowly forward.*]

IYALOJA   Daughters, please.

AMUSA [*squaring himself for defence*]   The first woman wey touch me . . .

IYALOJA   My children, I beg of you . . .

GIRL   Then tell him to leave this market. This is the home of our mothers. We don't want the eater of white left-overs at the feast their hands have prepared.

IYALOJA   You heard them Amusa. You had better go.

GIRL   Now!

AMUSA [*commencing his retreat*]   We dey go now, but make you no say we no warn you.

GIRL   Now!

GIRL   Before we read the riot act—you should know all about that.

AMUSA   Make we go. [*They depart, more precipitately.*]

[*The* WOMEN *strike their palms across in the gesture of wonder.*]

WOMEN   Do they teach you all that at school?

WOMAN   And to think I nearly kept Apinke away from the place.

WOMAN   Did you hear them? Did you see how they mimicked the
white man?

WOMAN   The voices exactly. Hey, there are wonders in this world!

IYALOJA   Well, our elders have said it: Dada may be weak, but he
has a younger sibling who is truly fearless.[6]

WOMAN   The next time the white man shows his face in this market
I will set Wuraola[7] on his tail.

> [A WOMAN *bursts into song and dance of euphoria*—'Tani
> l'awa o l'ogbeja? Kayi! A l'ogbeja. Omo Kekere l'ogbeja.'[8] *The
> rest of the* WOMEN *join in, some placing the* GIRLS *on their
> back like infants, others dancing round them. The dance be-
> comes general, mounting in excitement.* ELESIN *appears, in
> wrapper only. In his hands a white velvet cloth folded loosely
> as if it held some delicate object. He cries out.*]

ELESIN   Oh you mothers of beautiful brides! [*The dancing stops.
They turn and see him, and the object in his hands.* IYALOJA *approaches and gently takes the cloth from him.*] Take it. It is no
mere virgin stain, but the union of life and the seeds of passage.
My vital flow, the last from this flesh is intermingled with the
promise of future life. All is prepared. Listen! [*A steady drum-beat
from the distance.*] Yes. It is nearly time. The King's dog has been
killed. The King's favourite horse is about to follow his master.
My brother chiefs know their task and perform it well. [*He listens
again.*]

> [*The* BRIDE *emerges, stands shyly by the door. He turns to her.*]

Our marriage is not yet wholly fulfilled. When earth and passage
wed, the consummation is complete only when there are grains
of earth on the eyelids of passage. Stay by me till then. My faithful drummers, do me your last service. This is where I have chosen to do my leave-taking, in this heart of life, this hive which
contains the swarm of the world in its small compass. This is
where I have known love and laughter away from the palace.
Even the richest food cloys[9] when eaten days on end; in the market, nothing ever cloys. Listen. [*They listen to the drums.*] They
have begun to seek out the heart of the King's favourite horse.
Soon it will ride in its bolt of raffia[1] with the dog at its feet.

---

6. Dada, the mythical king of Oyo and patron god of newborns, is reputed to have abdicated
in favor of his fierce younger brother Shango, the god of thunder and lightning in the
Yoruba pantheon.
7. Translated as "rich gold," a common name for a girl.
8. "Who says we haven't a defender? Silence! We have our defenders. Little children are
our champions" [Soyinka's translation].
9. Becomes uninteresting or distasteful.
1. The fiber from raffia palms, used in making skirts for masks.

Together they will ride on the shoulders of the King's grooms through the pulse centres of the town. They know it is here I shall await them. I have told them. [*His eyes appear to cloud. He passes his hand over them as if to clear his sight. He gives a faint smile.*] It promises well; just then I felt my spirit's eagerness. The kite makes for wide spaces and the wind creeps up behind its tail; can the kite say less than—thank you, the quicker the better? But wait a while my spirit. Wait. Wait for the coming of the courier of the King. Do you know, friends, the horse is born to this one destiny, to bear the burden that is man upon its back. Except for this night, this night alone when the spotless stallion will ride in triumph on the back of man. In the time of my father I witnessed the strange sight. Perhaps tonight also I shall see it for the last time. If they arrive before the drums beat for me, I shall tell them to let the Alafin know I follow swiftly. If they come after the drums have sounded, why then, all is well for I have gone ahead. Our spirits shall fall in step along the great passage. [*He listens to the drums. He seems again to be falling into a state of semi-hypnosis; his eyes scan the sky but it is in a kind of daze. His voice is a little breathless.*] The moon has fed, a glow from its full stomach fills the sky and air, but I cannot tell where is that gateway through which I must pass. My faithful friends, let our feet touch together this last time, lead me into the other market with sounds that cover my skin with down yet make my limbs strike earth like a thoroughbred. Dear mothers, let me dance into the passage even as I have lived beneath your roofs. [*He comes down progressively among them. They make way for him, the* DRUMMERS *playing. His dance is one of solemn, regal motions, each gesture of the body is made with a solemn finality. The* WOMEN *join him, their steps a somewhat more fluid version of his. Beneath the* PRAISE-SINGER's *exhortations the women dirge 'Alẹ lẹ lẹ, awo mi lọ.'*[2]]

PRAISE-SINGER   Elesin Alafin, can you hear my voice?
ELESIN   Faintly, my friend, faintly.
PRAISE-SINGER   Elesin Alafin, can you hear my call?
ELESIN   Faintly my king, faintly.
PRAISE-SINGER   Is your memory sound Elesin?
    Shall my voice be a blade of grass and
    Tickle the armpit of the past?
ELESIN   My memory needs no prodding but
    What do you wish to say to me?
PRAISE-SINGER   Only what has been spoken. Only what concerns
    The dying wish of the father of all.

2. "Night has fallen, the seasoned initiate is leaving."

ELESIN   It is buried like seed-yam in my mind.
        This is the season of quick rains, the harvest
        Is this moment due for gathering.
PRAISE-SINGER   If you cannot come, I said, swear
        You'll tell my favourite horse. I shall
        Ride on through the gates alone.
ELESIN   Elesin's message will be read
        Only when his loyal heart no longer beats.
PRAISE-SINGER   If you cannot come Elesin, tell my dog.
        I cannot stay the keeper too long
        At the gate.
ELESIN   A dog does not outrun the hand
        That feeds it meat. A horse that throws its rider
        Slows down to a stop. Elesin Alafin
        Trusts no beasts with messages between
        A king and his companion.
PRAISE-SINGER   If you get lost my dog will track
        The hidden path to me.
ELESIN   The seven-way crossroads[3] confuses
        Only the stranger. The Horseman of the King
        Was born in the recesses of the house.
PRAISE-SINGER   I know the wickedness of men. If there is
        Weight on the loose end of your sash, such weight
        As no mere man can shift; if your sash is earthed
        By evil minds who mean to part us at the last . . .
ELESIN   My sash is of the deep purple *alari*;
        It is no tethering-rope. The elephant
        Trails no tethering-rope; that king
        Is not yet crowned who will peg an elephant—
        Not even you my friend and King.
PRAISE-SINGER   And yet this fear will not depart from me
        The darkness of this new abode is deep—
        Will your human eyes suffice?
ELESIN   In a night which falls before our eyes
        However deep, we do not miss our way.
PRAISE-SINGER   Shall I now not acknowledge I have stood
        Where wonders met their end? The elephant deserves
        Better than that we say 'I have caught
        A glimpse of something'. If we see the tamer
        Of the forest let us say plainly, we have seen
        An elephant.

---

3. In Yoruba cosmology, Esu Elegba, the god of confusion and doubleness, is often to be
found at the crossroads.

ELESIN [*his voice is drowsy*]
  I have freed myself of earth and now
  It's getting dark. Strange voices guide my feet.
PRAISE-SINGER   The river is never so high that the eyes
  Of a fish are covered. The night is not so dark
  That the albino fails to find his way. A child
  Returning homewards craves no leading by the hand.
  Gracefully does the mask regain his grove at the end of the
  day . . .
  Gracefully. Gracefully does the mask dance
  Homeward at the end of the day, gracefully . . .

  [ELESIN's *trance*[4] *appears to be deepening, his steps heavier.*]

IYALOJA   It is the death of war that kills the valiant,
  Death of water is how the swimmer goes
  It is the death of markets that kills the trader
  And death of indecision takes the idle away
  The trade of the cutlass blunts its edge
  And the beautiful die the death of beauty.
  It takes an Elesin to die the death of death . . .
  Only Elesin . . . dies the unknowable death of death . . .
  Gracefully, gracefully does the horseman regain
  The stables at the end of day, gracefully . . .
PRAISE-SINGER   How shall I tell what my eyes have seen? The
  Horseman gallops on before the courier, how shall I tell what my
  eyes have seen? He says a dog may be confused by new scents
  of beings he never dreamt of, so he must precede the dog to
  heaven. He says a horse may stumble on strange boulders and be
  lamed, so he races on before the horse to heaven. It is best, he
  says, to trust no messenger who may falter at the outer gate; oh
  how shall I tell what my ears have heard? But do you hear me
  still Elesin, do you hear your faithful one?

  [ELESIN *in his motions appears to feel for a direction of sound,
  subtly, but he only sinks deeper into his trance-dance.*]

  Elesin Alafin, I no longer sense your flesh. The drums are changing now but you have gone far ahead of the world. It is not yet
  noon in heaven; let those who claim it is begin their own journey
  home. So why must you rush like an impatient bride: why do you
  race to desert your Olohun-iyo?

  [ELESIN *is now sunk fully deep in his trance, there is no longer
  sign of any awareness of his surroundings.*]

---

4. A hypnotic condition or a state of being possessed; in another sense, the word refers to
a passageway.

Does the deep voice of *gbedu*[5] cover you then, like the passage of royal elephants? Those drums that brook no rivals, have they blocked the passage to your ears that my voice passes into wind, a mere leaf floating in the night? Is your flesh lightened Elesin, is that lump of earth I slid between your slippers to keep you longer slowly sifting from your feet? Are the drums on the other side now tuning skin to skin with ours in *osugbo*?[6] Are there sounds there I cannot hear, do footsteps surround you which pound the earth like *gbedu*, roll like thunder round the dome of the world? Is the darkness gathering in your head Elesin? Is there now a streak of light at the end of the passage, a light I dare not look upon? Does it reveal whose voices we often heard, whose touches we often felt, whose wisdoms come suddenly into the mind when the wisest have shaken their heads and murmured; It cannot be done? Elesin Alafin, don't think I do not know why your lips are heavy, why your limbs are drowsy as palm oil in the cold of harmattan.[7] I would call you back but when the elephant heads for the jungle, the tail is too small a handhold for the hunter that would pull him back. The sun that heads for the sea no longer heeds the prayers of the farmer. When the river begins to taste the salt of the ocean, we no longer know what deity to call on, the river-god or Olokun.[8] No arrow flies back to the string, the child does not return through the same passage that gave it birth. Elesin Oba, can you hear me at all? Your eyelids are glazed like a courtesan's, is it that you see the dark groom and master of life? And will you see my father? Will you tell him that I stayed with you to the last? Will my voice ring in your ears awhile, will you remember Olohun-iyo even if the music on the other side surpasses his mortal craft? But will they know you over there? Have they eyes to gauge your worth, have they the heart to love you, will they know what thoroughbred prances towards them in caparisons of honour? If they do not Elesin, if any there cuts your yam with a small knife, or pours you wine in a small calabash, turn back and return to welcoming hands. If the world were not greater than the wishes of Olohun-iyo, I would not let you go . . .

[*He appears to break down.* ELESIN *dances on, completely in a trance. The dirge wells up louder and stronger.* ELESIN's

---

5. A deep-timbred royal drum [Soyinka's glossary].
6. Secret 'executive' cult of the Yoruba; its meeting place [Soyinka's glossary].
7. In west Africa, a dry, parching seasonal breeze carrying dusty winds from the Sahara Desert.
8. God of the ocean, worshiped by fishermen and sailors.

dance does not lose its elasticity but his gestures become, if
possible, even more weighty. Lights fade slowly on the scene.]

4

A Masque.[1] *The front side of the stage is part of a wide corridor*
around the great hall of the Residency extending beyond vision
into the rear and wings. It is redolent of the tawdry decadence
of a far-flung but key imperial frontier. The couples in a va-
riety of fancy-dress are ranged around the walls, gazing in the
same direction. The guest-of-honour is about to make an ap-
pearance. A portion of the local police brass band with its
white conductor is just visible. At last, the entrance of Royalty.
The band plays 'Rule Britannia', badly, beginning long before
he is visible. The couples bow and curtsey as he passes by
them. Both he and his companions are dressed in seventeenth-
century European costume. Following behind are the RESI-
DENT *and his partner similarly attired. As they gain the end of*
the hall where the orchestra dais begins the music comes to
an end. The PRINCE *bows to the guests. The band strikes up a*
Viennese waltz and the PRINCE *formally opens the floor. Sev-*
eral bars later the RESIDENT *and his companion follow suit.*
Others follow in appropriate pecking order. The orchestra's
waltz rendition is not of the highest musical standard.

Some time later the PRINCE *dances again into view and is*
settled into a corner by the RESIDENT *who then proceeds to*
select couples as they dance past for introduction, sometimes
threading his way through the dancers to tap the lucky couple
on the shoulder. Desperate efforts from many to ensure that
they are recognised in spite of, perhaps, their costume. The
ritual of introductions soon takes in PILKINGS *and his wife.*
The PRINCE *is quite fascinated by their costume and they dem-*
onstrate the adaptations they have made to it, pulling down
the mask to demonstrate how the egungun *normally appears,*
then showing the various press-button controls they have in-
novated for the face flaps, the sleeves, etc. They demonstrate
the dance steps and the guttural sounds made by the egungun,
harass other dancers in the hall, MRS PILKINGS *playing the*
'restrainer'[2] to PILKINGS' *manic darts. Everyone is highly en-*
tertained, the Royal Party especially who lead the applause.

At this point a liveried footman comes in with a note on a

---

1. A formal European-style costume party with elaborate dress and masks.
2. The person who controls the movements of the dancing mask when its movements seem
   excessive.

salver and is intercepted almost absent-mindedly by the RESI-
DENT *who takes the note and reads it. After polite coughs he
succeeds in excusing the* PILKINGS *from the* PRINCE *and takes
them aside. The* PRINCE *considerately offers the* RESIDENT's
wife his hand and dancing is resumed.

  On their way out the RESIDENT *gives an order to his* AIDE-
DE-CAMP.[3] *They come into the side corridor where the* RESI-
DENT *hands the note to* PILKINGS.

RESIDENT   As you see it says 'emergency' on the outside. I took the
  liberty of opening it because His Highness was obviously enjoying
  the entertainment. I didn't want to interrupt unless really
  necessary.

PILKINGS   Yes, yes of course, sir.

RESIDENT   Is it really as bad as it says? What's it all about?

PILKINGS   Some strange custom they have sir. It seems because the
  King is dead some important chief has to commit suicide.

RESIDENT   The King? Isn't it the same one who died nearly a month
  ago?

PILKINGS   Yes sir.

RESIDENT   Haven't they buried him yet?

PILKINGS   They take their time about these things, sir. The pre-
  burial ceremonies last nearly thirty days. It seems tonight is the
  final night.

RESIDENT   But what has it got to do with the market women? Why
  are they rioting? We've waived that troublesome tax[4] haven't we?

PILKINGS   We don't quite know that they are exactly rioting yet sir.
  Sergeant Amusa is sometimes prone to exaggerations.

RESIDENT   He sounds desperate enough. That comes out even in
  his rather quaint grammar. Where is the man anyway? I asked
  my aide-de-camp to bring him here.

PILKINGS   They are probably looking in the wrong verandah. I'll
  fetch him myself.

RESIDENT   No no you stay here. Let your wife go and look for them.
  Do you mind my dear . . . ?

JANE   Certainly not, your Excellency. [*Goes.*]

RESIDENT   You should have kept me informed, Pilkings. You realise
  how disastrous it would have been if things had erupted while
  His Highness was here.

PILKINGS   I wasn't aware of the whole business until tonight sir.

RESIDENT   Nose to the ground Pilkings, nose to the ground. If we
  all let these little things slip past us where would the empire be
  eh? Tell me that. Where would we all be?

---

3. A military assistant to a civilian administrator.
4. Taxes levied on market women were often the sources of riots in colonial west Africa.

PILKINGS [*low voice*]   Sleeping peacefully at home I bet.

RESIDENT   What did you say Pilkings?

PILKINGS   It won't happen again sir.

RESIDENT   It mustn't Pilkings. It mustn't. Where is that damned sergeant? I ought to get back to His Highness as quickly as possible and offer him some plausible explanation for my rather abrupt conduct. Can you think of one, Pilkings?

PILKINGS   You could tell him the truth, sir.

RESIDENT   I could? No no no Pilkings, that would never do. What! Go and tell him there is a riot just two miles away from him? This is supposed to be a secure colony of His Majesty, Pilkings.

PILKINGS   Yes, sir.

RESIDENT   Ah, there they are. No, these are not our native police. Are these the ring-leaders of the riot?

PILKINGS   Sir, these are my police officers.

RESIDENT   Oh, I beg your pardon officers. You do look a little . . . I say, isn't there something missing in their uniform? I think they used to have some rather colourful sashes. If I remember rightly I recommended them myself in my young days in the service. A bit of colour always appeals to the natives, yes, I remember putting that in my report. Well well well, where are we? Make your report man.

PILKINGS [*moves close to* AMUSA, *between his teeth*]   And let's have no more superstitious nonsense from you Amusa or I'll throw you in the guardroom for a month and feed you pork!

RESIDENT   What's that? What has pork to do with it?

PILKINGS   Sir, I was just warning him to be brief. I'm sure you are most anxious to hear his report.

RESIDENT   Yes yes yes of course. Come on man, speak up. Hey, didn't we give them some colourful fez hats with all those wavy things, yes, pink tassels . . .

PILKINGS   Sir, I think if he was permitted to make his report we might find that he lost his hat in the riot.

RESIDENT   Ah yes indeed. I'd better tell His Highness that. Lost his hat in the riot, ha ha. He'll probably say well, as long as he didn't lose his head. [*Chuckles to himself.*] Don't forget to send me a report first thing in the morning young Pilkings.

PILKINGS   No sir.

RESIDENT   And whatever you do, don't let things get out of hand. Keep a cool head and—nose to the ground Pilkings. [*Wanders off in the general direction of the hall.*]

PILKINGS   Yes, sir.

AIDE-DE-CAMP   Would you be needing me sir?

PILKINGS   No thanks Bob. I think His Excellency's need of you is greater than ours.

AIDE-DE-CAMP We have a detachment of soldiers from the capital sir. They accompanied His Highness up here.

PILKINGS I doubt if it will come to that but, thanks, I'll bear it in mind. Oh, could you send an orderly with my cloak.

AIDE-DE-CAMP Very good sir. [*Goes.*]

PILKINGS Now sergeant.

AMUSA Sir . . . [*Makes an effort, stops dead. Eyes to the ceiling.*]

PILKINGS Oh, not again.

AMUSA I cannot against death to dead cult. This dress get power of dead.

PILKINGS Alright, let's go. You are relieved of all further duty Amusa. Report to me first thing in the morning.

JANE Shall I come Simon?

PILKINGS No, there's no need for that. If I can get back later I will. Otherwise get Bob to bring you home.

JANE Be careful Simon . . . I mean, be clever.

PILKINGS Sure I will. You two, come with me. [*As he turns to go, the clock in the Residency begins to chime. PILKINGS looks at his watch then turns, horror-stricken, to stare at his wife. The same thought clearly occurs to her. He swallows hard. An orderly brings his cloak.*] It's midnight. I had no idea it was that late.

JANE But surely . . . they don't count the hours the way we do. The moon, or something . . .

PILKINGS I am . . . not so sure.

> [*He turns and breaks into a sudden run. The two CONSTABLES follow, also at a run. AMUSA, who has kept his eyes on the ceiling throughout waits until the last of the footsteps has faded out of hearing. He salutes suddenly, but without once looking in the direction of the woman.*]

AMUSA Goodnight madam.

JANE Oh. [*She hesitates.*] Amusa . . . [*He goes off without seeming to have heard.*] Poor Simon . . . [*A figure emerges from the shadows, a young black man dressed in a sober western suit. He peeps into the hall, trying to make out the figures of the dancers.*] Who is that?

OLUNDE [*emerging into the light*] I didn't mean to startle you madam. I am looking for the District Officer.

JANE Wait a minute . . . don't I know you? Yes, you are Olunde, the young man who . . .

OLUNDE Mrs Pilkings! How fortunate. I came here to look for your husband.

JANE Olunde! Let's look at you. What a fine young man you've become. Grand but solemn. Good God, when did you return? Simon never said a word. But you do look well Olunde. Really!

OLUNDE   You are . . . well, you look quite well yourself Mrs Pilkings. From what little I can see of you.

JANE   Oh, this. It's caused quite a stir I assure you, and not all of
it very pleasant. You are not shocked I hope?

OLUNDE   Why should I be? But don't you find it rather hot in there?
Your skin must find it difficult to breathe.

JANE   Well, it is a little hot I must confess, but it's all in a good
cause.

OLUNDE   What cause Mrs Pilkings?

JANE   All this. The ball. And His Highness being here in person
and all that.

OLUNDE   [*mildly*]   And that is the good cause for which you dese-
crate an ancestral mask?

JANE   Oh, so you are shocked after all. How disappointing.

OLUNDE   No I am not shocked Mrs Pilkings. You forget that I have
now spent four years among your people. I discovered that you
have no respect for what you do not understand.

JANE   Oh. So you've returned with a chip on your shoulder. That's
a pity Olunde. I am sorry.

[*An uncomfortable silence follows.*]

I take it then that you did not find your stay in England altogether
edifying.

OLUNDE   I don't say that. I found your people quite admirable in
many ways, their conduct and courage in this war[5] for instance.

JANE   Ah yes, the war. Here of course it is all rather remote. From
time to time we have a black-out drill just to remind us that there
is a war on. And the rare convoy passes through on its way somewhere or on manoeuvres. Mind you there is the occasional bit of
excitement like that ship that was blown up in the harbour.

OLUNDE   Here? Do you mean through enemy action?

JANE   Oh no, the war hasn't come that close. The captain did it
himself. I don't quite understand it really. Simon tried to explain.
The ship had to be blown up because it had become dangerous
to the other ships, even to the city itself. Hundreds of the coastal
population would have died.

OLUNDE   Maybe it was loaded with ammunition and had caught
fire. Or some of those lethal gases they've been experimenting
on.

JANE   Something like that. The captain blew himself up with it.
Deliberately. Simon said someone had to remain on board to light
the fuse.

OLUNDE   It must have been a very short fuse.

5. World War II.

JANE [*shrugs*]   I don't know much about it. Only that there was no other way to save lives. No time to devise anything else. The captain took the decision and carried it out.

OLUNDE   Yes . . . I quite believe it. I met men like that in England.

JANE   Oh just look at me! Fancy welcoming you back with such morbid news. Stale[6] too. It was at least six months ago.

OLUNDE   I don't find it morbid at all. I find it rather inspiring. It is an affirmative commentary on life.

JANE   What is?

OLUNDE   That captain's self-sacrifice.

JANE   Nonsense. Life should never be thrown deliberately away.

OLUNDE   And the innocent people round the harbour?

JANE   Oh, how does one know? The whole thing was probably exaggerated anyway.

OLUNDE   That was a risk the captain couldn't take. But please Mrs Pilkings, do you think you could find your husband for me? I have to talk to him.

JANE   Simon? Oh. [*As she recollects for the first time the full significance of* OLUNDE'*s presence.*] Simon is . . . there is a little problem in town. He was sent for. But . . . when did you arrive? Does Simon know you're here?

OLUNDE [*suddenly earnest*]   I need your help Mrs Pilkings. I've always found you somewhat more understanding than your husband. Please find him for me and when you do, you must help me talk to him.

JANE   I'm afraid I don't quite . . . follow you. Have you seen my husband already?

OLUNDE   I went to your house. Your houseboy told me you were here. [*He smiles.*] He even told me how I would recognise you and Mr Pilkings.

JANE   Then you must know what my husband is trying to do for you.

OLUNDE   For me?

JANE   For you. For your people. And to think he didn't even know you were coming back! But how do you happen to be here? Only this evening we were talking about you. We thought you were still four thousand miles away.

OLUNDE   I was sent a cable.

JANE   A cable? Who did? Simon? The business of your father didn't begin till tonight.

OLUNDE   A relation sent it weeks ago, and it said nothing about my father. All it said was, Our King is dead. But I knew I had to return home at once so as to bury my father. I understood that.

6. Old or out of date.

JANE Well, thank God you don't have to go through that agony. Simon is going to stop it.

OLUNDE That's why I want to see him. He's wasting his time. And since he has been so helpful to me I don't want him to incur the enmity of our people. Especially over nothing.

JANE [*sits down open-mouthed*] You . . . you Olunde!

OLUNDE Mrs Pilkings, I came home to bury my father. As soon as I heard the news I booked my passage home. In fact we were fortunate. We travelled in the same convoy as your Prince, so we had excellent protection.

JANE But you don't think your father is also entitled to whatever protection is available to him?

OLUNDE How can I make you understand? He *has* protection. No one can undertake what he does tonight without the deepest protection the mind can conceive. What can you offer him in place of his peace of mind, in place of the honour and veneration of his own people? What would you think of your Prince if he refused to accept the risk of losing his life on this voyage? This . . . showing-the-flag[7] tour of colonial possessions.

JANE I see. So it isn't just medicine you studied in England.

OLUNDE Yet another error into which your people fall. You believe that everything which appears to make sense was learnt from you.

JANE Not so fast Olunde. You have learnt to argue I can tell that, but I never said you made sense. However clearly you try to put it, it is still a barbaric custom. It is even worse—it's feudal! The king dies and a chieftain must be buried with him. How feudal-istic can you get!

OLUNDE [*waves his hand towards the background. The* PRINCE *is dancing past again—to a different step—and all the guests are bowing and curtseying as he passes*] And this? Even in the midst of a devastating war, look at that. What name would you give to that?

JANE Therapy, British style. The preservation of sanity in the midst of chaos.

OLUNDE Others would call it decadence. However, it doesn't really interest me. You white races know how to survive; I've seen proof of that. By all logical and natural laws this war should end with all the white races wiping out one another, wiping out their so-called civilisation for all time and reverting to a state of primitiv-ism the like of which has so far only existed in your imagination when you thought of us. I thought all that at the beginning. Then I slowly realised that your greatest art is the art of survival. But at least have the humility to let others survive in their own way.

---

7. Bolstering-of-confidence.

JANE   Through ritual suicide?

OLUNDE   Is that worse than mass suicide? Mrs Pilkings, what do you call what those young men are sent to do by their generals in this war? Of course you have also mastered the art of calling things by names which don't remotely describe them.

JANE   You talk! You people with your long-winded, roundabout way of making conversation.

OLUNDE   Mrs Pilkings, whatever we do, we never suggest that a thing is the opposite of what it really is. In your newsreels[8] I heard defeats, thorough, murderous defeats described as strategic victories. No wait, it wasn't just on your newsreels. Don't forget I was attached to hospitals all the time. Hordes of your wounded passed through those wards. I spoke to them. I spent long evenings by their bedsides while they spoke terrible truths of the realities of that war. I know now how history is made.

JANE   But surely, in a war of this nature, for the morale of the nation you must expect . . .

OLUNDE   That a disaster beyond human reckoning be spoken of as a triumph? No. I mean, is there no mourning in the home of the bereaved that such blasphemy is permitted?

JANE   [after a moment's pause]   Perhaps I can understand you now. The time we picked for you was not really one for seeing us at our best.

OLUNDE   Don't think it was just the war. Before that even started I had plenty of time to study your people. I saw nothing, finally, that gave you the right to pass judgement on other peoples and their ways. Nothing at all.

JANE   [hesitantly]   Was it the . . . colour thing? I know there is some discrimination.

OLUNDE   Don't make it so simple, Mrs Pilkings. You make it sound as if when I left, I took nothing at all with me.

JANE   Yes . . . and to tell the truth, only this evening, Simon and I agreed that we never really knew what you left with.

OLUNDE   Neither did I. But I found out over there. I am grateful to your country for that. And I will never give it up.

JANE   Olunde please . . . promise me something. Whatever you do, don't throw away what you have started to do. You want to be a doctor. My husband and I believe you will make an excellent one, sympathetic and competent. Don't let anything make you throw away your training.

OLUNDE   [genuinely surprised]   Of course not. What a strange idea.

---

8. Tapes of news and features shown in movie houses before the main features. This was common before the age of television and prominent during World War II.

I intend to return and complete my training. Once the burial of my father is over.

JANE   Oh, please . . . !

OLUNDE   Listen! Come outside. You can't hear anything against that music.

JANE   What is it?

OLUNDE   The drums. Can you hear the changes? Listen.

[*The drums come over, still distant but more distinct. There is a change of rhythm, it rises to a crescendo and then, suddenly, it is cut off. After a silence, a new beat begins, slow and resonant.*]

There, it's all over.

JANE   You mean he's . . .

OLUNDE   Yes, Mrs Pilkings, my father is dead. His will-power has always been enormous; I know he is dead.

JANE   [*screams*]   How can you be so callous! So unfeeling! You announce your father's own death like a surgeon looking down on some strange . . . stranger's body! You're just a savage like all the rest.

AIDE-DE-CAMP   [*rushing out*]   Mrs Pilkings. Mrs Pilkings. [*She breaks down, sobbing.*] Are you all right, Mrs Pilkings?

OLUNDE   She'll be all right. [*Turns to go.*]

AIDE-DE-CAMP   Who are you? And who the hell asked your opinion?

OLUNDE   You're quite right, nobody. [*Going.*]

AIDE-DE-CAMP   What the hell! Did you hear me ask you who you were?

OLUNDE   I have business to attend to.

AIDE-DE-CAMP   I'll give you business in a moment you impudent nigger. Answer my question!

OLUNDE   I have a funeral to arrange. Excuse me. [*Going.*]

AIDE-DE-CAMP   I said stop! Orderly!

JANE   No, no, don't do that. I'm alright. And for heaven's sake don't act so foolishly. He's a family friend.

AIDE-DE-CAMP   Well he'd better learn to answer civil questions when he's asked them. These natives put a suit on and they get high opinions of themselves.

OLUNDE   Can I go now?

JANE   No no don't go. I must talk to you. I'm sorry about what I said.

OLUNDE   It's nothing, Mrs Pilkings. And I'm really anxious to go. I couldn't see my father before, it's forbidden for me, his heir and successor, to set eyes on him from the moment of the king's death. But now . . . I would like to touch his body while it is still warm.

JANE   You will. I promise I shan't keep you long. Only, I couldn't possibly let you go like that. Bob, please excuse us.

AIDE-DE-CAMP   If you're sure . . .

JANE   Of course I'm sure. Something happened to upset me just then, but I'm alright now. Really.

[*The* AIDE-DE-CAMP *goes, somewhat reluctantly.*]

OLUNDE   I mustn't stay long.

JANE   Please, I promise not to keep you. It's just that . . . oh you saw yourself what happens to one in this place. The Resident's man thought he was being helpful, that's the way we all react. But I can't go in among that crowd just now and if I stay by myself somebody will come looking for me. Please, just say something for a few moments and then you can go. Just so I can recover myself.

OLUNDE   What do you want me to say?

JANE   Your calm acceptance for instance, can you explain that? It was so unnatural. I don't understand that at all. I feel a need to understand all I can.

OLUNDE   But you explained it yourself. My medical training perhaps. I have seen death too often. And the soldiers who returned from the front, they died on our hands all the time.

JANE   No. It has to be more than that. I feel it has to do with the many things we don't really grasp about your people. At least you can explain.

OLUNDE   All these things are part of it. And anyway, my father has been dead in my mind for nearly a month. Ever since I learnt of the King's death. I've lived with my bereavement so long now that I cannot think of him alive. On that journey on the boat, I kept my mind on my duties as the one who must perform the rites over his body. I went through it all again and again in my mind as he himself had taught me. I didn't want to do anything wrong, something which might jeopardise the welfare of my people.

JANE   But he had disowned you. When you left he swore publicly you were no longer his son.

OLUNDE   I told you, he was a man of tremendous will. Sometimes that's another way of saying stubborn. But among our people, you don't disown a child just like that. Even if I had died before him I would still be buried like his eldest son. But it's time for me to go.

JANE   Thank you. I feel calmer. Don't let me keep you from your duties.

OLUNDE   Goodnight, Mrs Pilkings.

JANE Welcome home. [*She holds out her hand. As he takes it foot-steps are heard approaching the drive. A short while later a woman's sobbing is also heard.*]

PILKINGS [*off*] Keep them here till I get back. [*He strides into view, reacts at the sight of* OLUNDE *but turns to his wife.*] Thank goodness you're still here.

JANE Simon, what happened?

PILKINGS Later Jane, please. Is Bob still here?

JANE Yes, I think so. I'm sure he must be.

PILKINGS Try and get him out here as quickly as you can. Tell him it's urgent.

JANE Of course. Oh Simon, you remember . . .

PILKINGS Yes yes. I can see who it is. Get Bob out here. [*She runs off.*] At first I thought I was seeing a ghost.

OLUNDE Mr Pilkings, I appreciate what you tried to do. I want you to believe that. I can tell you it would have been a terrible calamity if you'd succeeded.

PILKINGS [*opens his mouth several times, shuts it*] You . . . said what?

OLUNDE A calamity for us, the entire people.

PILKINGS [*sighs*] I see. Hm.

OLUNDE And now I must go. I must see him before he turns cold.

PILKINGS Oh ah . . . em . . . but this is a shock to see you. I mean er thinking all this while you were in England and thanking God for that.

OLUNDE I came on the mail boat. We travelled in the Prince's convoy.

PILKINGS Ah yes, a-ah, hm . . . er well . . .

OLUNDE Goodnight. I can see you are shocked by the whole business. But you must know by now there are things you cannot understand—or help.

PILKINGS Yes. Just a minute. There are armed policemen that way and they have instructions to let no one pass. I suggest you wait a little. I'll er . . . give you an escort.

OLUNDE That's very kind of you. But do you think it could be quickly arranged?

PILKINGS Of course. In fact, yes, what I'll do is send Bob over with some men to the er . . . place. You can go with them. Here he comes now. Excuse me a minute.

AIDE-DE-CAMP Anything wrong sir?

PILKINGS [*takes him to one side*] Listen Bob, that cellar in the disused annexe of the Residency, you know, where the slaves were stored before being taken down to the coast . . .[9]

9. The Atlantic coast of west Africa was at one time known as the slave coast.

AIDE-DE-CAMP   Oh yes, we use it as a storeroom for broken furniture.

PILKINGS   But it's still got the bars on it?

AIDE-DE-CAMP   Oh yes, they are quite intact.

PILKINGS   Get the keys please. I'll explain later. And I want a strong guard over the Residency tonight.

AIDE-DE-CAMP   We have that already. The detachment from the coast . . .

PILKINGS   No, I don't want them at the gates of the Residency. I want you to deploy them at the bottom of the hill, a long way from the main hall so they can deal with any situation long before the sound carries to the house.

AIDE-DE-CAMP   Yes of course.

PILKINGS   I don't want His Highness alarmed.

AIDE-DE-CAMP   You think the riot will spread here?

PILKINGS   It's unlikely but I don't want to take a chance. I made them believe I was going to lock the man up in my house, which was what I had planned to do in the first place. They are probably assailing it by now. I took a roundabout route here so I don't think there is any danger at all. At least not before dawn. Nobody is to leave the premises of course—the native employees I mean. They'll soon smell something is up and they can't keep their mouths shut.

AIDE-DE-CAMP   I'll give instructions at once.

PILKINGS   I'll take the prisoner down myself. Two policemen will stay with him throughout the night. Inside the cell.

AIDE-DE-CAMP   Right sir. [*Salutes and goes off at the double.*]

PILKINGS   Jane. Bob is coming back in a moment with a detachment. Until he gets back please stay with Olunde. [*He makes an extra warning gesture with his eyes.*]

OLUNDE   Please, Mr Pilkings . . .

PILKINGS   I hate to be stuffy old son, but we have a crisis on our hands. It has to do with your father's affair if you must know. And it happens also at a time when we have His Highness here. I am responsible for security so you'll simply have to do as I say. I hope that's understood. [*Marches off quickly, in the direction from which he made his first appearance.*]

OLUNDE   What's going on? All this can't be just because he failed to stop my father killing himself.

JANE   I honestly don't know. Could it have sparked off a riot?

OLUNDE   No. If he'd succeeded that would be more likely to start the riot. Perhaps there were other factors involved. Was there a chieftancy dispute?

JANE   None that I know of.

ELESIN [*an animal bellow*[1] *from off*] Leave me alone! Is it not enough that you have covered me in shame! White man, take your hand from my body!

[OLUNDE *stands frozen to the spot.* JANE, *understanding at last, tries to move him.*]

JANE   Let's go in. It's getting chilly out here.

PILKINGS [*off*]   Carry him.

ELESIN   Give me back the name you have taken away from me you ghost from the land of the nameless!

PILKINGS   Carry him! I can't have a disturbance here. Quickly! stuff up his mouth.

JANE   Oh God! Let's go in. Please Olunde. [OLUNDE *does not move.*]

ELESIN   Take your albino's[2] hand from me you . . .

[*Sounds of a struggle. His voice chokes as he is gagged.*]

OLUNDE [*quietly*]   That was my father's voice.

JANE   Oh you poor orphan, what have you come home to?

[*There is a sudden explosion of rage from off-stage and powerful steps come running up the drive.*]

PILKINGS   You bloody fools, after him!

[*Immediately* ELESIN, *in handcuffs, comes pounding in the direction of* JANE *and* OLUNDE, *followed some moments afterwards by* PILKINGS *and the* CONSTABLES. ELESIN, *confronted by the seeming statue of his son, stops dead.* OLUNDE *stares above his head into the distance. The* CONSTABLES *try to grab him.* JANE *screams at them.*]

JANE   Leave him alone! Simon, tell them to leave him alone.

PILKINGS   All right, stand aside you. [*Shrugs.*] Maybe just as well. It might help to calm him down.

[*For several moments they hold the same position.* ELESIN *moves a step forward, almost as if he's still in doubt.*]

ELESIN   Olunde? [*He moves his head, inspecting him from side to side.*] Olunde! [*He collapses slowly at* OLUNDE's *feet.*] Oh son, don't let the sight of your father turn you blind!

---

1. A loud, hollow sound usually associated with animals, especially cows; in some cases, it was considered to be a feature of the language of *egungun* and other masked figures.
2. An albino is a person born without pigmentation; *albino* a term of abuse when used in reference to a white person.

OLUNDE [*he moves for the first time since he heard his voice, brings his head slowly down to look on him*]   I have no father, eater of left-overs.

[*He walks slowly down the way his father had run. Light fades out on* ELESIN, *sobbing into the ground.*]

5

A wide iron-barred gate stretches almost the whole width of the cell in which ELESIN *is imprisoned. His wrists are encased in thick iron bracelets, chained together; he stands against the bars, looking out. Seated on the ground to one side on the outside is his recent bride, her eyes bent perpetually to the ground. Figures of the two* GUARDS *can be seen deeper inside the cell, alert to every movement* ELESIN *makes.* PILKINGS *now in a police officer's uniform, enters noiselessly, observes him a while. Then he coughs ostentatiously and approaches. Leans against the bars near a corner, his back to* ELESIN. *He is obviously trying to fall in mood with him. Some moments' silence.*

PILKINGS   You seem fascinated by the moon.
ELESIN [*after a pause*]   Yes, ghostly one. Your twin-brother up there engages my thoughts.
PILKINGS   It is a beautiful night.
ELESIN   Is that so?
PILKINGS   The light on the leaves, the peace of the night . . .
ELESIN   The night is not at peace, District Officer.
PILKINGS   No? I would have said it was. You know, quiet . . .
ELESIN   And does quiet mean peace for you?
PILKINGS   Well, nearly the same thing. Naturally there is a subtle difference . . .
ELESIN   The night is not at peace, ghostly one. The world is not at peace. You have shattered the peace of the world for ever. There is no sleep in the world tonight.
PILKINGS   It is still a good bargain if the world should lose one night's sleep as the price of saving a man's life.
ELESIN   You did not save my life, District Officer. You destroyed it.
PILKINGS   Now come on . . .
ELESIN   And not merely my life but the lives of many. The end of the night's work is not over. Neither this year nor the next will see it. If I wished you well, I would pray that you do not stay long enough on our land to see the disaster you have brought upon us.

PILKINGS   Well, I did my duty as I saw it. I have no regrets.

ELESIN   No. The regrets of life always come later.

[*Some moments' pause.*]

You are waiting for dawn white man. I hear you saying to yourself: only so many hours until dawn and then the danger is over. All I must do is to keep him alive tonight. You don't quite understand it all but you know that tonight is when what ought to be must be brought about. I shall ease your mind even more, ghostly one. It is not an entire night but a moment of the night, and that moment is past. The moon was my messenger and guide. When it reached a certain gateway in the sky, it touched that moment for which my whole life has been spent in blessings. Even I do not know the gateway. I have stood here and scanned the sky for a glimpse of that door but, I cannot see it. Human eyes are useless for a search of this nature. But in the house of *osugbo*, those who keep watch through the spirit recognised the moment, they sent word to me through the voice of our sacred drums to prepare myself. I heard them and I shed all thoughts of earth. I began to follow the moon to the abode of the gods . . . servant of the white king, that was when you entered my chosen place of departure on feet of desecration.

PILKINGS   I'm sorry, but we all see our duty differently.

ELESIN   I no longer blame you. You stole from me my first-born, sent him to your country so you could turn him into something in your own image. Did you plan it all beforehand? There are moments when it seems part of a larger plan. He who must follow my footsteps is taken from me, sent across the ocean. Then, in my turn, I am stopped from fulfilling my destiny. Did you think it all out before, this plan to push our world from its course and sever the cord that links us to the great origin?

PILKINGS   You don't really believe that. Anyway, if that was my intention with your son, I appear to have failed.

ELESIN   You did not fail in the main thing ghostly one. We know the roof covers the rafters,[1] the cloth covers blemishes; who would have known that the white skin covered our future, preventing us from seeing the death our enemies had prepared for us. The world is set adrift and its inhabitants are lost. Around them, there is nothing but emptiness.

PILKINGS   Your son does not take so gloomy a view.

ELESIN   Are you dreaming now, white man? Were you not present at the reunion of shame? Did you not see when the world reversed itself and the father fell before his son, asking forgiveness?

---

1. Timbers supporting the roof of a house.

PILKINGS That was in the heat of the moment. I spoke to him and
. . . if you want to know, he wishes he could cut out his tongue
for uttering the words he did.

ELESIN No. What he said must never be unsaid. The contempt of
my own son rescued something of my shame at your hands. You
have stopped me in my duty but I know now that I did give birth
to a son. Once I mistrusted him for seeking the companionship
of those my spirit knew as enemies of our race. Now I understand. One should seek to obtain the secrets of his enemies. He
will avenge my shame, white one. His spirit will destroy you and
yours.

PILKINGS That kind of talk is hardly called for. If you don't want
my consolation . . .

ELESIN No white man, I do not want your consolation.

PILKINGS As you wish. Your son, anyway, sends his consolation.
He asks your forgiveness. When I asked him not to despise you
his reply was: I cannot judge him, and if I cannot judge him, I
cannot despise him. He wants to come to you and say goodbye
and to receive your blessing.

ELESIN Goodbye? Is he returning to your land?

PILKINGS Don't you think that's the most sensible thing for him to
do? I advised him to leave at once, before dawn, and he agrees
that is the right course of action.

ELESIN Yes, it is best. And even if I did not think so, I have lost
the father's place of honour. My voice is broken.

PILKINGS Your son honours you. If he didn't he would not ask your
blessing.

ELESIN No. Even a thoroughbred is not without pity for the turf
he strikes with his hoof. When is he coming?

PILKINGS As soon as the town is a little quieter. I advised it.

ELESIN Yes white man, I am sure you advised it. You advise all our
lives although on the authority of what gods, I do not know.

PILKINGS [opens his mouth to reply, then appears to change his mind.
Turns to go. Hesitates and stops again] Before I leave you, may
I ask just one thing of you?

ELESIN I am listening.

PILKINGS I wish to ask you to search the quiet of your heart and
tell me—do you not find great contradictions in the wisdom of
your own race?

ELESIN Make yourself clear, white one.

PILKINGS I have lived among you long enough to learn a saying or
two. One came to my mind tonight when I stepped into the market and saw what was going on. You were surrounded by those
who egged you on with song and praises. I thought, are these not
the same people who say: the elder grimly approaches heaven

and you ask him to bear your greetings yonder; do you really think he makes the journey willingly? After that, I did not hesitate.

[*A pause.* ELESIN *sighs. Before he can speak a sound of running feet is heard.*]

JANE [*off*] Simon! Simon!
PILKINGS What on earth . . . ! [*Runs off.*]

[ELESIN *turns to his new wife, gazes on her for some moments.*]

ELESIN My young bride, did you hear the ghostly one? You sit and sob in your silent heart but say nothing to all this. First I blamed the white man, then I blamed my gods for deserting me. Now I feel I want to blame you for the mystery of the sapping of my will. But blame is a strange peace offering for a man to bring a world he has deeply wronged, and to its innocent dwellers. Oh little mother, I have taken countless women in my life but you were more than a desire of the flesh. I needed you as the abyss across which my body must be drawn, I filled it with earth and dropped my seed in it at the moment of preparedness for my crossing. You were the final gift of the living to their emissary to the land of the ancestors, and perhaps your warmth and youth brought new insights of this world to me and turned my feet leaden on this side of the abyss. For I confess to you, daughter, my weakness came not merely from the abomination of the white man who came violently into my fading presence, there was also a weight of longing on my earth-held limbs. I would have shaken it off, already my foot had begun to lift but then, the white ghost entered and all was defiled.

[*Approaching voices of* PILKINGS *and his wife.*]

JANE Oh Simon, you will let her in won't you?
PILKINGS I really wish you'd stop interfering.

[*They come into view.* JANE *is in a dressing-gown.* PILKINGS *is holding a note to which he refers from time to time.*]

JANE Good gracious, I didn't initiate this. I was sleeping quietly, or trying to anyway, when the servant brought it. It's not my fault if one can't sleep undisturbed even in the Residency.
PILKINGS He'd have done the same thing if we were sleeping at home so don't sidetrack the issue. He knows he can get round you or he wouldn't send you the petition in the first place.
JANE Be fair Simon. After all he was thinking of your own interests. He is grateful you know, you seem to forget that. He feels he owes you something.
PILKINGS I just wish they'd leave this man alone tonight, that's all.

JANE   Trust him Simon. He's pledged his word it will all go peace-fully.

PILKINGS   Yes, and that's the other thing. I don't like being threat-ened.

JANE   Threatened? [*Takes the note.*] I didn't spot any threat.

PILKINGS   It's there. Veiled, but it's there. The only way to prevent serious rioting tomorrow—what a cheek!

JANE   I don't think he's threatening you Simon.

PILKINGS   He's picked up the idiom alright. Wouldn't surprise me if he's been mixing with commies or anarchists over there. The phrasing sounds too good to be true. Damn! If only the Prince hadn't picked this time for his visit.

JANE   Well, even so Simon, what have you got to lose? You don't want a riot on your hands, not with the Prince here.

PILKINGS   [*going up to* ELESIN]   Let's see what he has to say. Chief Elesin, there is yet another person who wants to see you. As she is not a next-of-kin I don't really feel obliged to let her in. But your son sent a note with her, so it's up to you.

ELESIN   I know who that must be. So she found out your hiding-place. Well, it was not difficult. My stench of shame is so strong, it requires no hunter's dog to follow it.

PILKINGS   If you don't want to see her, just say so and I'll send her packing.

ELESIN   Why should I not want to see her? Let her come. I have no more holes in my rag of shame. All is laid bare.

PILKINGS   I'll bring her in. [*Goes off.*]

JANE   [*hesitates, then goes to* ELESIN]   Please, try and understand. Everything my husband did was for the best.

ELESIN   [*he gives her a long strange stare, as if he is trying to under-stand who she is*]   You are the wife of the District Officer?

JANE   Yes. My name, is Jane.

ELESIN   That is my wife sitting down there. You notice how still and silent she sits? My business is with your husband.

[PILKINGS *returns with* IYALOJA.]

PILKINGS   Here she is. Now first I want your word of honour that you will try nothing foolish.

ELESIN   Honour? White one, did you say you wanted my word of honour?

PILKINGS   I know you to be an honourable man. Give me your word of honour you will receive nothing from her.

ELESIN   But I am sure you have searched her clothing as you would never dare touch your own mother. And there are these two liz-ards of yours who roll their eyes even when I scratch.

PILKINGS   And I shall be sitting on that tree trunk watching even how you blink. Just the same I want your word that you will not let her pass anything to you.

ELESIN You have my honour already. It is locked up in that desk in which you will put away your report of this night's events. Even the honour of my people you have taken already; it is tied together with those papers of treachery which make you masters in this land.

PILKINGS Alright. I am trying to make things easy but if you must bring in politics we'll have to do it the hard way. Madam, I want you to remain along this line and move no nearer to the cell door. Guards! [*They spring to attention.*] If she moves beyond this point, blow your whistle. Come on Jane. [*They go off.*]

IYALOJA How boldly the lizard struts before the pigeon when it was the eagle itself he promised us he would confront.

ELESIN I don't ask you to take pity on me Iyaloja. You have a message for me or you would not have come. Even if it is the curses of the world, I shall listen.

IYALOJA You made so bold with the servant of the white king who took your side against death. I must tell your brother chiefs when I return how bravely you waged war against him. Especially with words.

ELESIN I more than deserve your scorn.

IYALOJA [*with sudden anger*] I warned you, if you must leave a seed behind, be sure it is not tainted with the curses of the world. Who are you to open a new life when you dared not open the door to a new existence? I say who are you to make so bold? [*The* BRIDE *sobs and* IYALOJA *notices her. Her contempt noticeably increases as she turns back to* ELESIN.] Oh you self-vaunted[2] stem of the plantain, how hollow it all proves. The pith[3] is gone in the parent stem, so how will it prove with the new shoot?[4] How will it go with that earth that bears it? Who are you to bring this abomination on us!

ELESIN My powers deserted me. My charms, my spells, even my voice lacked strength when I made to summon the powers that would lead me over the last measure of earth into the land of the fleshless. You saw it, Iyaloja. You saw me struggle to retrieve my will from the power of the stranger whose shadow fell across the doorway and left me floundering and blundering in a maze I had never before encountered. My senses were numbed when the touch of cold iron[5] came upon my wrists. I could do nothing to save myself.

---

2. Excessively self-praising, vain.
3. The inner part of a plant, its fiber or core.
4. The young plant that grows directly from the parent, not from a seed.
5. A reference to a very sharp knife or razor.

IYALOJA   You have betrayed us. We fed you sweetmeats[6] such as we
  hoped awaited you on the other side. But you said No, I must
  eat the world's left-overs. We said you were the hunter who
  brought the quarry down; to you belonged the vital portions of
  the game. No, you said, I am the hunter's dog and I shall eat the
  entrails of the game and the faeces of the hunter. We said you
  were the hunter returning home in triumph, a slain buffalo pressing down on his neck; you said wait, I first must turn up this
  cricket hole with my toes. We said yours was the doorway at
  which we first spy the tapper when he comes down from the tree,
  yours was the blessing of the twilight wine,[7] the purl that brings
  night spirits out of doors to steal their portion before the light of
  day. We said yours was the body of wine whose burden shakes
  the tapper like a sudden gust on his perch. You said, No, I am
  content to lick the dregs[8] from each calabash when the drinkers
  are done. We said, the dew on earth's surface was for you to
  wash your feet along the slopes of honour. You said No, I shall
  step in the vomit of cats and the droppings of mice; I shall fight
  them for the left-overs of the world.
ELESIN   Enough Iyaloja, enough.
IYALOJA   We called you leader and oh, how you led us on. What
  we have no intention of eating should not be held to the nose.
ELESIN   Enough, enough. My shame is heavy enough.
IYALOJA   Wait. I came with a burden.
ELESIN   You have more than discharged it.
IYALOJA   I wish I could pity you.
ELESIN   I need neither your pity nor the pity of the world. I need
  understanding. Even I need to understand. You were present at
  my defeat. You were part of the beginnings. You brought about
  the renewal of my tie to earth, you helped in the binding of the
  cord.
IYALOJA   I gave you warning. The river which fills up before our
  eyes does not sweep us away in its flood.
ELESIN   What were warnings beside the moist contact of living
  earth between my fingers? What were warnings beside the renewal of famished embers lodged eternally in the heart of man.
  But even that, even if it overwhelmed one with a thousandfold
  temptations to linger a little while, a man could overcome it. It
  is when the alien hand pollutes the source of will,[9] when a
  stranger force of violence shatters the mind's calm resolution,
  this is when a man is made to commit the awful treachery of

6. Sweet delicacies made with sugar or honey; pastries or candies.
7. Palm wine tapped before dawn is considered fresh and potent.
8. The sediment of leftover liquids; hence, considered impure.
9. In Yoruba cosmology, will is the life source that makes everything happen.

relief, commit in his thought the unspeakable blasphemy of seeing the hand of the gods in this alien rupture of his world. I know it was this thought that killed me, sapped my powers and turned me into an infant in the hands of unnamable strangers. I made to utter my spells anew but my tongue merely rattled in my mouth. I fingered hidden charms and the contact was damp; there was no spark left to sever the life-strings that should stretch from every finger-tip. My will was squelched in the spittle of an alien race, and all because I had committed this blasphemy of thought—that there might be the hand of the gods in a stranger's intervention.

IYALOJA Explain it how you will, I hope it brings you peace of mind. The bush-rat fled his rightful cause, reached the market and set up a lamentation. 'Please save me!'—are these fitting words to hear from an ancestral mask? 'There's a wild beast at my heels' is not becoming language from a hunter.

ELESIN May the world forgive me.

IYALOJA I came with a burden I said. It approaches the gates which are so well guarded by those jackals whose spittle will from this day be on your food and drink. But first, tell me, you who were once Elesin Oba, tell me, you who know so well the cycle of the plantain: is it the parent shoot which withers to give sap[1] to the younger or, does your wisdom see it running the other way?

ELESIN I don't see your meaning Iyaloja?

IYALOJA Did I ask you for a meaning? I asked a question. Whose trunk withers to give sap to the other? The parent shoot or the younger?

ELESIN The parent.

IYALOJA Ah. So you do know that. There are sights in this world which say different Elesin. There are some who choose to reverse the cycle of our being. Oh, you emptied bark[2] that the world once saluted for a pith-laden being, shall I tell you what the gods have claimed of you?

> [*In her agitation she steps beyond the line indicated by* PILK-INGS *and the air is rent by piercing whistles. The two* GUARDS *also leap forward and place safe-guarding hands on* ELESIN. IYALOJA *stops, astonished.* PILKINGS *comes racing in, followed by* JANE.]

PILKINGS What is it? Did they try something?

GUARD She stepped beyond the line.

ELESIN [*in a broken voice*] Let her alone. She meant no harm.

---

1. The vital liquid or juice circulating in a tree or plant, the equivalent of blood.
2. The external covering or skin of a tree.

IYALOJA   Oh Elesin, see what you've become. Once you had no need to open your mouth in explanation because evil-smelling goats, itchy of hand and foot, had lost their senses. And it was a brave man indeed who dared lay hands on you because Iyaloja stepped from one side of the earth onto another. Now look at the spectacle of your life. I grieve for you.

PILKINGS   I think you'd better leave. I doubt you have done him much good by coming here. I shall make sure you are not allowed to see him again. In any case we are moving him to a different place before dawn, so don't bother to come back.

IYALOJA   We foresaw that. Hence the burden I trudged here to lay beside your gates.

PILKINGS   What was that you said?

IYALOJA   Didn't our son explain? Ask that one. He knows what it is. At least we hope the man we once knew as Elesin remembers the lesser oaths he need not break.

PILKINGS   Do you know what she is talking about?

ELESIN   Go to the gates, ghostly one. Whatever you find there, bring it to me.

IYALOJA   Not yet. It drags behind me on the slow, weary feet of women. Slow as it is Elesin, it has long overtaken you. It rides ahead of your laggard[3] will.

PILKINGS   What is she saying now? Christ! Must your people forever speak in riddles?

ELESIN   It will come white man, it will come. Tell your men at the gates to let it through.

PILKINGS   [*dubiously*]   I'll have to see what it is.

IYALOJA   You will. [*Passionately.*] But this is one oath he cannot shirk. White one, you have a king here, a visitor from your land. We know of his presence here. Tell me, were he to die would you leave his spirit roaming restlessly on the surface of earth? Would you bury him here among those you consider less than human? In your land have you no ceremonies of the dead?

PILKINGS   Yes. But we don't make our chiefs commit suicide to keep him company.

IYALOJA   Child, I have not come to help your understanding. [*Points to* ELESIN.] This is the man whose weakened understanding holds us in bondage to you. But ask him if you wish. He knows the meaning of a king's passage; he was not born yesterday. He knows the peril to the race when our dead father, who goes as intermediary, waits and waits and knows he is betrayed. He knows when the narrow gate was opened and he knows it will not stay for laggards who drag their feet in dung and vomit, whose lips

---

3. Slow, sluggish, spent.

are reeking of the left-overs of lesser men. He knows he has condemned our King to wander in the void of evil with beings who are enemies of life.

PILKINGS Yes er . . . but look here . . .

IYALOJA What we ask is little enough. Let him release our King so he can ride on homewards alone. The messenger is on his way on the backs of women. Let him send word through the heart that is folded up within the bolt. It is the least of all his oaths, it is the easiest fulfilled.

[*The* AIDE-DE-CAMP *runs in.*]

PILKINGS Bob?

AIDE-DE-CAMP Sir, there's a group of women chanting up the hill.

PILKINGS [*rounding on* IYALOJA] If you people want trouble . . .

JANE Simon, I think that's what Olunde referred to in his letter.

PILKINGS He knows damned well I can't have a crowd here! Damn it, I explained the delicacy of my position to him. I think it's about time I got him out of town. Bob, send a car and two or three soldiers to bring him in. I think the sooner he takes his leave of his father and gets out the better.

IYALOJA Save your labour white one. If it is the father of your prisoner you want, Olunde, he who until this night we knew as Elesin's son, he comes soon himself to take his leave. He has sent the women ahead, so let them in.

[PILKINGS *remains undecided.*]

AIDE-DE-CAMP What do we do about the invasion? We can still stop them far from here.

PILKINGS What do they look like?

AIDE-DE-CAMP They're not many. And they seem quite peaceful.

PILKINGS No men?

AIDE-DE-CAMP Mm, two or three at the most.

JANE Honestly, Simon, I'd trust Olunde. I don't think he'll deceive you about their intentions.

PILKINGS He'd better not. Alright then, let them in Bob. Warn them to control themselves. Then hurry Olunde here. Make sure he brings his baggage because I'm not returning him into town.

AIDE-DE-CAMP Very good, sir. [*Goes.*]

PILKINGS [*to* IYALOJA] I hope you understand that if anything goes wrong it will be on your head. My men have orders to shoot at the first sign of trouble.

IYALOJA To prevent one death you will actually make other deaths? Ah, great is the wisdom of the white race. But have no fear. Your Prince will sleep peacefully. So at long last so ours. We will disturb you no further, servant of the white King. Just let Elesin fulfil his oath and we will retire home and pay homage to our King.

JANE   I believe her Simon, don't you?

PILKINGS   Maybe.

ELESIN   Have no fear ghostly one. I have a message to send my King and then you have nothing more to fear.

IYALOJA   Olunde would have done it. The chiefs asked him to speak the words but he said no, not while you lived.

ELESIN   Even from the depths to which my spirit has sunk, I find some joy that this little has been left to me.

> [*The* WOMEN *enter, intoning the dirge 'Alę lę lę' and swaying from side to side. On their shoulders is borne a longish object roughly like a cylindrical bolt, covered in cloth. They set it down on the spot where* IYALOJA *had stood earlier, and form a semi-circle round it. The* PRAISE-SINGER *and* DRUMMER *stand on the inside of the semi-circle but the drum is not used at all. The* DRUMMER *intones under the* PRAISE-SINGER's *invocations.*]

PILKINGS [*as they enter*]   What is *that*?

IYALOJA   The burden you have made white one, but we bring it in peace.

PILKINGS   I said *what* is it?

ELESIN   White man, you must let me out. I have a duty to perform.

PILKINGS   I most certainly will not.

ELESIN   There lies the courier of my King. Let me out so I can perform what is demanded of me.

PILKINGS   You'll do what you need to do from inside there or not at all. I've gone as far as I intend to with this business.

ELESIN   The worshipper who lights a candle in your church to bear a message to his god bows his head and speaks in a whisper to the flame. Have I not seen it ghostly one? His voice does not ring out to the world. Mine are no words for anyone's ears. They are not words even for the bearers of this load. They are words I must speak secretly, even as my father whispered them in my ears and I in the ears of my first-born. I cannot shout them to the wind and the open night-sky.

JANE   Simon . . .

PILKINGS   Don't interfere. Please!

IYALOJA   They have slain the favourite horse of the King and slain his dog. They have borne them from pulse to pulse centre of the land receiving prayers for their King. But the rider has chosen to stay behind. Is it too much to ask that he speak his heart to heart of the waiting courier? [PILKINGS *turns his back on her.*] So be it,

Elesin Oba, you see how even the mere leavings[4] are denied you.
[*She gestures to the* PRAISE-SINGER.]

PRAISE-SINGER   Elesin Oba! I call you by that name only this last
time. Remember when I said, if you cannot come, tell my horse.
[*Pause.*] What? I cannot hear you? I said, if you cannot come,
whisper in the ears of my horse. Is your tongue severed from the
roots Elesin? I can hear no response. I said, if there are boulders
you cannot climb, mount my horse's back, this spotless black
stallion, he'll bring you over them. [*Pauses.*] Elesin Oba, once you
had a tongue that darted like a drummer's stick. I said, if you get
lost my dog will track a path to me. My memory fails me but I
think you replied: My feet have found the path, Alafin.

[*The dirge rises and falls.*]

I said at the last, if evil hands hold you back, just tell my horse
there is weight on the hem of your smock. I dare not wait too
long.

[*The dirge rises and falls.*]

There lies the swiftest ever messenger of a king, so set me free
with the errand of your heart. There lie the head and heart of
the favourite of the gods, whisper in his ears. Oh my companion,
if you had followed when you should, we would not say that the
horse preceded its rider. If you had followed when it was time,
we would not say the dog has raced beyond and left his master
behind. If you had raised your will to cut the thread of life at the
summons of the drums, we would not say your mere shadow fell
across the gateway and took its owner's place at the banquet. But
the hunter, laden with slain buffalo, stayed to root in the cricket's
hole with his toes. What now is left? If there is a dearth of bats,
the pigeon must serve us for the offering. Speak the words over
your shadow which must now serve in your place.

ELESIN   I cannot approach. Take off the cloth. I shall speak my
message from heart to heart of silence.

IYALOJA [*moves forward and removes the covering*]   Your courier Elesin, cast your eyes on the favoured companion of the King.

[*Rolled up in the mat, his head and feet showing at either end,
is the body of* OLUNDE.]

There lies the honour of your household and of our race. Because
he could not bear to let honour fly out of doors, he stopped it

---

4. Remains or leftovers, usually of food.

with his life. The son has proved the father, Elesin, and there is nothing left in your mouth to gnash but infant gums.

PRAISE-SINGER　Elesin, we placed the reins of the world in your hands yet you watched it plunge over the edge of the bitter precipice. You sat with folded arms while evil strangers tilted the world from its course and crashed it beyond the edge of emptiness—you muttered, there is little that one man can do, you left us floundering in a blind future. Your heir has taken the burden on himself. What the end will be, we are not gods to tell. But this young shoot has poured its sap into the parent stalk, and we know this is not the way of life. Our world is tumbling in the void of strangers, Elesin.

> [ELESIN *has stood rock-still, his knuckles taut on the bars, his eyes glued to the body of his son. The stillness seizes and paralyses everyone, including* PILKINGS *who has turned to look. Suddenly* ELESIN *flings one arm round his neck, once, and with the loop of the chain, strangles himself in a swift, decisive pull. The* GUARDS *rush forward to stop him but they are only in time to let his body down.* PILKINGS *has leapt to the door at the same time and struggles with the lock. He rushes within, fumbles with the handcuffs and unlocks them, raises the body to a sitting position while he tries to give resuscitation. The* WOMEN *continue their dirge, unmoved by the sudden event.*]

IYALOJA　Why do you strain yourself? Why do you labour at tasks for which no one, not even the man lying there, would give you thanks? He is gone at last into the passage but oh, how late it all is. His son will feast on the meat and throw him bones. The passage is clogged with droppings from the King's stallion; he will arrive all stained in dung.

PILKINGS　[*in a tired voice*]　Was this what you wanted?

IYALOJA　No child, it is what you brought to be, you who play with strangers' lives, who even usurp the vestments of our dead, yet believe that the stain of death will not cling to you. The gods demanded only the old expired plantain but you cut down the sap-laden shoot to feed your pride. There is your board, filled to overflowing. Feast on it. [*She screams at him suddenly, seeing that* PILKINGS *is about to close* ELESIN's *staring eyes.*] Let him alone! However sunk he was in debt he is no pauper's carrion abandoned on the road. Since when have strangers donned clothes of indigo before the bereaved cries out his loss?

> [*She turns to the* BRIDE *who has remained motionless throughout.*]

Child.

[*The girl takes up a little earth, walks calmly into the cell and closes* ELESIN's *eyes. She then pours some earth over each eyelid and comes out again.*]

IYALOJA   Now forget the dead, forget even the living. Turn your mind only to the unborn.

[*She goes off, accompanied by the* BRIDE. *The dirge rises in volume and the* WOMEN *continue their sway. Lights fade to a black-out.*]

THE END

Glossary

alari	a rich, woven cloth, brightly coloured
egungun	ancestral masquerade
etutu	placatory rites or medicine
gbedu	a deep-timbred royal drum
opele	string of beads used in Ifa divination
osugbo	secret 'executive' cult of the Yoruba; its meeting place
robo	a delicacy made from crushed melon seeds, fried in tiny balls
sanyan	a richly valued woven cloth
sigidi	a squat, carved figure, endowed with the powers of an incubus

BACKGROUNDS AND CONTEXTS

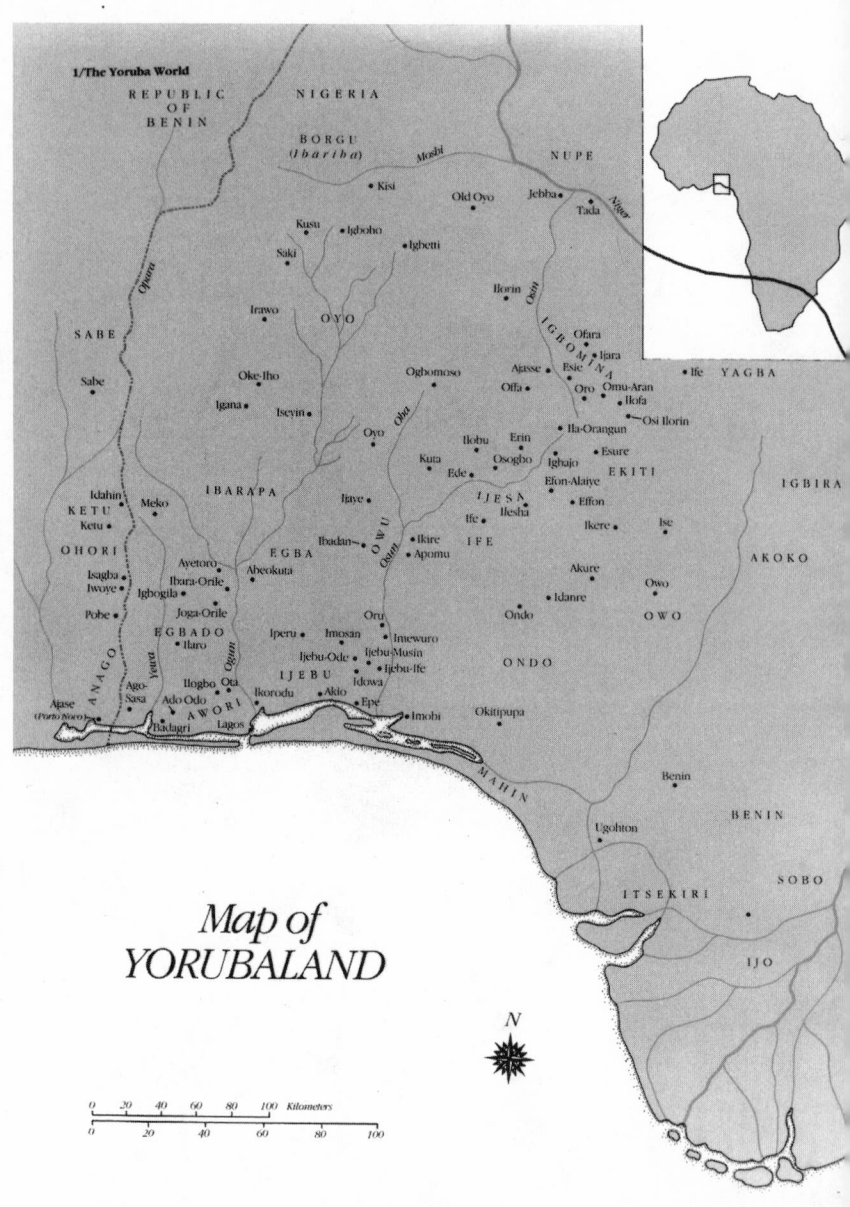

1/The Yoruba World

Map of
YORUBALAND

N

0   20   40   60   80   100 Kilometers
0   20   40   60   80   100

† From Henry John Drewal, John Pemberton III, and Rowland Abiodun, *Yoruba: Nine Centuries of African Art and Thought* (New York: The Center for African Art in association with Harry N. Abrams, 1989).

HENRY JOHN DREWAL, JOHN PEMBERTON III, AND ROWLAND ABIODUN

The Yoruba World†

The Yoruba-speaking peoples of Nigeria and the Popular Republic of Benin, together with their countless descendants in other parts of Africa and the Americas, have made remarkable contributions to world civilization.[1] Their urbanism is ancient and legendary, probably dating to A.D. 800–1000, according to the results of archeological excavations at two ancient city sites, Oyo and Ife.[2] These were only two of numerous complex city-states headed by sacred rulers (both women and men) and councils of elders and chiefs. Many have flourished up to our own time. The dynasty of kings at Ife, for example, regarded by the Yoruba as the place of origin of life itself and of human civilization, remains unbroken to the present day.

In the arts, the Yoruba are heirs to one of the oldest and finest artistic traditions in Africa, a tradition that remains vital and influential today. By A.D. 1100 the artists at Ife had already developed an exquisitely refined and highly naturalistic sculptural tradition in terracotta and stone that was soon followed by works in copper, brass and bronze. Large figures portraying an array of social roles have been found in the region of Esie.

Of the series of remarkable Yoruba kingdoms over the last nine centuries, one of the earliest was Oyo, sited near the Niger River, the "Nile" of West Africa. Straddling this important trading corridor Oyo and its feared cavalry flourished between 1600 and 1830 and came to dominate a vast territory that extended northward to Borgu country, eastward to the Edo, westward to the Fon, and southward to the coast at Whydah, Ajase, and Allada. In Allada the presence of the Yoruba divination system known as Ifa was documented in an early divining tray.

Another Yoruba kingdom in the southeast, Owo, maintained

---

† From Henry John Drewal, John Pemberton III, and Rowland Abiodun, *Yoruba: Nine Centuries of African Art and Thought* (New York: The Center for African Art in association with Harry N. Abrams, 1989). Copyright © The Center for African Art. Reprinted by permission of the authors.
1. Throughout this book we use the term Yoruba as shorthand for Yoruba-speaking peoples who historically identified themselves by their independent but interactive city-states, such as Ife, Ijebu, Owo, Ekiti, Oyo, and others. Despite significant cultural diversity, Yoruba-speaking peoples assert their common origins at Ile-Ife and share certain fundamental social, political, religious, philosophical, and artistic concepts that justify the now widely used and accepted designation of Yoruba.
2. See R. S. Smith, *Kingdoms of the Yoruba* (London: Methuen, 1969).

close ties to Ife and also experienced the powerful artistic and cultural influences of Benin between the fifteenth and nineteenth centuries. Both were changed in the process—Owo artists supplying fine ivory work to the court at Benin, and Owo royalty adapting and transforming many Benin titles, institutions, and the regalia of leadership in the process.

The Ijebu Yoruba kingdoms (1400–1900) of the coastal plain were shaped by many of these same factors. These Yoruba became masters of trade along the lagoons, creeks, and rivers as well as masters of bronze casting and cloth weaving. They were the first Yoruba to establish trading ties with Europeans in the late fifteenth century. Over the next four centuries, the Yoruba kingdoms prospered and then declined as the devastating effects of the slave trade and internecine warfare of the nineteenth century took their toll. The stage was set for the ascendancy of the British and the advent of colonial rule at the end of the nineteenth century.

One of the effects of eighteenth- and nineteenth-century disruptions was the dispersal of millions of Yoruba peoples over the globe, primarily to the Americas—Haiti, Cuba, Trinidad, and Brazil— where their late arrival and enormous numbers ensured a strong Yoruba character in the artistic, religious, and social lives of Africans in the New World. That imprint persists today in many arts and in a variety of African-American faiths that have arisen not only in the Caribbean and South America, but also in urban centers across the United States.[3] Yoruba philosophical, religious, and artistic tenets, ideas, and icons have transformed and continue to transform religious beliefs and practices and the arts of persons far beyond Africa's shores.

There are several fundamental concepts that are distinctive to a Yoruba world view. They provide a foundation for comprehending the dynamics of Yoruba art and culture through time and space. Furthermore, these concepts are expressed in words, images, and actions. All three modes of expression contribute to the shaping of Yoruba culture and our understanding of it. Here, we concentrate on concepts conveyed in words and images that seem to permeate a wide variety of forms, media, and contexts. In the Yoruba view, all the arts are closely related and are often meant to be understood and seen as images in the mind's eye. Such mental images (*iran*) are related to *oju inu* (literally "inner eye" or "insight"). Thus, both the words and the forms considered in this chapter embody concepts that are pervasive and enduring markers of Yoruba civilization.

---

3. The African-American religious communities include Lucumi, Candomble, Shango, Santeria, Vodun, Umbanda, and Macumba.

The Yoruba Cosmos

The Yoruba conceive of the cosmos as consisting of two distinct yet inseparable realms—*aye* (the visible, tangible world of the living) and *orun* (the invisible, spiritual realm of the ancestors, gods, and spirits) (Figure [1]). Such a cosmic conception is often visualized as either a spherical gourd, whose upper and lower hemispheres fit tightly together, or as a divination tray with a raised figurated border enclosing a flat central surface. The images clustered around the perimeter of the tray refer to mythic events and persons as well as everyday concerns. They depict a universe populated by countless competing forces. The intersecting lines inscribed on the surface by a diviner at the outset of divination symbolize metaphoric cross-roads, *orita meta* (the point of intersection between the cosmic realms). The manner in which they are drawn (vertical from bottom to top, center to right, center to left) shows them to be three paths—a symbolically significant number. These lines are always drawn by Yoruba priests at the outset of divination to "open" chan-nels of communication before beginning to reveal the forces at work and to interpret their significance for a particular individual, family, group, or community. Thus the Yoruba world view is a circle with intersecting lines.

Such an image also has temporal implications since the Yoruba conceive of the past as accessible and essential as a model for the present. They believe that persons live, depart, and are reborn and that every individual comes from either the gods or one's ancestors on the mother's or the father's side. In addition, rituals are effica-cious only when they are performed regularly according to tenets from the past and creatively re-presented to suit the present.

Orun: The Otherworld

Olodumare (also known as Odumare, Olorun, Eleda, Eleemi) is conceived as the creator of existence, without sexual identity and generally distant, removed from the affairs of both divine and worldly beings. Olodumare is the source of *ase*, the life force pos-sessed by everything that exists. *Orun* (the otherworld), the abode of the sacred, is populated by countless forces such as *orisa* (gods), *ara orun* (ancestors) and *oro, iwin, ajogun,* and *egbe* (various spirits), who are close to the living and frequently involved in human affairs.

The *orisa* are deified ancestors and/or personified natural forces. They are grouped broadly into two categories depending upon their personalities and modes of action—the "cool, temperate, symboli-cally white gods" (*orisa funfun*), and the "hot, temperamental gods"

YORUBA COSMOS

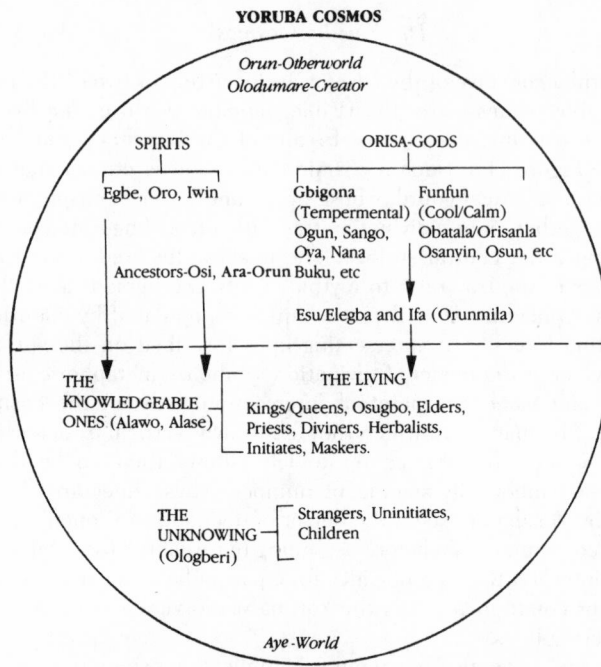

A diagram of some of the key elements of the Yoruba cosmos. It consists of two distinct yet interactive realms—*aye*, the tangible world of the living and *orun*, the invisible realm of spiritual forces such as the gods, ancestors, and spirits. All beings, whether living or spiritual, possess life force, *ase*. Those wise individuals such as priests, initiates, diviners, rulers and elders who learn to use it for the benefit of themselves and those around them are known as *alase* or *alawo*. Drawing by H. J. Drewal.

(*orisa gbigbona*). The former tend to be gentle, soothing, calm, and reflective and include: Obatala/Orisanla, the divine sculptor; Osoosi/Eyinle, hunter and water lord; Osanyin, lord of leaves and medicines; Oduduwa, first monarch at Ile-Ife; Yemoja, Osun, Yewa, and Oba, queens of their respective rivers; Olosa, ruler of the lagoon; and Olokun, goddess of the sea. Many of the "hot gods" are male, although some are female. They include: Ogun, god of Iron; Sango, former king of Oyo and lord of thunder; Obaluaye, lord of pestilence; and Oya, Sango's wife and queen of the whirlwind. The latter tend to be harsh, demanding, aggressive and quick-tempered.

This characterization of the *orisa* has nothing to do with issues of good and evil. All gods, like humans, possess both positive and negative values—strengths as well as foibles. Only their modes of action differ, which is the actualization of their distinctive *ase* (life force), as expressed by their natures or personalities (*iwa*). Furthermore, the gods are not ranked in any hierarchy. Their relative importance in any given part of the Yoruba world reflects their relative local popularity, reputation, and influence, and the order in which they are invoked in ceremonies has to do with their roles in the ritual and their relationships to each other.

The gods regularly enter the world through their mediums—worshippers who have been trained and prepared to receive the spirit of their divinities during possession trances in the course of religious ceremonies. When the gods are made manifest in this way, they speak through their devotees, praying and giving guidance.

While all the gods periodically journey to the world, two sacred powers, Ifa and Esu/Elegba, stand at the threshold between the realms of *orun* and *aye*, assisting in communication between the divine and human realms. Ifa, actually a Yoruba system of divination, is presided over by Orunmila, its deified mythic founder, who is also sometimes called Ifa. Esu/Elegba is the divine messenger and activator.

Ifa offers humans the possibility of knowing the forces at work in specific situations in their lives and of influencing the course of events through prayer and sacrifice. The diviner, or *babalawo* ("father of ancient wisdom") uses the rituals and poetry of Ifa to identify cosmic forces: the gods, ancestors, and spirits, and the machinations of the enemies of humankind personified as Death, Disease, Infirmity, and Loss; certain troublesome entities such as *egbe abiku* (spirit children), who may cause newborn children to die and be reborn frequently thus plaguing their parents until rituals and offerings can set matters right; and the sometimes evil-intentioned persons known collectively as *araye* ("people-of-the-world") who include *aje* (witches), *oso* (wizards), and others.

While Ifa symbolizes the revealable, Esu/Elegba is the agent of effective action, who also reminds one of the unpredictable nature of human experience. Esu's constant and often unsettling activity reminds humans of the need for guidance in lives of engaged action. Esu, who bears the sacrifices of humans to the *orisa* and other spirits, is the guardian of the ritual process. A verse from Ifa warns that if Esu is not acknowledged, "life is the bailing of waters with a sieve."

The ancestors (*oku orun, osi, babanla, iyanla*) constitute another major category of beings in *orun*. They are departed but not deceased. They can be contacted by their descendants for support and guidance and can return to the world either for short stays in the form of maskers called *egungun*, or as part of new persons in their lineages who are partially their reincarnation. A young female child revealed to be the incarnation of her grandmother, for example, will be named Yetunde ("Mother-has-returned"). The grandmother continues to exist in *orun*, but part of her spirit, or breath, *emi*, is a constituent element of the new child.

Aye: The World of the Living

Aye, the world, is the visible, tangible realm of the living, including those invisible otherworldly forces that visit frequently and strongly influence human affairs. The importance and omnipresence of the otherworld in this world is expressed in a Yoruba saying: "The world is a marketplace [we visit], the otherworld is home" (Aye l'oja, orun n'ile). A variant of this phrase, Aye l'ajo, orun n'ile ("The world [life] is a journey, the otherworld [afterlife] is home"), contrasts the movement and unpredictability of life with the haven of the afterworld that promises spiritual existence for eternity.[4] Individual goals and aspirations in the world include long life, peace, prosperity, progeny, and good reputation. Ideally, these can be achieved through the constant search for ogbon (wisdom), imo (knowledge), and oye (understanding).

Yoruba society is traditionally open, but with a long history of monarchical and hierarchical organization. Nevertheless, decision making is shared widely—consensual rather than autocratic or dictatorial—and an elaborate series of checks and balances ensures an essentially egalitarian system. Just as all the gods are equal in relation to Olodumare, so too all lineages are structurally equal in their relation to the sacred king. At the same time, the possibility of mobility is fundamental, depending on how one marshals the forces in the environment. The situation is remarkably fluid and dynamic. Within this context, there is some recognition of rank, yet distribution of responsibilities and authority are given more importance than hierarchy. Seniority is based on the age of the person, the antiquity of the title, and the person's tenure in office. Such an ideal for social interaction is rooted in the concept of ase, the life force possessed by all individuals and unique to each one. Thus ase must be acknowledged and used in all social matters and in dealings with divine forces as well.

Ase: Life Force

Ase is given by Olodumare to everything—gods, ancestors, spirits, humans, animals, plants, rocks, rivers, and voiced words such as songs, prayers, praises, curses, or even everyday conversation. Existence, according to Yoruba thought, is dependent upon it; it is the power to make things happen and change. In addition to its sacred characteristics, ase also has important social ramifications, reflected in its translation as "power, authority, command." A person who,

---

4. For the importance of the metaphor of the "journey" in Yoruba thought and in ritual practice, see M. T. Drewal, "Performer, Play, and Agency: Yoruba Ritual Process." Ph.D Thesis, New York University, 1989.

through training, experience, and initiation, learns how to use the essential life force of things is called an *alaase*. Theoretically, every individual possesses a unique blend of performative power and knowledge—the potential for certain achievements. Yet because no one can know with certainty the potential of others, *eso* (caution), *ifarabale* (composure), *owo* (respect), and *suuru* (patience) are highly valued in Yoruba society and shape all social interactions and organization.

Social processes encourage the participation of all and the contribution of the *ase* of every person. For example, members of the council of elder men and women, known as Osugbo among the Ijebu Yoruba and Ogboni in the Oyo area, have hereditary titles that rotate among many lineages, and there are other positions that are open to all in the society, as well as honorary titles bestowed on those who have made special contributions to the community. Members stress the equality of such positions in emphasizing their distinctive rights and responsibilities. All are seen as crucial to the successful functioning of the society as evident in Osugbo rituals. The members share kola nut, the drummers play the praises of titles, individuals take turns hosting a series of celebrations, each person has the opportunity to state opinions during debates, and all decisions are consensual. Osugbo members stress the autonomy of their individual roles while at the same time asserting their equality in decision making. At various times some will dominate while others acquiesce, which is entirely in keeping with Yoruba notions of the distinctive *ase* of individuals and the fluid social reality of competing powers that continually shape society.

Rituals to invoke divine forces reflect this same concern for the autonomous *ase* of particular entities. Those invoked first are not more important or higher in rank, rather they are called first in order to perform specific tasks—such as the divine mediator Esu/Elegba who "opens the way" for communication between humans and gods. The recognition of the uniqueness and autonomy of the *ase* of persons and gods is what structures society and its relationship with the otherworld.

* * *

DURO LADIPO

Oba Waja†
(The King Is Dead)

(Based on a true incident that happened in Oyo in 1946)

Characters

OLORI ELESIN	*Commander of the King's Horse*
DAWUDU, HIS SON	*A Trader in Ghana.*
DAWUDU'S WIFE	
DISTRICT OFFICER	
DISTRICT OFFICER'S WIFE	
ELDERS, MARKET WOMEN ETC.	

ACT ONE:	*The District Officer's House, at Night.*
ACT TWO:	*Oyo Market.*
ACT THREE:	*The House of the Olori Elesin.*
ACT FOUR:	*A Highlife Bar in Ghana.*
ACT FIVE:	*The House of the Olori Elesin.*

Act I: The District Officer's Bedroom

The scene is dark. The D.O. *and his* WIFE *are visible as silhouettes against large windows. Through the windows* DANCERS *and* DRUMMERS *can be seen in the moonlight.*

ELDERS [*outside*]   We must not see it.
  It is forbidden.
  The king is dead
  And never shall we see him
  Leaving the palace in procession.
CHORUS & AGOGO   We must not see it.
  It is forbidden.
ELDERS   The coconut is lost
  Under the huge silk cotton tree.
CHORUS   Yeeeee!

---

† From *Three Yoruba Plays: Oba Koso, Oba Moro, Oba Waja*, English adaptation by Ulli Beier (Ibadan: Mbari Publications, 1964). Reprinted by permission of Ulli Beier.

The coconut has failed
To bear another fruit.
The iron gongs resound.
The funeral gongs
Make us tremble with fear.

ELDERS Farewell, farewell,
We shall never set eyes on him again,
Unless we meet his double.

CHORUS Ye, ye, ye, ye!
The king has gone
The owner of the palace is dead.
Our father returned home,
He entered into a deep forest.
We shall not see him return from there,
Except in our dreams.

ELDERS We must not see it
It is forbidden.
The king is dead
He has crossed the river of life.
He has crossed the river into darkness.
The owner of the palace
Shall be buried with the beating of gongs.
The sound of the funeral gongs makes us tremble,
When wild animals scatter in fear.
Saworo, ye, ye, saworo.

WOMEN Ololade, my great husband,
Ogurogbe, my great husband
They say it is forbidden
To see you.
We must not see you, we must not see you.
The road death travelled on to capture you
Lies hidden in the bush.
Alafin has become a burning sun,
Shining like red hot iron.
Warn all strangers to leave this town,
Steep all your brooms in magic potions.
The eyes of the dead are gleaming in the darkness
Their backs are glittering in the shadows
Alafin has become a spirit
Hot like a burning sun,
Shining like a red hot iron.

D.O.'S WIFE For God's sake, John!
Can't you stop this noise?
Can these people never keep quiet?

D.O. I am sorry, Jane. These people are burying their king.

There is nothing I can do about it. We'll have to put up with it.

D.O.'S WIFE   Burying their king?

What are you talking about! I thought they'd buried him last week!

Can these fellows never stop celebrating?

D.O.   The Alafin of Oyo never dies alone.

These people believe that a king must be accompanied by his dignitaries.

Tomorrow, the commander of the king's horse will die a voluntary death, in order to accompany his king.

D.O.'S WIFE   What?

Do you mean to say that in the twentieth century we still have human sacrifices in this town—and under British rule?

D.O.   This is not a human sacrifice. Nobody will kill the man. He will die by simple act of will.

D.O.'S WIFE   And you tolerate that under your own jurisdiction? Are you not here to bring civilization to this people?

And you allow these barbaric things to happen?

D.O.   I am here to maintain law and order, not to interfere in people's lives.

D.O.'S WIFE   You are here to prevent this type of savagery. I am disgusted with you. You are letting down the side. I promise you that if you will not stop this ugly business then I will take the next boat home.

D.O.   Now don't get excited. I will see what I can do tomorrow— I'll do it for your sake. But I assure you that these things are better left alone.

> *Their conversation is then drowned by the loud singing and dancing that goes on outside.*

ELDERS   Shall the owner of the palace cross the river alone?
Shall he confront the gate-keeper of heaven unaccompanied?
Ojurongbe Aremu, commander of the King's horse,
You will row him across the river;
You will enforce his entry into heaven.
Ojurongbe Aremu,
Tomorrow you will be a burning sun, like Alafin,
Tomorrow your eyes will gleam in the shadows,
Tomorrow you will shine like a red hot iron.

Act II: King's Market in Oyo

WOMEN TRADERS *sit on the left of the stage.*

FIRST SELLER   Come and buy maize gruel;
  Come and buy my bean cakes.
  Come and trade with us.
SECOND SELLER   Handwoven cloths I sell:
  Etu, Lumumba and the latest styles.
  Make your gowns from my handwoven cloth,
  Your Danshikis, Gbaries and Agbadas.
TWO CUSTOMERS [*crossing the stage*]   Rich people trading in the
    market,
  Jalolo Jalolo
  People trading in the market,
  You hope to get rich quickly.
  Jalolo Jalolo
  Let us see the Kichikpa cloth
  That is good for a farmer's gown.
  Give us a reasonable price:
  A house is not built in one day.
  Jalolo Jalolo
CUSTOMERS   You people trading in the market:
  Remember that money is scarce these days
  Money is the cause of all evil.
  Don't you know, that it is money
  That caused two brothers to fight,
  That money caused them to kill each other?
SELLERS   Stop all this irrelevant talk,
  And buy what you want to buy.
  All handwoven cloths we sell:
  Etu, Lumumba and all the latest styles.

  Enter WOMEN *with drums.*

WOMEN   One hand by itself cannot lift the load on the head
  Ajeje—it is a fact.
  Alafin must not cross the river alone.
  Ojurongbe Aremu, commander of the king's horse;
  Follow in your father's footsteps.
  The forest will be ashamed,
  If the elephant eats and he is not satisfied.
  If the red camwood is used up in the calabash,
  The child cannot anoint its body for the feast.
  If your courage runs out,
  How shall the king confront the gateman of heaven?

You, owner of crown, born into a big house,
Ojurongbe Aremu
Do not allow the world to spoil
In your own time.
Will you stay behind to eat earthworms and centipedes?
Follow your king and
Share his meal in heaven.
Commander of the horse,
Come forth, come forth,
We are expecting you.
Today you are the owner of the market,
Today the town belongs to you.
Follow the footsteps of your fathers.
The forest will be ashamed,
If the elephant eats and is not satisfied.
The forest will be ashamed.

OLORI ELESIN   Eeeh, eeeh, eeeh, eeeh!
  The child is weeping.

CHORUS   Eeeh, eeeh, eeeh, eeeh!
  The child is weeping.

OLORI ELESIN   I Ojurongbe, owner of crown,
  I am going to heaven to rest.

CHORUS   Eeeh, eeeh, eeeh, eeeh!
  The child is weeping.

OLORI ELESIN   No oracle can cure a hunchback
  No medicine can heal a cripple
  No doctor can cure hunger.

CHORUS   Eeeh, eeeh, eeeh, eeeh!
  The child is weeping.

OLORI ELESIN   Who can obstruct the elephant?
  He is not an ordinary animal
  That could be beheaded with a matchet.
  He is not an ordinary animal
  That can be trapped by the hunter.
  If thick creepers try to obstruct his road,
  The elephant and the creepers will go together.

CHORUS   Eeeh, eeeh, eeeh, eeeh!
  The child is weeping.

WOMEN   Ojurongbe Aremu, Owner of crown,
  Commander of the king's horse
  When one reaches the door of one's father's house,
  One's courage fails.
  But you are the strong wizard
  Whose heart has learnt
  To resist the thrust of a knife.

You are a spirit
Who drinks water from the foot of the plantain.
Your chest is brown
Like the rat that lives at the foot of the palm,
Arise and stand!
Follow your father's footsteps.
Whether you bring sacrifices,
Or prepare magic potions—
What you are destined to do today
You must do.
Today is your day:
Walk freely, owner of the market.
Rejoice, owner of the town.
Do not stay behind to eat earthworms and centipedes.
Today you shall share the king's meal in heaven.

OLORI ELESIN   Today I shall accompany my king across the river.
No gate-keeper shall bar his way
When I am at his side.
Today I shall fly to heaven like the fruit pidgeon.
Today I shall leave you to walk the ground like the hornbill.

OYO PEOPLE   Eeeh, eeeh, eeeh, eeeh!
The child is weeping.
The hornbill is sad.
When the pidgeon rises to heaven,
Leaving him to stalk the ground!

OLORI ELESIN   Alantere O! Antere
This day belongs to me
Antere
Nothing can stop me now
Antere
In dreams we shall meet
In riches
And with children
We shall meet
Where there is no more punishment.
Alantere O! Antere.

Enter DISTRICT OFFICER *with* POLICEMEN.

D.O.   STOP, STOP, STOP!

OYO PEOPLE   Oyinbo Ajele
What are you trying to do?

D.O.   Are you trying to commit suicide?
Don't you know this is a criminal offence?
Leave the dead alone.
You must not die!

OYO PEOPLE When Ojurongbe took his title
He knew he would die like this.
He knew he would die like his father.
He knew he would die like his grandfather.
Let not the world spoil in our own time!
Eeeh, eeeh, eeeh, eeeh!
The child is weeping.
D.O. Arrest him! Arrest him!
Lock him up!
Bring the man to court tomorrow
For trial.
OYO PEOPLE The world is spoilt in the white man's time
Shall the commander of the horse
Remain behind to eat earthworms and centipedes?
And who will give food to the king
On his way to heaven?
Alafin, owner of the palace,
The white man's rule has spoiled our world.
Vengeance is in your hands.

Act III: *In the House of the* Commander of the Horse

> OLORI ELESIN *alone in his house.*
> OYO PEOPLE *rush in.*

OYO PEOPLE We made you Commander of the King's horse,
We trusted you; our eyes were upon you today:
But you obeyed the European.
Our town has spoiled in your time!
Yesterday's stale yam
Is good enough for you.
Yesterday's shit—
You shitted it.
Yesterday's piss in the room—
You pissed it.
Carry your shit!
Carry your piss!
Feeeeeee!
May this disaster break over your own head!
We had confidence in you.
You promised, to put your cloth on your head
And walk naked through the market.
You promised to strip yourself
Of all your belongings

To wade naked through the river into darkness.
Your courage failed,
Your king is left to wander in darkness.
How could he present himself
At the gate of heaven unattended?
May this disaster break over your head.

Exit OYO PEOPLE.

OLORI ELESIN   Ha, ha, ha,
What have I seen,
Why should this happen within my own life time.
During the life of Adekanbi
The king died and he died with him.
During the life of Sekoni Akangbe
The king died and his servant followed him.
But to the toothless man
The softest bean cake is as hard as bone.
My charms were rendered impotent
By the European;
My medicines have gone stale in their calabash.
Help me people of Oyo
Lest this disaster will break over my head.
OYO PEOPLE [*back stage*]   Eeeh, eeeh, eeeh!
Commander of the king's horse
The world has spoilt in your time,
We must leave you to your fate.
OLORI ELESIN   My head whom I worshipped in the morning
My head whom I praised in the morning.
Why did you allow this to happen in my time?
The white man rendered my charms impotent,
He drained the power of my medicine.
He has deprived me of a glorious death.
Now I can die of the matchet
Like a cow slaughtered in the market
I can bleed to death.
Now I can burn myself alive
Smouldering away like a rubbish dump.
But the glorious road to heaven is closed.
The elephant has been beheaded like a common hyena,
The elephant has been trapped like a common antelope.
People of Oyo.
Help me to repair the life that was spoiled
By the white man's rule.
OYO PEOPLE [*behind the scene*]   Commander of the king's horse,

Your sacrifice has been rejected.
You can die of the matchet
Bleeding to death like a cow
Slaughtered in the market-place.
You can burn alive in fire
Smouldering away like a rubbish dump.
But the glorious road to heaven is closed to you.
How the king is hungry.
He is wandering in the dark.
He cannot face the gate of heaven alone.
May this calamity break over your head.

Enter dead ALAFIN.

ALAFIN [*Oro sounds accompany his speech*]
    To to to to
    Let me cry over this world
    To to to to
    The world is spoilt in my time.
    You Ojurongbe Aperu
    Commander of my horse:
    When I was alive, we ate together
    We drank together, we lived together.
    Why are you staying behind!
OLORI ELESIN   Haaa! Haaa! Haaa!
    This is Alafin!
DEAD ALAFIN   You have failed to come and give me food.
    Alone I wander in darkness, unattended.
    Let earth, the mother of all, judge between you and me.
OLORI ELESIN   Eeeh, eeeh, eeeh, eeeh!
    Our times have spoilt.
    The white man's rule has spoilt our world.
    Do not curse me, it is not my fault:
    The white man's power
    He has drained the medicines from my calabash;
    And my magic charms he rendered impotent.
    He has brought with him a new law
    A white man's law to which I have succumbed.
ALAFIN   Ojurongbe
    You have forgotten your birthright.
    Cruel man, you have forgotten tomorrow.
    Know then; that I shall not enter the gate of heaven unattended,
    I have chosen my new attendant
    And you will pay for your betrayal.
    The white man's law will not protect you from my wrath!

Exit ALAFIN.

OYO PEOPLE [*back stage*]   Haaa, Haaa, Haaa! Ojurongbe
  The elephant was beheaded like the common antelope.
  The elephant was trapped like the common hyena.
  Haaa, Haaa, Haaa! Ojurongbe!
  The world breaks over your head.

Act IV: A Highlife Bar in Ghana

HIGHLIFE CHORUS   *Vomfo Araga Vamfo Noyede*
  Let us be happy and enjoy ourselves.

> *The music continues while men are drinking beer at a table
> and others are dancing with prostitutes.*

NEWSVENDOR   Ghana Times, Nigerian Times, Daily Mirror, Daily
  Express!
A GHANAIAN   Vendor, vendor, come here, *brawa didi.*

  [*He looks at the headlines.*]

  O what a pity, the king of Oyo is dead.
  You son of Nigeria, a king has died in your country.
  Look at the news.
  The Alafin of Oyo is dead—did you know that man?
DAWUDU   Stop music! Stop!
  This is bad news indeed!
CHORUS   This king who died
  Is he your father?
DAWUDU   No! But my father too, must die today.
  He is the commander of the king's horse,
  Who must follow the king to his grave.
  O heaven,
  May God allow the dead to rest in peace.
CHORUS   Heaven o Heaven,
  May God allow the king to rest in peace.
DAWUDU   O merciless death.
  The house of joy collapses when you arrive.
  You break the honeycomb and spill its sweetness.
  You do not allow a man to pack his loads before he follows you.
  You kill the king of Ara, you do not respect the king of Esa either!
CHORUS   Heaven o Heaven,
  May God allow the dead to rest in peace.
DAWUDU   O merciless death,
  You are the short man in the afternoon

You are the tall man at night.
When you enter the house
The whole compound breaks out into noise.
When you enter the back-yard,
The entire house begins to shake in its foundations.
Death, you turn the house into a forest,
You turn the verandah into a pile of rubble
Death, you cross the river,
And wailing is your companion.
CHORUS   Heaven o Heaven!
May God allow the dead to rest in peace.
DAWUDU   Listen my friends!
I must leave you. Today my father must die
To accompany his king.
Let me return to my town.
For I must bury my father.
CHORUS   Heaven o Heaven!
May God allow the dead to rest in peace.

Enter DAWUDU'S WIFE.

DAWUDU'S WIFE   Dawudu, Dawudu, Dawudu! Let us rush home!
The news has come: Alafin is dead!
Let us return to Oyo, let us bury your father!
Dawudu, let us rush home.

DAWUDU *and* WIFE *leave*.

A DRUNKEN GHANAIAN   Let our Nigerian friend go and follow his
strange custom!
And let us remember, that death respects no king.
Tomorrow it may be our turn: therefore let us be happy
And enjoy ourselves today.
Music!

Vomfo Araga Vomfo Nayede.

CHORUS AND HIGHLIFE ORCHESTRA   *Vomfo Araga Vomfo Nayede!*

Act V: *The* Olori Elesin*'s House*

DAWUDU *enters and meets* ELESIN'S *household*.

WOMEN   Welcome, welcome!
You are the true son of your father!
When you speak, the ground opens its mouth.
Dawudu, son of Elesin, welcome.

We have long been expecting you.
We wrote to you—
We had no reply.
Welcome First Born of the Elesin.
DAWUDU   I greet you for the loss of the Alafin.
I greet you above all for the loss of my father.
Commander of the king's horse.
Who followed his king across the river.
The day our mother dies,
Our gold turns to trash.
The day our father dies,
Our mirror sinks into the deep sea.
Today Oyo must weep for the loss of my father.

Enter ELESIN.

OLORI ELESIN   Welcome my son, Dawudu,
Welcome back from Ghana!
DAWUDU [*screams*]   Why are you alive,
Is the Alafin not dead?
OLORI ELESIN   The white man's power
Rendered impotent my charms
My medicines were drained from their calabash.
Then the bean cake was bone in my toothless mouth!
My son:
The white man brought us a new law
A law that will not allow you to lose your father.
Let us thank God then, that we can still see each other.
DAWUDU   Shame, shame on you my father, shame!
Is it in your time that world is spoilt?
CHORUS   Shame on the servant who betrays his master.
Shame on the servant
Who remains behind to eat earthworms and centipedes.
DAWUDU   Do you forget history?
Do you forget how Abidogun followed the Alafin?
How Olanipekun died with the Alafin
Who was killed in war?
CHORUS   Another Alafin has died
But the bean cake has turned to bone in your mouth!
OLORI ELESIN   My son, my son,
The times have changed.
Then let us thank our God
That we still see each other.
DAWUDU   Ooooh!
Today a child must carry a father's burden.
The falling leaf does not stop to rest

Before it touches the ground.
The river will never return to its source.
Today will I face the gatekeeper of heaven
Preparing the glorious entry of my king!

He stabs himself!

OYO PEOPLE   O pain, o pain! O cruel death!
Death breaks the honeycomb
And spills its sweetness.
Commander of the horse!
Weep!
For the Alafin is revenged!
Weep!
For the world has broken over your head!
OLORI ELESIN   Save me, save me, my people!
I must witness the ruin of my life!
O my child, my child!
No one can say he has a child,
Until his child has buried him!
This is the white man's doing,
The white man with his new law!
Let him never return to his town well!
The monkey will never have the chance
To rub camwood on his child's bottom.
Let the white man never have the chance
To continue his evil doings in my town!
Owner of the world come near me
And have mercy on me.
CHORUS   The bride will never weep
For leaving her father's house.
Continue to weep over your own folly.
OLORI ELESIN   If the dove is annoyed in the house
He flies into the bush.
I must leave this town
The scene of my shame!
CHORUS   Continue to weep over your folly.
OLORI ELESIN   The foolish man threw his cutlass at the rat,
The cutlass broke and the rat escaped!
What use is my life, since my son is dead?
Oyo people—the world is spoilt in my time
The world has broken over my head.
OYO PEOPLE   Commander of the horse.
Continue to weep over your folly.
But rejoice in your son's courage.
Even now he is leading the king across the river.

The eyes of the dead are gleaming in the shadows.
They have become hot like burning suns,
They shine in the shadows like red hot iron.

    Enter DISTRICT OFFICER.

OYO PEOPLE We speak—you do not hear us.
  We shout—you turn away.
  We beat the drum—you do not understand.
  Look now—the evil of your work has been exposed.
  The unspeakable has happened.
  The unpronounceable has come to pass.
  The head of the family is shitting like a toothing child.
  The palm tree should die, being weighed down by his fruit
  See now the old stem erect, and his fruit rotting on the ground.
  Oyinbo Ajele—this is your work.
DISTRICT OFFICER What mockery is this!
  Can good intentions turn to evil?
  Can justice turn into crime?
  Must the son pay, because the father was saved?
DAWUDU'S WIFE There stands the hunter over his prey.
  You have hunted down your game—
  Why don't you carry it home in triumph!
  The stranger thought he was wiser than the owner of the house.
  The child thought it was wiser than his father.
  The farmer thought he could teach the oracle priest.
  Woe to you Olori Elesin, Commander of the king's horse.
  Did you believe in the white man's wisdom?
  You behaved like the child that bites its mother's breast.
  You acted like the son who points to his father's house
  With his left hand!
  We talked—you did not hear!
  We shouted—you turned away!
  We beat the drum—you did not understand!
  Your son has cleared the name of your house.
  Dawudu rose to heaven like the eagle—
  But will never return to his nest.
  Even now his eyes are gleaming in the darkness.
  He leads his king through the gates of heaven.
  Even now he is with the king, the owner of the palace.
  He has become a burning sun; glowing like red hot iron.
OLORI ELESIN The blind man is sure to walk into trouble.
  How can the deaf man heed the warning of his friends?
  I was like a stranger in this my country:
  I had eyes but did not understand what I saw.
  I had ears but did not understand what I heard.

I believed in a new time: in a new law!
White man: where is your power now?
Can you call Dawudu back to life?
Oh the disgrace!
We kill the elder in the sun
And we carry his head into the shade.
I had to step down for my son.
My greatest glory did I surrender to him.
Shall the old palm tree remain erect in the wind,
When its fruit have rotted on the ground?
My glorious death I have forfeited.
I shall not carry my head to heaven
In front of the Alafin.
Yet I must follow Dawudu.
Today I shall see the king of the river
And the king of the sun.
Today I shall see my king
Gleaming in the darkness like a red hot sun.

      OLORI ELESIN *kills himself.*

DISTRICT OFFICER   O God!
Can I be blamed for doing justice?
Is kindness my crime?
I was trying to save a life—
And I have caused a double death.
Man only understands the good he does unto himself,
When he acts for others,
Good is turned into evil; evil is turned into good!

OYO PEOPLE   White man, bringer of new laws.
White man, bringer of new times.
Your work was confounded by Eshu, confuser of men.
Nobody can succeed against the will of Eshu
The god of fate.
Having thrown a stone today—he kills a bird yesterday.
Lying down, his head hits the roof—
Standing up he cannot look into the cooking pot.
With Eshu
Wisdom counts for more than good intentions,
And understanding is greater than justice.

WOMEN   Olori Elesin, Commander of the Horse:
You believed the stranger
And the world broke over your head.
You believed in the new time—
As yet we cannot tell
How much of our world you have destroyed

Cross now the river in peace.
Today you shall see the king of the river.
Today you shall face the king of the sun.
Alafin's eyes will gleam in the darkness.
He has become a burning sun, glowing in the darkness.

THE END

WOLE SOYINKA

Theatre in African Traditional Cultures: Survival Patterns†

Even where other resources of pre-colonial society are unevenly shared, culture tends to suggest a comparatively even-handed distribution or—perhaps more simply—mass appropriation. This may help to explain why it is always a primary target of assault by an invading force. As an instrument of self-definition, its destruction or successful attrition reaches into the reserves of racial/national will on a comprehensive scale. Conversely, the commencement of resistance and self-liberation by the suppressed people is not infrequently linked with the survival strategies of key cultural patterns, manifested through various art forms. The experience of West Africa has been no different. The history of West African theatre in the colonial period reveals itself therefore as largely a history of cultural resistance and survival. Confronted by the hostility of both Islamic and Christian values, in addition to the destructive imperatives of colonialism, it has continued until today to vitalise contemporary theatrical forms both in the tradition of 'folk opera' and in the works of those playwrights and directors commonly regarded as 'Westernised'.

We must not lose sight of the fact that drama, like any other art form, is created and executed within a specific physical environment. It naturally interacts with that environment, is influenced by it, influences that environment in turn and acts together with the environment in the larger and far more complex history of society. The history of a dramatic pattern or its evolution is therefore very much the history of other art forms of society. And when we consider art forms from the point of view of survival strategies, the dynamics of cultural interaction with society become even more aesthetically challenging and fulfilling. We discover, for instance,

---

† From *Art, Dialogue, and Outrage: Essays on Literature and Culture*, ed. Biodun Jeyifo. (Ibadan: New Horn Press, 1988). Copyright © Wole Soyinka.

that under certain conditions some art forms are transformed into others—simply to assure the survival of the threatened forms. Drama may give way to poetry and song in order to disseminate dangerous sentiments under the watchful eye of the oppressor, the latter forms being more easily communicable. On the other hand, drama may become more manifestly invigorated in order to counteract the effect of alienating an environment.

Nigeria offers a valuable example of the dual process of cultural attenuation and resurgence. For example, theatrical professionalism was synonymous by the middle nineteenth century with the artistic proficiency and organisation of a particular theatrical form which had emerged from the burial rituals associated with the Oyo monarchy, the *egungun*. The question of when a performed event became theatre as ritualism is of course a vexed one that we need not bother about in this context. It is, however, commonly agreed that what started out—probably—as a ritualistic ruse to effect the funeral obsequies of an Oyo king had, by the mid-century, evolved into a theatrical form in substance and practice. From an annual celebration rite of the smuggling-in of the corpse of that king and its burial, the *egungun* ancestral play became, firstly, a court re-enactment, then a secular form of performance which was next appropriated by the artists themselves. Its techniques were perfected by family guilds and township cults. About this time, however, Islam had begun its push southwards. The Oyo empire, already in disintegration from internal rivalries and other stresses, found itself under increasing military pressure from the Hausa-Fulani in the north, a situation which came on the heels of a rebellion of tributary states to the south. The fall of Oyo took down with it the security which the theatrical art had enjoyed under its patronage. The Muslims, victorious in northern Yorubaland, banned most forms of theatrical performance as contrary to the spirit of Islam. The *Agbejijo, Alarinjo* and allied genres, with their dramatic use of the paraphernalia of carved masks and other representations of ancestral spirits, came most readily under religious disapproval. It did not matter that, by now, they had lost most of their pretence to the mysterious or numinous.

Southern Nigeria and its neighbouring territories were, however, only temporary beneficiaries from this disruption of political life in the old Oyo empire. The Christian missionaries had also begun their northward drive, usually only a few steps ahead of the colonial forces. The philistine task begun by the Moslems was rounded out by the Christians' ban on the activities of suspect cults. The Christians went further. They did not content themselves with banning just the dramatic performance; they placed their veto also on indigenous musical instruments—*bata, gangan, dundun* and so on—

the very backbone of traditional theatre. It was into this vacuum that the returned slaves stepped with their Western (and therefore Christian) instruments, their definitely Christian dramatic themes and their Western forms.

Another historical factor aided the temporary eclipse of indigenous theatre forms: the slave trade and its supply which involved inter-state wars, raids and casual kidnappings. The missionary compounds often offered the securest havens from these perennial hazards, just as did (in West Africa) submission to the protective spheres of the Muslim overlords. It is difficult to imagine a group of refugees from the old Oyo empire encouraged by their Muslim or Christian protectors to revert to the ways of their 'pagan art'. The records do not reveal any such acts of disinterested artistic patronage. Artistic forms might be appropriated, but only in the cause of religious promotion; thus, for example, the appropriation of musical forms by the nineteenth-century Christian missionaries in Buganda for hymns. This, however, was only a later refinement, a sensible strategy for rendering the patently alien words and sentiments less abrasive to the indigenes by coating them in traditional harmonies.

It is difficult to trace, at present, the effect of the Oyo *egungun* dispersal on the development of theatrical forms in neighbouring areas. This is always the case with any situation of artistic hiatus —a period, that is, when a particular form of art goes underground or disappears temporarily, especially under the pressures of a dominant political and artistic ethos. The records simply ignore them, or treat them merely as isolated nuisances. The substitution of new forms belonging to the dominant culture takes pride of place in records, and this is the situation we encounter in the development of Western 'concerts' and variety shows in the colonised territories of West Africa.

At this point, therefore, let us clarify in our minds what theatre is. That this is more than a merely academic exercise is easily grasped if we refer to a sister art, sculpture, an achievement which the missionary-coloniser pioneers found convenient to deny to the African. The redressing assessment was made by other Europeans —the artists themselves, notably the Expressionists; they had no overriding reasons to deny the obvious, to ignore what was even a potential source of inspiration to their own creative endeavours. The vexed question of what constitutes drama and what is merely ritual, ceremony, festival and so on, while it continues to be legitimately argued, must always be posed against an awareness of early prejudiced reading of the manifestations encountered by culture denigrators, definitions which today still form the language of orthodox theatre criticism. To assist our own definition we need look only at any one cultural event within which diversified forms are found, forms which—through their visual impact—tend towards the creation of differing categories for a comparative description. In other words if, within one performance or cluster of performances (say, a festival or a celebration) in any given community, we discover consciously differing qualitative enactments, we are obliged to rummage around in our artistic vocabulary for categories that reflect such differences. Thus we find that, sooner or later, we arrive at the moment when only the expression 'drama' or 'theatre' seems apposite, and then the search is over. We will take an example from the Afikpo masquerades of south-east Nigeria.

A contrast between the *okumkpa* event and the *oje ogwu*, both being components of this Afikpo festival, actually furnishes us with the basic definition we need. This masquerade, which is the professional handiwork of a male initiation society, varies, we discover, from basically balletic sequences as contained in the oje ogwu to the *mimetic* as contained in the okumkpa. The latter is indeed performed as a climax to what appears to be the prominent oje ogwu turn by the masquerades. Both are basically audience-oriented—in other words, we are not really concerned here with the complication of a *ritual* definition but one of performance and reception. The audience plays a prominent appreciative role in this outdoor performance, judging, booing or approving on purely aesthetic grounds. Whatever symbolism may be contained in the actual movement of the oje ogwu is of no significance in the actual judgement. What the audience looks for and judges are the finer points of leaps, turns, control and general spatial domination. The poorer performers are soon banished to the group sessions—which demonstrates the importance given to individual technical mastery.

The okumkpa event, by contrast, consists of satirical mimesis. Masks are also used but the *action* forms the basis of performance. This action consists of a satirical rendition of actual events both in neighbouring settlements and in the village itself. Personalities are ridiculed, the events in which they were involved are re-enacted. In short, events are transformed artistically both for audience delectation and for the imparting of moral principles. Additionally, however, one standard repertoire consists of the taking of female roles by the young male initiates, this role being of a rather derogatory character. The satirised female is invariably what we might call 'the reluctant bride'. As the young actor minces and prances around, sung dialogues accompany him, built around the same theme: 'How much longer are you going to reject all suitors on the grounds that they are not sufficiently handsome/strong/industrious etc., etc.?' Competition is keen among the initiates for the honour of playing this central female impersonator. The various sketches in this vein are rounded off in the end by a massed parade of the various actors in the *njenji* where the less accomplished actors have their own hour of glory and the entire female world is satirically lectured on the unkindness of keeping the male rooster waiting too long.

We will not examine the sociological motivation of this kind of drama except to point out that this example is actually more rewarding, in our search for an explanation of man's motives in *dramatising*, than, for instance, the theory of the origin in the Oyo masquerade. Clearly, in the Afikpo masquerade we encounter a male-prejudiced device. It ensures man's claim to social superiority and creates guilt in the woman for not fulfilling on demand man's need for female companionship. It is of no more mystifying an order of things than, for instance, the disparagement by male undergraduates in their press of female undergraduates who have not submitted to their own desires—except, of course, that traditional society imposed heavy penalties on libellous fabrication (which is, by the way, a reliable indication of artistic barrenness). What we obtain from one, therefore, is genuine art; from their modern progeny, alas, only dirty pictures and fevered fantasies. The okumkpa provides us with drama—variety, satire. We are left with no other definition when we contrast it with its consciously differentiated companion piece—the oje ogwu.

Similarly, festivals such as the Ogun or Osun (River) festivals in Yorubaland provide us with multi-media and multi-formal experiences within which it is not at all difficult to find unambiguous examples of dramatic enactments. The high point of the festival of the Yoruba hero-deity Obatala is, for instance, undoubted drama, consisting of all the elements that act on the emotions, the expectations of conflict and resolution and the human appreciation of spectacle. We begin to understand now why dating the origin of African drama, locating it in a specific event, time and place is an impossible task—indeed, a meaningless one. In the study of art forms, it is clearly more appealing to look into extant material for what may be deduced as primitive or early forms of the particular art, noting along the way what factors have contributed to their survival in the specific forms. Festivals, comprising as they do such a variety of forms, from the most spectacular to the most secretive and emotionally charged, offer the most familiar hunting-ground. What is more, they constitute in themselves *pure theatre* at its most prodigal and resourceful. In short, the persistent habit of dismissing festivals as belonging to a 'spontaneous' inartistic expression of communities demands re-examination. The level of organisation involved, the integration of the sublime with the mundane, the endowment of the familiar with properties of the unique (and this, spread over days) all indicate that it is into the heart of many African festivals that we should look for the most stirring expressions of man's instinct and need for drama at its most comprehensive and community-involving. Herbert M. Cole renders this point of view in penetrating terms:

> A festival is a relatively rare climatic event in the life of any community. It is bounded by a definite beginning and end, and is unified thereby, as well as being set apart from the above daily life. Its structure is built on a core or armature of ritual. The festival brings about a suspension of ordinary time, a transformation of ordinary space, a formaliser of ordinary behaviour. It is as if a community becomes a stage set and its people actors with a battery of seldom-seen props and costumes. Meals become feasts, and greetings, normally simple, become ceremonies. Although dependent upon life-sustaining rituals, the festival is an elaborated and stylised phenomenon which far surpasses ritual necessity. It often becomes the social, ritual and political apotheosis of community life in a year. At festival time one level of reality—the common and everyday—gives way to another, a more intense, symbolic and expressive level of reality.[1]

What this implies is that instead of considering festivals from one point of view only—that of providing, in a primitive form, the ingredients of drama—we may even begin examining the opposite point of view: that contemporary drama, as we experience it today, is a contraction of drama, necessitated by the productive order of society in other directions. That is, drama undergoes parallel changes with other structuring mechanisms of society. As communities outgrow certain patterns of producing what they require to sustain themselves or of transforming what exists around them, the structures which sustain the arts are affected in parallel ways, affecting in turn the very forms of the arts. That the earlier forms are not necessarily more 'primitive' or 'crude' is borne out by the fact that more and more of the highly developed societies are turning to the so-called 'primitive' forms of drama as representing the significant dramatic forms for contemporary society. These societies, which vary from such ideologically disparate countries as the United States and East European countries, are re-introducing on stage, in both formal theatre structures and improvised spaces, dramatic forms such as we have described, from the macro-conceptual (as represented in festivals) to the micro-conceptual, as ritual may be held to epitomise.

In this vein, what are we to make of the famous Return-to-the Village Festival of the Koumina canton in Bobo-Dioulasso, Upper

---

1. Herbert Cole, "The Art of Festival in Ghana," *African Arts* 8, no. 3 (1975): 12–23, 60–92 [adapted from author's note].

Volta?[2] Here we encounter a people who, like many others in West Africa, have experienced the culturally disrupting influences of Muslim and Christian cultures. The traders came first, the Mande traders, in the early sixteenth century. In their next significant migration, the mid-eighteenth century, they were accompanied by Muslim clerics, with the cultural results with which we are by now familiar. By 1775 proselytisation had become so successful that an Imamate had been established by the famous Saghnughu family of scholars. The late nineteenth century saw the take-over by colonial administrators and Christian missionaries. Yet under this double assault, Bobo traditional arts have survived until today, and nowhere is it given more vital expression than in the 'Tagaho' season festival which marks the return of the Bobo to their village after their seasonal migrations to their farmsteads. The festival, which has for its core the funeral ceremonies for those who died during the period of farmland migration, has a far more important function for the living: the re-installation of the cohering, communal spirit and existential reality. Costumes are elaborately prepared, formal patterns both of 'ritual' and 'pageant' worked out and rehearsed, individual events enacted by masked figures for a delayed participation by the community as one entity. It is all of course a conscious performance, informed and controlled by aesthetic ideas, by the competitive desire also of 'showing off' dramatic skills. Simultaneously it is an affirmation of social solidarity. Can this form of theatre, considered in its most fundamental purpose and orientation, be viewed much differently from the theatre of 'happenings' which began in America and Europe in the sixties and is still encountered in parts of those societies today? To be sure, the former is more disciplined, formal and community-inspired, which are all attributes that we experience from unalienating forms of theatre.

At this point, it may be useful to consider instances where an art form evolves into another art form in one geographical/cultural area but fails to do so in another. The heroic tradition is one that is common to most parts of Africa (and, indeed, to most societies). Within this tradition may be grouped, at any level of its development, the epic, saga, praise-chants, ballads and so on, but here we are concerned with the performance aspect from which dramatisation most naturally evolves. East, Central and South Africa are particularly rich in the tradition of the heroic recitative. Among the Luo of Kenya and Uganda, for instance, we may note the form known as the *pakrouk*, a kind of virtue-boasting which takes place at ceremonial gatherings, usually to the accompaniment of a harp. The individual performer emerges from the group, utters praises of

---

2. Now renamed Burkina Faso.

his own person and his achievements, and is replaced or contended with by another. Similar manifestations are found among the Ankole tribes, while further south, among the Sotho and the Zulu, sustained lyrical recitations on important historical events have become highly developed.

Among the Ijaw people of south-eastern Nigeria, however, the same tradition has actually developed dramatic variants, has moved beyond the merely recited to the enacted, a *tour de force* sustained by a principal actor for over three days. The saga of *Ozidi*, the principal source for J. P. Clark's play of the same name, is an example. By contrast, the history of the performance arts in Central and Southern Africa reveals a tendency towards virtual stasis of the putative dramatic elements. Even the dramatic potential of such rituals as the *Nyasi-iye*, the boat-building and launching ceremonies of the Luo, with its symbolic cutting of the 'umbilical cord' as the boat is freed from its moorings, even the abundant parallelisms with nuptial rites, have somehow failed to move towards a truly dramatic rendering of the significance and life-intertwining role of the boats in the daily pre-occupations of the Luo. One need only contrast this with the various rites and festivals of the coastal and riverine peoples of West Africa, where both religious observances and economic practicalities of the same activity have taken on, over the centuries, a distinctly dramatic ordering. One may speculate at length on the reasons for this contrast; the reality remains, however, that drama as an integral phenomenon in the lives of the peoples of Central and Southern Africa has followed a comparatively meagre development.

Well then, let us, using one of our early examples, follow how traditional theatre forms adjusted or re-surfaced from the preliminary repressions of alien cultures. We find that the 'pagan' theatre ultimately withstood the onslaught, not only preserving its forms but turning itself consciously into a base of resistance against both dominating systems. We are able to witness the closing of a cycle of cultural substitution in a curious irony of this slavery-colonial experience. Having first broken up the cultural life of the people, the slave era, now in its dying phase in the first half of the nineteenth century, brought back the sons of the land with a new culture in place of the old. The returnees constituted a new elite: they possessed after all the cultural tools of the colonial masters. But—and now we emphasise the place of theatre among these cultural tools—even where they were fully assimilated into the cultural values of their erstwhile masters (or saviours), they found on their return company servants, civil servants, missionary converts who belonged in the same social class as themselves, but were culturally unalienated. These stay-at-homes had had what was more or less an equivalent colonial education, yet had also acquired a nationalist awareness which manifested itself in cultural attitudes. As the nineteenth century entered its last quarter, the stay-at-homes were able to provide a balancing development pattern to cultural life on the West coast which came predominantly under the creative influence of the returnee Christians, despite the latter's confidence in the superiority of their acquired arts and their eagerness to prove to the white population that the black man was capable not only of receiving but also of practising the refined arts of the European.

The cultural difference between the settlers of Liberia and Sierra Leone on the one hand, and the coastal societies of Ghana and Nigeria on the other can be translated in terms of the degree of cultural identification with, and adaptation of the authentic resources of the hinterland. To the former—mostly returnee slaves —the indigenous people remained savage, crude and barbaric, to be regarded only as material for missionary conversion and possible education. The converts who had remained at home, however, set off a process of schisms within social and religious institutions whose value-system was Eurocentric, delving again and again into the living resources of indigenous society. Naturally there were exceptions on both sides, but this dichotomy did hold in general. The direction of *new* forms of theatrical entertainment therefore followed an eastward pattern from the new returnee settlements; inevitably it received increasing native blood-transfusion as it moved further east away from the bastardised vaudeville of the 'Nova Scotians', so that by the time it arrived in Ghana, Dahomey (now Benin) and Nigeria, both in form and content, a distinct West African theatrical idiom had evolved.

'Academies', to begin with, were formed for the performance of concerts which were modelled on the Victorian music hall or the American vaudeville. The Christian churches organised their own concerts, schools were drawn into the concert rage—prize-giving days, visits of the District Officer, Queen Victoria's birthday and so on. The black missionaries refused to be outdone; Rev. Ajayi Crowther was a famous example, a black prelate who patronised and encouraged this form of the arts, while the Rev. James Johnson turned the famous Breadfruit church in Lagos into a springboard for theatrical performances. The Brazilian returnees added an exotic yet familiar flavour, their music finding a ready echo in the traditional melodies of the West Coast and the Congo whose urban suppression had not occurred long enough ago for such melodies to be totally forgotten. At the turn of the century and in the first decades of the twentieth century, Christmas and New Year saw the streets of the capital cities of Freetown and Lagos transformed by mini-pageants reminiscent of Latin fiestas, of which the 'caretta', a kind of satyr masquerade, appears to have been the most durable.

Cultural nationalism was, however, constantly at work against a total usurpation by imported forms. Once again religion and its institutions provided the base. Unable to accept the excesses of the Christian cultural imperialism, such as the embargo on African instruments and tunes in a 'universal' church, and the prohibition of drumming on tranquil Anglican Sundays, the breakaway movements began. The period 1888 to the early 1930s witnessed a proliferation of secessionist movements, mostly inspired by a need to worship God in the cultural mode of the forefathers. And now began also a unique 'operatic' tradition in West Africa, but especially Lagos, beginning with church cantatas which developed into dramatisations of biblical stories until it asserted its independence in secular stories and the development of professional touring troupes. The process, reminiscent of the evolution of the 'miracle' or 'mystery' plays of medieval Europe, is identical with the evolution of the Agbegijo theatre (then temporarily effaced) from the sacred funeral rites of the Alafin of Oyo to court entertainment and, thereafter, independent existence and geographical dispersion. From the genteel concerts of classical music and English folk songs by the 'Academy' of the 1880s to the historical play *King Elejigbo* of the Egbe Ife Church Dramatic Society in 1902, a transformation of thought and sensibility had recognisably taken place even among the Westernised elite of southern Nigeria. The Churches did not take kindly to it. They closed their churchyards and schools to the evolving art. Alas, they only succeeded in accelerating the defiant erection of theatre halls, specifically designed for the performing arts. It was in reality a tussle between groups of colonial elite, fairly balanced in the matter of resources. By 1912 the secularisation of theatrical entertainment in southern Nigeria was sufficiently advanced for the colonial government to gazette a 'Theatre and Public Performance Regulations Ordinance', which required that performing groups obtain a licence before going before the public. In the climate of cultural nationalism which obtained in Lagos at that time, it is doubtful whether this disguised attempt at political censorship would have worked; it is significant that the ordinance was never made into law.

Ironically, yet another breakaway church, the Cherubim and Seraphim movement, swung the pendulum back towards a rejection of traditional forms and was followed shortly by other emulators in the Christian re-consecration of theatrical forms. The furthest these churches would go in the use of musical instruments was the tambourine; local instruments which had created a new tonality in the operettas now touring the West Coast—sekere, dundun, gangan, and so on—were damned as instruments of the Devil. Secular stories, even of historic personages and events, were banned and the new theatre halls, church halls and schoolrooms echoed once more to the Passion of Christ, the anguish of Nebuchadnezzar, the trials of Job, and other dramatic passages from the Bible. The Aladura, Cherubim and Seraphim, and their adherents did not however stop there. These 'prophetist' cults spread rapidly along the West Coast waging a crusade against all 'pagan' worship and their sacred objects. Descending on the provinces of the established churches, they ignited bonfires with their hot-gospelling in which perished thousands of works of art, especially in Nigeria, Cameroons, Ghana and the Ivory Coast. The vision of a fifteen-year-old girl, Abiodun Akinsowon, about 1921, was to prove a costly dream for the cultural heritage of West Africa, the heaviest brunt of which was borne by Yoruba sculpture. This period may also be justly said to constitute the lowest ebb in the fortunes of traditional theatre, their participation in the cultural life even of the villages being subjected to lightning descents from the fanatical hordes of the prophetic sects. In the physical confrontations that often took place, the position of authority was predictable. Embarrassed as they sometimes were by the excesses of the sectarians, the European missionaries and their black priests had no hesitation about their alliances—and their voice was weighty in the processes of imposing the colonial peace.

But the 'vaudeville' troupes prospered. Names of groups such as we encounter in 'Two Bobs and their Carolina Girl' tell us something of the inspiration of much of these. Master Yalley, a schoolteacher, is credited with having begun the tradition of the vaudeville variety act in Ghana. His pupil Bob Johnson and his 'Axim Trio' soon surpassed the master and became a familiar figure on Ghana's cultural landscape, also later in Nigeria. More important still, Bob Johnson's innovations must be credited with having given birth to the tradition of the 'concert party' of Ghana, groups which specialise in variety routine: songs, jokes, dances, impersonations, comic scenes. However, the most notable achievement in the sense of cultural continuity was their thrusting on to the fore-stage of contemporary repertoire a stock character from traditional lore, the wily trickster Anansi. This quickly developed into a vehicle for social and political commentary, apart from its popularity in comic situations.

The Jaguar Jokers, for example, transformed Anansi into the more urban character of Opia, while Efua Sutherland's more recent *The Marriage of Anansewa* takes this tradition into an even more tightly-knit and disciplined play format—the term 'disciplined' being employed here merely in the sense of reducing the areas of spontaneous improvisation, without however eliminating them. Those who saw this piece during Festac 77 will have observed how attractively the element of formal discipline and free improvisation blended together to encourage a controlled audience interaction. By the middle 1930s, Bob Johnson had become sufficiently established to take his brand of vaudeville to other West African cities. West Africa in this decade could boast of a repertoire of shows displaying the most bizarre products of eclectic art in the history of theatre. Even cinema, an infant art, had by then left its mark on West African theatre: some of Bob Johnson's acts were adaptations of Charlie Chaplin's escapades, not omitting his costume and celebrated shuffle. And the thought of Empire Day celebration concerts at which songs like 'Mini the Moocher' formed part of the evening musical recitals, side by side with 'God's Gospel is our Heritage' and vignettes from the life of a Liberian stevedore, stretches the contemporary imagination, distanced from the historical realities of colonial West Africa.

Again, another irony of colonial intentions: while Bob Johnson was preparing his first West African tour and Hubert Ogunde, later to become Nigeria's foremost 'concert party' leader, was undergoing his aesthetic formation from the vying forces of a clergyman father and a grandmother who was a priestess of the *Osugbe* cult, a European educationist, Charles Beart in Senegal, was beginning to reverse the policy of European acculturation in a leading secondary school in Senegal. The extent of this development—including also an appreciation of the slow pace of such an evolution—will be better grasped by recalling the educational charter of assimilationism, spelt in diverse ways by the publications of such dedicated African Francophiles as the Abbe Boillat, Paul Holle and so on. Boillat, in spite of extensive sociological research, the result of his examination of the culture and philosophy of the Bambara, Sarakole, Wolof, Serer, the Tukulor and Moorish groups in Senegal, found no lessons to be drawn from African society for modern cultural development, no future but to witness the fall of all those gross, if not dishonourable, ways known as the *custom of the country*.[3] If his addresses to the metropolitan centre of the French world did not become the cornerstone of French assimilationist policies, they undoubtedly played a key role in their formulation. Against this background, and ensuing decades of such conservatism, the Ecole William Ponty was founded. A famous teachers' college, it served Francophone Africa in the same way as did Achimota College in the Anglophone West and Makerere College in East Africa. They were all designed to provide a basic European education for would-be teachers and low-echelon civil servants. Such humanistic education as came into the curriculum of the Ecole William Ponty was of ne-

---

3. Abbe Boillat, *Esquisses sénégalaises* (Paris: Editions Karthala, [1858], 1984) [adapted from author's note].

cessity French—French plays, poetry, music, art, history. Charles Beart, during his principalship, embarked however on a new orientation of the students' cultural instructions. From 1930 onwards the students were encouraged to return to their own societies for cultural directions. Assignments were given which resulted in the students' exploration of both the form and the substance of indigenous art. Groups from every colonial territory represented at William Ponty were then expected to return from vacation armed with a theatrical presentation based on their researches, the entire direction being left in the hands of the students themselves. Since the new theatrical sociology did not confine itself to the usual audiences of European officials and 'educated' Africans nor to Senegal alone, its influence spread widely through different social strata of French-speaking Africa. Was it, however, a satisfying development of the culture from which it derived?

The answer must be in the negative, though the experiment was not without its instructive values. It would be too much to expect that, at that period, the classic model of French theatre could yield completely to the expression of traditional forms. The community represented by William Ponty was an artificial one. It was distanced from the society whose cultural hoard it rifled both in qualitative thought and material product. The situation was of course not peculiar to William Ponty since it also obtained in the other schools and institutions set up by the coloniser for the fulfilment of his own mission in Africa. Thus the theatre of William Ponty served the needs of exotic satisfaction for the community of French colonials. Even when it 'went to the people', and with their own material, it remained a curiosity that left the social life and authentic cultural awareness of the people untouched.

We will conclude with the 'new' theatre form which has proved the most durable; hybrid in its beginnings, the 'folk opera' has become the most expressive language of theatre in West Africa. What were the themes that mostly engaged the various groups spread along the Coast? The Nigerian Hubert Ogunde provides a convenient compendium since he does appear to be more consistently varied in his dramatic fare than any comparable group to date in West Africa. His repertoire ranges from outright fantasy through biblical dramatisations to social commentary and political protest, both in the colonial and post-colonial era. A comparative study of the repertoire of the Jaguar Jokers, the Axim Trio, or the current Anansekrom groups of Ghana for example would reveal that these concentrate almost exclusively on social commentary, mostly with a moralistic touch—the evils of witchcraft, maladjustment in the social status of the cash-crop *nouveaux riches*, generational problems, changing status of women in society, sexual mores and so on, all of which also preoccupy the pamphlet drama of the Onitsha market literatures. Hubert Ogunde explored these themes in his plays and more. His biblical adaptations became in effect a vehicle for direct commentaries on contemporary society. Reference is hardly necessary to those plays which have earned him the ire of colonial and post-colonial governments: *Bread and hunger*, a play not merely on the famous Iva Valley strike by miners in eastern Nigeria but on the general inequity of labour exploitation; and *Yoruba Ronu*, an indictment of the corruption and repression of the government of the then Western Region. Both plays were proscribed by the affected governments. They have entered the lore of theatrical commitment in Nigeria.

And additionally, Hubert Ogunde exemplifies what we have referred to up until now as the survival patterns of traditional theatrical art. From the outset of his theatrical career, Ogunde's theatre belonged only partially to what we have described as the 'Nova Scotian' tradition. His musical instrumentation was all borrowed from the West, movement on stage was pure Western chorus-line, nightclub variety. Nevertheless, the attachment to traditional musical forms (albeit with Western impurities) gradually became more assertive. Encouraged no doubt by the appearance of more tradition-grounded groups such as Kola Ogunmola and Duro Ladipo, Hubert Ogunde in the early sixties began to employ traditional instruments in his performance, his music delved deeper into home melodies, and even his costumes began to eschew the purely fabricated, theatrically glossy, for recognisable local gear. Rituals appeared with greater frequency and masquerades became a frequent feature— often, it must be added, as gratuitous insertions. Ogunde's greatest contribution to West African drama—quite apart from his innovative energy and his commitment to a particular political line—lies in his as yet little appreciated musical 'recitative' style, one which he has made unique to himself. It has few imitators, but the success of his records in this genre of 'dramatic monologue' testifies to the responsive chord it elicits from his audience. Based in principle on the Yoruba *rara* style of chanting, but in stricter rhythm, it is melodically a modernistic departure, flexibly manipulated to suit a variety of themes. Once again, we find that drama draws on other art forms for its own survival and extension. It is no exaggeration to claim that Hubert Ogunde's highest development of the chanted dramatic monologue can be fixed at the period of the political ban on his *Yoruba Ronu*. Evidently all art forms flow into one another, confirming, as earlier claimed, that the temporary historic obstacles to the flowering of a particular form sometimes lead to its transformation into other media of expression, or even the birth of totally different genres.

This survey stops at the emergence of the latest forms of traditional drama. The finest representatives of this to date have been the late Kola Ogunmola (comedy and satire) and Duro Ladipo (history and tragedy). Their contribution to contemporary drama and their innovations from indigenous forms require a far more detailed study, just as Moses Olaiya (Baba Sala) demands a chapter on his own iconoclastic brand of theatrical wit. The foregoing attempts to highlight ways in which artistic forms return to life again and again after their seeming demise, ways by which this process emphasises the fundamental unity of various art forms and the social environment that gives expression to them; how certain creative ideas are the very offspring of historic convulsions. Finally, while for purposes of demarcation we may speak of Nigerian, Ghanaian or perhaps Togolese drama, it must constantly be borne in mind that, like the economic intercourse of the people themselves, the various developments we have touched upon here in drama and the arts do not obey the laws of political boundaries though they might respond to the events within them. The various artistes we have mentioned had, and still enjoy, instant *rapport* with audiences far from their national and linguistic boundaries. Their art finds a ready response in most audiences since their themes are rooted in everyday experience, fleshed out in shared idioms of cultural adjustment.

ANTHONY APPIAH

[Wole Soyinka and the Myth of an African World]†

* * *

I want to try to identify a problem in Soyinka's account of his cultural situation: a problem with the account he offers of what it is to be an African writer de nos jours, a problem that appears in the tension between what his plays show and what he says about them.

We could start in many places in his dramatic oeuvre; I have chosen *Death and the King's Horseman*. "The play," Soyinka says, "is based on events which took place in Oyo, ancient Yoruba city of Nigeria, in 1946. That year, the lives of Elesin (Olori Elesin), his son, and the Colonial District Officer intertwined with the disastrous results set out in the play."[1] The first scene opens with a praise

---

† From *In My Father's House: Africa in the Philosophy of Culture* (New York: Oxford University Press, 1992). Copyright © 1992 by Anthony Appiah. Used by permission of Oxford University Press, Inc.
1. Wole Soyinka, *Death and the King's Horseman* (London: Methuen, 1975).

singer and drummers pursuing Elesin Oba as he marches through
the marketplace. We gradually discover that he is the "King's
Horseman"—whose pride and duty is to follow the dead king to
ride with him to the "abode of the gods."[2] In the words of Joseph,
the "houseboy" of the British district officer, "It is native law and
custom. The King die last month. Tonight is his burial. But before
they can bury him, the Elesin must die so as to accompany him to
heaven."[3] When a colonial official intervenes to stop Elesin Oba's
"ritual suicide," his son, newly returned from England for the king's
funeral, dies for him, and the Elesin responds by strangling himself
in his cell with the chain with which the colonial police have bound
his hands. The district officer's intervention to save one life ends
with the loss of two and, as the people of Oyo believe, with a threat
to the cosmic order.

The issue is complicated by the fact that Elesin Oba has chosen
to marry on the eve of his death—so that, as he puts it, "My vital
flow, the last from this flesh is intermingled with the promise of
future life."[4] We are aware from the very first scene that this
act raises doubts—expressed by Iyaloja, mother of the market—
about the Elesin's preparedness for his task. When the Elesin
fails, he himself addresses this issue, as he speaks to his young
bride:

> First I blamed the white man, then I blamed my gods for
> deserting me. Now I feel I want to blame you for the mystery
> of the sapping of my will. But blame is a strange peace of-
> fering for a man to bring a world he has deeply wronged, and
> to its innocent dwellers. Oh little mother, I have taken count-
> less women in my life, but you were more than a desire of
> the flesh. I needed you as the abyss across which my body
> must be drawn, I filled it with earth and dropped my seed in
> it at the moment of preparedness for my crossing. . . . I con-
> fess to you, daughter, my weakness came not merely from the
> abomination of the white man who came violently into my fad-
> ing presence, there was also a weight of longing on my earth-
> held limbs. I would have shaken it off, already my foot had
> begun to lift but then, the white ghost entered and all was
> defiled.[5]

There are so many possible readings here, and the Elesin's un-
certainties as to the meaning of his own failure leave us scope to

2. Soyinka, *Death and the King's Horseman*, 62.
3. Soyinka, *Death and the King's Horseman*, 28.
4. Soyinka, *Death and the King's Horseman*, 40.
5. Soyinka, *Death and the King's Horseman*.

wonder whether the intervention of the colonizer provides only a pretext. But what is Soyinka's own reading?

In his author's note to the play Soyinka writes:

> The bane of themes of this genre is that they are no sooner employed creatively than they acquire the facile tag of "clash of cultures," a prejudicial label, which, quite apart from its frequent misapplication, presupposes a potential equality *in every given situation* of the alien culture and the indigenous, on the actual soil of the latter. (In the area of misapplication, the overseas prize for illiteracy and mental conditioning undoubtedly goes to the blurb-writer for the American edition of my novel *Season of Anomy* who unblushingly declares that this work portrays the "clash between the old values and new ways, between Western methods and African traditions"!) . . . I find it necessary to caution the would-be producer of this play against a sadly familiar reductionist tendency, and to direct his vision instead to the far more difficult and risky task of eliciting the play's threnodic essence. . . .
>
> The Colonial Factor is an incident, a catalytic incident merely. . . . The confrontation in the play is largely metaphysical.[6]

I find the tone of this passage strained, the claim disingenuous. We may, of course, make distinctions more carefully than blurb writers and scribblers of facile tags: Soyinka feels that talk of the clash of cultures suggests that colonizer and colonized meet on culturally equal terms. We may reject the implication. There is, as Soyinka says, something so oversimple as to be thoroughly misleading in the claim that the novel is "about," that it "portrays," the relation between European methods and African traditions.

Still, it is absurd to deny that novel and play have something to say about that relationship. The "Colonial Factor" is not a catalytic incident merely; it is a profound assault on the consciousness of the African intellectual, on the consciousness that guides this play. And it would be irresponsible, which Soyinka is not, to assert that novel and play do not imply a complex (and nonreductionist) set of attitudes to the problem. It is one thing to say (as I think correctly) that the drama in Oyo is driven ultimately by the logic of Yoruba cosmology, another to deny the existence of a dimension of power in which it is the colonial state that forms the action.

So that after all the distinctions have been drawn, we still need to ask why Soyinka feels the need to conceal his purposes. Is it

6. Soyinka, *Death and the King's Horseman*, 65.

perhaps because he has not resolved the tension between the desire that arises from his *enracinement* in the European tradition of authorship to see his literary work as, so to speak, authentic, "metaphysical," and the desire that he must feel as an African in a once-colonized and merely notionally decolonized culture to face up to and reflect the problem at the level of ideology? Is it, to put it briskly, because Soyinka is torn between the demands of a private authenticity and a public commitment? Between individual self-discovery and what he elsewhere calls the "social vision"?

It is this problem, central to Soyinka's situation as the archetypical African writer, that I wish to go on to discuss.

The "social vision" is, of course, the theme of two of the lectures in Soyinka's *Myth, Literature, and the African World*, and it was in this work that the tensions I have mentioned first caught my attention. Soyinka's essays are clearly not directed particularly to an African audience (hardly surprising when we remember that they are based on lectures given in England at Cambridge University). References to Peter Brook and Brecht, to Robbe-Grillet and Lorca, are intended to help locate the Western reader. Indeed, the introduction of Lorca is glossed with the observation that it is "for ease of reference."[7] And it is clear from the way in which the first chapter (on Yoruba theology and its transformations in African and African-American drama) tells us much that it would be absurd to tell to any Yoruba, and a certain amount that it would be gratuitous to mention for almost any African readership.

Yet, it is intended (and to a large extent this intention is achieved) that *Myth, Literature, and the African World* should be a work that, like Soyinka's plays (and unlike, say, Achebe's novels) takes its African—its Yoruba—background utterly for granted. Soyinka is not arguing that modern African writers should be free to draw on African, and, in his case, Yoruba, mythology; rather, he is simply showing us how this process can and does take place. He tells us in his preface, for example, that the literature of the "secular social vision" reveals that the "universal verities" of "the new ideologue" can be "elicited from the world-view and social structure of his own [African] people."[8] I have every sympathy with the way Soyinka tries to take the fact of Africa for granted. But this taking for granted is doubly paradoxical.

First, the readership for his dramatic texts and theoretical writings—*unlike* the audience for his performances—is largely not

7. Wole Soyinka, *Myth, Literature, and the African World* (Cambridge: Cambridge Univ. Press, 1976), 50.
8. Soyinka, *Myth, Literature, and the African World*, xii.

African. *Myth, Literature, and the African World* is largely to be read by people who see Soyinka as a guide into what remains for them from a literary point of view (and this is, of course, a reflection of political realities) the Dark Continent. How can we ask people who are not African, do not know Africa, to take us for granted? And, more importantly, why *should* we? (Observe how odd it would be to praise Norman Mailer—to take a name entirely at random—for taking America for granted.)

It is part of the curious problematic of the African intellectual that taking his culture for granted—as politics, as history, as culture, and, more abstractly yet, as mind—is, absurdly, something that does require an effort. So that, inevitably—and this is the second layer of paradox—what Soyinka does is to take Africa for granted in reaction to a series of self-misunderstandings in Africa that are a product of colonial history and the European imagination, and this despite Soyinka's knowledge that it is Europe's fictions of Africa that we need to forget. In escaping Europe's Africa, the one fiction that Soyinka as theorist cannot escape is that Africans can only take their cultural traditions for granted by an effort of mind.

Yet in Soyinka's plays Yoruba mythology and theology, Yoruba custom and tradition *are* taken for granted. They may be reworked, as Shakespeare reworked English or Wagner German traditions, but there is never any hesitation, when, as in *Death and the King's Horseman*, Soyinka draws confidently on the resources of his tradition. We outsiders need surely have no more difficulty in understanding Soyinka's dramas because they draw on Yoruba culture than we have in understanding Shakespeare because he speaks from within what used to be called the "Elizabethan world picture," and Soyinka's dramas show that he knows this.

I think we should ask what leads Soyinka astray when it comes to his accounting for his cultural situation. And part of the answer must be that he is answering the wrong question. For what he needs to do is not to take an *African* world for granted but to take for granted his own culture—to speak freely not as an African but as a Yoruba and a Nigerian. The right question, then, is not "Why Africa shouldn't take its traditions for granted?" but "Why I shouldn't take mine?" The reason that Africa cannot take an African cultural or political or intellectual life for granted is that there is no such thing: there are only so many traditions with their complex relationships—and, as often, their lack of any relationship—to each other.

For this reason, Soyinka's situation is even more complex than it is likely to appear to the Westerner—or to the African enmeshed in unanimist mythologies. For even if his writing were addressed solely to other Africans, Soyinka could not presuppose a knowledge

of Yoruba traditions—and these are precisely what we need to understand if we are to follow the arguments of his first lecture. Even
when addressing other Africans, that is, he can only take for granted
an interest in his situation, and a shared assumption that he has
the right to speak from within a Yoruba cultural world. He cannot
take for granted a common stock of cultural knowledge.

*   *   *

We can approach Soyinka's presuppositions by asking ourselves a
question: what has Yoruba cosmology, the preoccupation of the first
lecture of *Myth, Literature, and the African World*, to do with African literature? It is not enough to answer that Yoruba cosmology
provides both the characters and the mythic resonances of some
African drama—notably, of course, Soyinka's—as it does of some
of the Afro-Caribbean and African-American drama that Soyinka
himself discusses in *Myth, Literature, and the African World*. For
this is no answer for the Akan writer or reader who is more familiar
with Ananse than Esu-Elegba as trickster, and who has no more
obligations to Ogun than he does to Vishnu. "Africa minus the
Sahara North"—and this is an observation of Soyinka's—"is still a
very large continent, populated by myriad races and cultures."[9]

It is natural, after reading the first lecture of *Myth, Literature,
and the African World*, to suppose that Soyinka's answer to our
question must be this: "Yoruba mythology is taken by way of example because, as a Yoruba, it happens to be what I know about."
In his interesting discussion of the differences (and similarities)
between Greek myth and drama and Yoruba, for example, he says:
"that Greek religion shows persuasive parallels with, *to stick to our
example*, the Yoruba, is by no means denied"[1]—as if the Yoruba
case is discussed as an example of (what else?) the African case.
Many other passages would support this interpretation.

Now if this is Soyinka's presupposition—and if it is not, it is
certainly a presupposition of his text—then it is one that we must
question. For, I would suggest, the assumption that this system of
Yoruba ideas is—that it *could* be—typical, is too direct a reaction
to the European conception of Africa as what Soyinka elsewhere
nicely terms a "metaphysical vacuum":[2] and the correct response to
this absurdity is not to claim that what appears to Europe as a
vacuum is in fact a uniform medium populated with certain typical
metaphysical notions, of which Yoruba conceptions would be one
particularization, but rather to insist that it is a plenum richly pop-

9. Soyinka, *Myth, Literature, and the African World*, 97.
1. Soyinka, *Myth, Literature, and the African World*, 14 [editor's italics].
2. Soyinka, *Myth, Literature, and the African World*, 97.

ulated with the metaphysical thought worlds of (in his own harmless hyperbole) "myriad races and cultures."

I do not want to represent Soyinka's apparent position as a kind of Yoruba imperialism of the thought world. The motive is nobler, and I think it is this: Soyinka recognizes that, despite the differences between the histories of British, French, and Portuguese ex-colonies, there is a deep and deeply self-conscious continuity between the problems and projects of decolonized Africans, a continuity that has, as he shows, literary manifestations, and he wants to give an account of that continuity that is both metaphysical and endogenous. The desire to give an account that is endogenous is, I think, primary. As we saw with Du Bois, there is something disconcerting for a Pan-Africanist in the thesis (which I here state at its most extreme) that what Africans have in common is fundamentally that European racism failed to take them seriously, that European imperialism exploited them. Soyinka will not admit the presupposition of Achebe's question: "When you see an African what does it mean to a white man?"—the presupposition that the African identity is, in part, the product of a European gaze.

I had better insist once more that I do not think that this *is* all that Africans have culturally in common. It is obvious that, like Europe before the Renaissance and much of the modern Third World, African cultures are formed in important ways by the fact that they had until recently no high technology and relatively low levels of literacy. And, despite the introduction of high technology and the rapid growth of literacy, these facts of the recent past are still reflected in the conceptions even of those of us who are most affected by economic development and cultural exposure to the West. I shall return to these issues in the final essays. But even if these economic and technical similarities were to be found only in Africa—and they aren't—they would not, even with the similarities in colonial history, justify the assumption of metaphysical or mythic unity, except on the most horrifyingly determinist assumptions.

In denying a metaphysical and mythic unity to African conceptions, then, I have *not* denied that "African literature" is a useful category. I have insisted from the very beginning that the social-historical situation of African writers generates a common set of problems. But notice that it is precisely not a metaphysical consensus that creates this shared situation. It is, inter alia, the transition from traditional to modern loyalties; the experience of colonialism; the racial theories and prejudices of Europe, which provide both the language and the text of literary experience; the growth of both literacy and the modern economy. And it is, as I say, because these are changes that were to a large extent thrust upon African peoples by European imperialism, precisely because they are exogenous, that Soyinka, in my view, revolts against seeing them as the major determinants of the situation of the African writer.

Once he is committed to an endogenous account of this situation, what is left by unity in metaphysics? Shaka and Osei Tutu— founders, respectively, of the Zulu and the Asante nations—do not belong in the same narrative, spoke different languages, and had conceptions of kinship (to bow to an ethnographer's idol) that were centrally patrilineal and matrilineal, respectively. Soyinka could have given an account of what they had in common that was racial. But, as I have argued and Soyinka knows well, we have passed the time when black racism is possible as an intelligent reaction to white racism. So, as I say, we are left with common metaphysical conceptions.

Though I think that the appeal of the myth of Africa's metaphysical solidarity is largely due to Soyinka's wish for an endogenous account, there is, I suspect, another reason why he is tempted by this story. Soyinka, the man of European letters, is familiar with the literature of authenticity and the account of it as an exploration of the metaphysics of the individual self, and he is tempted, by one of those rhetorical oppositions that appeal to abstract thinkers, to play against this theme an African exploration of the metaphysics of the community.

But in accepting such an account Soyinka is once more enmeshed in Europe's myth of Africa. Because he cannot see either Christianity or Islam as endogenous (even in their more syncretic forms), he is left to reflect on African traditional religions, and these have always seemed from Europe's point of view to be much of a muchness.

Some threads need tying together. I began this chapter by asserting that the central project of that Pan-African literary culture to which Soyinka belongs could be characterized as the search for a culture—a search for the relation of the author to the social world. I then suggested that we could detect in a preface of Soyinka's a tension between a private "metaphysical" account of his play *Death and the King's Horseman* and its obvious ideological implications. Soyinka, I went on to claim, rejects any obviously "political" account of his literary work, because he wishes to show how an African writer can take Africa for granted in his work, drawing on "the world-view . . . of his own people," and because he wishes to represent what is *African* about his and other African writing as arising endogenously out of Africa's shared metaphysical resources. Most recently I have argued that we cannot accept a central presupposition of this view, namely the presupposition that there is, even at quite a high level of abstraction, *an* African worldview.

My argument will be complete when I have shown why Soyinka's view of African metaphysical solidarity is an answer to the search for a culture, and what, since we must reject his answer, should replace it. To this latter question, I shall offer the beginnings of an answer that is sketched out further in later chapters.

African writers share, as I have said, both a social-historical situation and a social-historical perspective. One aspect of the situation is the growth both of literacy and of the availability of printing. This generates the now-familiar problem of the transition from fundamentally oral to literary cultures, and in doing so it gives rise to that peculiar privacy that is associated with the written and persistent text, a privacy associated with a new kind of property in texts, a new kind of authorial authority, a new kind of creative persona. It is easy to see now that, in generating the category of the individual in the new world of the public—*published*—text, in creating the private "metaphysical" interiority of the author, this social-historical situation tears the writer out of his social-historical perspective; the authorial "I" struggles to displace the "we" of the oral narration.

This struggle is as central to Soyinka's situation as it is to that of African writers generally. At the same time, and again typically, Soyinka, the individual, a Nigerian outside the traditional, more certain world of his Yoruba ancestors, struggles with the Soyinka who experiences the loss of that world, of these gods of whom he speaks with such love and longing in the first lecture. Once again the "I" seeks to escape the persistent and engulfing "we."

And with this dialectic of self-as-whole and self-as-part, we reach the core: for this struggle is, I suggest, the source of the tension in his author's note—the tension between Soyinka's account of his drama and the drama itself. But it is also at the root of the project of *Myth, Literature, and the African World*.

For Soyinka's search for a culture has led him, as the title of the book indicates, away from the possibility of a Yoruba or a Nigerian "we" to an African, a continental community. His solution to the problem of what it is that individuates African culture (which he senses as a problem because he realizes that Africans have so much in common) is that African literature is united in its drawing on the resources of an African conception of community growing out of an African metaphysics. The tension in *Myth, Literature, and the African World* is between this thesis and the Soyinka of the dramas, implicit in his account of Yoruba cosmology in the first lecture, the Soyinka whose account of Yoruba cosmology is precisely not the Yoruba account; who has taken sometimes Yoruba mythology, but sometimes the world of a long-dead Greek, and demythologized them to his own purposes, making of them something new, more "metaphysical," and, above all, more private and individual.

Once we see that Soyinka's account of his literary project is in tension with his literary corpus, we can see why he has to conceal, as I have suggested he does, the ideological role that he sees for the writer. If African writers were to play their social role in creating a new African literature of the "secular social vision" drawing on an African metaphysics, then the colonial experience *would* be a "catalytic incident merely"—it could only be the impetus to uncover this metaphysical solidarity. Furthermore, his own work, viewed as an examination of the "abyss of transition," serves its ideological purpose just by being a *metaphysical* examination, and loses this point when reduced to an account of the colonial experience. Paradoxically, its political purpose—in the creation of an African literary culture, the declaration of independence of the African mind—is served only by concealing its political interpretation.

We cannot, then, accept Soyinka's understanding of the purposes of Africa's literatures today. And yet his *oeuvre* embodies, perhaps more than any other body of modern African writing, the challenge of a new mode of individuality in African intellectual life. In taking up so passionately the heritage of the printed word, he has entered inevitably into the new kind of literary self that comes with print, a self that is the product, surely, of changes in social life as well as in the technology of the word. This novel self is more individualist and atomic than the self of precapitalist societies; it is a creature of modern economic relations. I do not know that this new conception of the self was inevitable, but it is no longer something that we in Africa could escape even if we wanted to. And if we cannot escape it, let us celebrate it—there is surely a Yoruba proverb with this moral—and celebrate it in the work of Wole Soyinka, who has provided in his plays a literary experience whose individuality is an endless source of insight and pleasure.[3]

3. My discussion of *Death and the King's Horseman* is much influenced by the Soyinka production at Lincoln Center in early 1987.

GERALD MOORE

Soyinka's New Play†

On a wide, bare stage a lone figure dances to the antiphonal singing of male and female choruses. He dances from the condition of life towards the condition of death. He has moved beyond words and is now "darkening homeward" to the urgent music of other voices. From the balcony above him the Praise-Singer, who had earlier spurred him along the path of transition his dancing feet must tread, now seems at the last to hold him back:

> Elesin Alafin. I no longer sense your flesh. The drums are changing now but you have gone far ahead of the world. It is not yet noon in heaven: let those who claim it is begin their own journey home. So why must you rush like an impatient bride: Why do you race to desert your Olohun-iyo?

This long scene is the center of Soyinka's new play and it is compelling theatre. Here is the purest expression to date of that African form of the tragic trance which Soyinka has long striven to realize in his art. The physical isolation of the Elesin upon the stage matches his psychic isolation as he prepares to abandon life and join his dead lord. But the Elesin, the King's Horseman, does not yet die. For the play is based on that well-known episode when the intervention of the District Officer prevented the Alafin's chief attendant from following him into the ancestral world.

The chief about to die takes the young bride intended for his son; and the son, about to live, embraces the death intended for the father. Only when confronted with the body of the son who has died to redeem the honor of his blood, does the Elesin strangle himself with the chains of his new bondage. For the alien intervention is not so much the cause as the precipitant of the tragedy. It collaborates with the sensual weakness which has already caused the Elesin to take a young bride on the very threshold of his own death, thus postponing the embrace of the shadows to embrace human flesh once more. As the Iyaloja, leader of the women, reminds him:

> I warned you, if you must leave a seed behind, be sure it is not tainted with the curses of the world.

† From *Critical Perspectives on Wole Soyinka*, ed. James Gibbs (London: Heinemann, 1980). Copyright © Three Continents Press/Heinemann.

This carnal involvement with his son's betrothed is one of the details Soyinka has added to the historical event, not only to heighten its dramatic content but to enrich its meaning. By making the Elesin a collaborator in his own undoing, Soyinka leads the audience away from sterile cliches about "culture conflict" towards a more subtle understanding of the event, turning it into a critique of the whole process by which Africans consented to the undermining of their vision of the world. The Elesin himself puts his finger on the wound:

> We know the roof covers the rafters, the cloth covers blemishes: who would have known that the white skin covered our future, preventing us from seeing the death our enemies had prepared for us.

Soyinka's premiere production makes bold use of the magnificent new theatre at Ife, which was initiated with this event. He has opened out the play, exploiting the Elesin's isolation on the forestage and pushing his choruses of marketwomen and praise-singers into the side balconies. The effect is to heighten the Elesin's role as carrier of a chosen death for the community. His failure is thus a communal catastrophe, evoking more anger than pity. The Masque scene in which a spooky parade of colonial dummies in "white-face" greet a visiting English prince to the excruciating strains of a local brass band, is also played to splendid advantage on this big stage. But the sheer volume of air separating the players from each other and from us did create problems of audibility on this first night.

Fortunately Jimi Solanke, who has to carry the bulk of the play in the role of the Elesin, turned in what must be the performance of his life. His expressive body and eloquent dancing were matched by a voice of great range and flexibility. Not a word was lost, and each word in the rich verbal texture of this beautiful play was made to work within our understanding. Other fine performances gave promise that the revival of the play early in the New Year will be an event which should send many trekking back to their origins in Ile-Ife.

TANURE OJAIDE

[*Death and the King's Horseman* in the Classroom]†

Set in the colonial era (1946), written by Nigerian Wole Soyinka when a fellow at Cambridge, England in the early 1970s, and published in 1975, *Death and the King's Horseman* is not typical of works written in Africa in the 1970s, which generally deal with sociopolitical protest against government corruption. It is more like works of the late 1950s and early 1960s, which express cultural conflict between the African and European (Western) worlds.

Teaching *Death and the King's Horseman* at the University of Maiduguri in Nigeria before teaching it at both Whitman College in Walla Walla, Washington and The University of North Carolina at Charlotte, I have had the opportunity of exposing the play to a diverse student population. Ironically African literary works are classified in the West as postcolonial, but never construed so by African writers and their primary audience of Africans. In Maiduguri, as I expect in other African universities, the postcolonial discourse invented by critics in the Western academy has not caught up with teachers of African literature. African critics of African literature in Africa and some more nationalistic ones abroad speak of "post-independence African literature" instead of the postcolonial. A Nigerian poet and scholar teaching in the United States, I favor the "post-independence" classification, which emphasizes the people's responsibilities to themselves over the never-ending "postcolonial," which seems paternalistic by comparison. Writers in Africa have moved from putting blame for their fate on colonialists to taking their fate in their own hands, a sort of self-criticism.

The focus of this note is to articulate my experience of teaching *Death and the King's Horseman* at both Whitman College and The University of North Carolina at Charlotte, to bring out problems of the teacher and students, which are sometimes symbiotic, and share strategies and techniques I adopted to make the play accessible. In my experience, racial, cultural, feminist, and ideological tendencies, among others, tend to condition student responses to the play.

I have encountered two types of responses in my teaching of *Death and the King's Horseman* in America, whose academy, with others in the West, has been promoting postcoloniality. These problems are both general and specific. General problems have to do

† From *College Literature* 19/20, nos. 3–1 (October 1992): 210–14. Copyright © Tanure Ojaide. Reprinted by permission of the author.

with the reception of any African literary work in America, and the specific relates to *Death and the King's Horseman* as a text.

The first general problem concerns teaching an African play in English to students used to the Euro-American literary tradition. I complicated issues in both colleges by calling Wole Soyinka "our W. S.," which reminded students of the English "W. S.," William Shakespeare. In the spring 1992 class, mainly of sophomores and seniors, a British female student and the remaining American students saw everything in the light of Shakespeare, the touchstone of English drama. My strategy was to show Soyinka as having a double heritage of African and Western dramatic traditions. I had to explain that Soyinka is very familiar with classical Greek drama and that he studied at Leeds under the famous Shakespearean scholar Wilson Knight, who became his mentor. But in addition, the African drama in traditional terms integrates music, poetry, and dance with conventional aspects of festival or ritual. I made the students aware of Greek, Shakespearean, and modern concepts of tragedy and had to approach *Death and the King's Horseman* from the angle they understood, while showing how the play is different in being African. The tragedy in the play has on one level to do with a son superseding his father in doing his duty; this involves Olunde dying in the place of his father to save his family from disgrace. In traditional African culture, a son buries his father, not the other way around. Elesin's son dies before him. So he symbolically eats leftovers, and will have to ride through dung to the afterworld. That is his tragic failure. Seeing this, students are able to extend their knowledge of concepts of tragedy.

The second general problem I have to tackle in *Death and the King's Horseman* concerns language. Soyinka has his own indigenous African language, Yoruba, before English. A Yoruba writing in English poses problems to the American reader because of what Abiola Irele calls "the problematic relation that obtains between an African work in a European language and the established conventions of Western literature."[1] While Soyinka is able to blend Yoruba thoughts into English effortlessly, students have problems with the indigenous background of his voice. Familiar with African language systems and proverbs, I have to decode the language of the play for the students. I explain the nature and function of ritual language and the significance of proverbs in African sociocultural discourse. This language issue directly leads to problems and strategies specific to *Death and the King's Horseman* as a unique text.

1. See Abiola Irele, Introduction, in *The Collected Plays and Poems of J. P. Clark–Bekederomo* (Washington, D.C.: Howard University Press, 1991), p. xiii.

A white student at The University of North Carolina at Charlotte asked: "Is it okay to commit wrong acts in the name of tradition?" This question, illustrative of students' initial ignorance of other cultures, shows the difficulty of teaching a "postcolonial" non-Western text to American students. Students ask: "What are praise-singers?" They do not know how to pronounce the names of characters. In both Whitman College and The University of North Carolina at Charlotte the students unanimously found Act 1 difficult. A black female student at Charlotte has expressed this difficulty succinctly: "I felt thrown into the midst of a cultural event, knowing absolutely nothing." The ritualistic language poses a difficulty to the students for the first time. The symbolism of the market, which is central to the play, is not discerned when it should be, nor is that of the egungun costume.

Students need background materials about the Yoruba people and/or traditional Africa—especially the place of traditional religion in the lives of the people—to give them a gradual induction into the world of the Old Oyo Kingdom in which the play is set. (Showing a feature film on African culture can help with this.) The living and the dead in traditional Africa are closely related, and the social set-up in Africa is such that the community takes precedence over the individual: the sacrifice of an individual for the harmony of the group is traditional in many areas. A brief historical survey of Old Oyo, British colonization of Nigeria and other parts of Africa with its "Indirect Rule" system, and World War II will also be helpful, as students will then be in a position not only to know the cultural background but also the historical setting of the play. After all, modern African literature directly reflects African history. Once students know the sanctity of the egungun cult and its costume, it will be easier for them to understand the colonialist insensitivity to African culture as displayed by the wearing of the cultic dress by the District Officer and his wife, the Pilkings.

The cultural dimension of the play raises both general and specific problems. How will American students grasp the full meaning of an African play which has so much to do with culture? Soyinka chooses the mystical mode in *Death and the King's Horseman*. To American students reading the play, he seems to be talking a mystical language to a secular people not used to the African sense of religious ritual. My strategy at Charlotte in two different African literature courses, after my experience at Whitman College, is to explain the mystical nature of African life. Without doing this, the mystical focus of the dramatist on the "numinous passage" and "transition" will be lost on students, black and white, male and female.

Olunde killing himself in place of his father is not a total surprise to the African reader as it is to the Euro-American. Like the Pilkings, my students tend to believe that Olunde as a medical student who has been educated abroad would not kill himself, in fact, would not support the customary practice of the king's horseman ritually killing himself so as to accompany his master-king to the spirit world. However, if students are exposed to the Yoruba world-view, as I have been through study and living with them, they would understand that Olunde would not abandon his culture for any other one. Generally, the Yoruba are absorptive and borrow from other cultures what can strengthen theirs. Olunde's stay in England and his medical training only convinced him more about his father's responsibility of self-sacrifice. His experience of war casualties in English hospitals, the captains' self-sacrifice, and the British Prince's braving the seas in war time for a "showing-the-flag tour of colonial possessions" reinforce his faith in his culture and people. He has to perform the ultimate sacrifice for his family honor and the harmony of the Oyo State.

The culture conflict in the play evokes racism in the United States. The play has consistently specially appealed to Southern African-American students. When the play is taught in a Colloquium course that includes John Edgar Wideman's *Fever*, black students are thrilled by Olunde's intelligence and high self-esteem. They like Olunde, a black man, who is more than a match for Jane Pilkings, who had at first appeared condescending to him. The students relish Olunde's statements to Jane that "I discovered that you have no respect for what you do not understand." The racist remarks of both Simon Pilkings and his aide-de-camp remind African-Americans of racism in America. A white colleague, Dr. Susan Gardner, with whom I co-taught a course that included *Death and the King's Horseman*, complained of the stereotypical way the British characters are portrayed. I agreed with her and the students, but explained that Simon Pilkings is portrayed as a typical district officer rather than as an individual. Jane is more individualized. The cultural and racist concerns bring out different perspectives that are valid readers' responses to the text.

A feminist or women-oriented dimension is strongly brought out in the play, so that gender matters very much in determining responses. My female students, black and white, like the market women's teasing of Amusa. Black female students relate Amusa to Uncle Tom and feel he deserves his humiliation. The entire class (and female students in particular) are ecstatic at the girls' mimicking of the English accent and mannerisms. Women generally, black and white, like Iyaloja who seems to be in command of events, especially at the end when she chastises Elesin for failing to perform his duty. Her dominant character is also borne out by her forbidding Mr. Pilkings from closing dead Elesin's eyes and asking the Bride to do it.

Identification makes students respond to the play in their own ways. The part in Act 4 where Olunde talks with Jane Pilkings elicits this. The exchange especially appeals to black students, male and female, with a nationalistic inclination. It is as if Olunde, an educated African confronting Western imperialism, is speaking for them as African-Americans who have been dominated by whites. There is also the appeal to African-American women of a black male, Olunde, who is not only intelligent, "sharp" and "smart," but also talks of his family honor. Seeing in him an ideal of a black male who is not easy to come by in America, they talk passionately of him.

Similarly, black and white women students prefer Jane to her husband Simon Pilkings. It seems they see in her the humane and sensitive aspects of womanhood that are lacking in Simon. In both instances, there is solidarity on the basis of race and gender. Black and white male students have not shown any liking for Simon Pilkings, who is portrayed as symbolic of the colonial administrator rather than just a male character.

The most difficult and perhaps debatable aspect of the play in my teaching at both Walla Walla and Charlotte for some three years is that many students cannot understand why Iyaloja, the market women, the Praise Singer, Olunde, and others blame Elesin for not doing his duty when already arrested. I link this problem to notions of tragedy and time in cultural perspectives. To many students, Elesin goes very far in the trance and has no way of killing himself once arrested. I counter this argument with: "But he kills himself in spite of chains when he really wants to!" In other words, earlier he hadn't the will to die because of his attachment to material things—market, fine clothes, and a young woman. To understand the play as a tragedy, I impress it on my students that Elesin's failure is not refusing to die, but not dying at the appropriate moment. It is a ritual and there is a time for everything. However, Elesin delays and provides the opportunity for his arrest and the excuse not to die. Interestingly, white students sympathize with Elesin, saying it is difficult for any human being willingly to take his or her life. Black students tend to feel that Elesin knows from the beginning what his position as the King's Horseman entails, and that since he has enjoyed the privileges of the position he should, as the custom demands, perform his duty properly. Students tend to defend or condemn Elesin.

I have adopted a part-seminar part-lecture strategy of teaching the text, which encourages students' questioning and my own as well. In lecture I may explain, for instance, that African time follows the rhythm of nature, like the moon, and is not precise as Western Swiss-watch time. Still, frequent inquiry as to why we should blame Elesin for not dying after being arrested, since the ritual was disrupted by Amusa and his fellow police, has led me to look more critically at the passage of time in this play whose classical structure entails a unity of time. It appears to me that there is a structural problem about the time that Elesin is supposed to die. There is a gap that the content of the play as it stands does not fill. While drums tell when Elesin is supposed to die, a time that the position of the moon is expected to manifest, and Olunde knows, there is the question as to whether Elesin was already arrested or not at that crucial time. Soyinka might have deliberately made it vague for suspense or unconsciously to leave gray areas in this play of the "numinous passage," but it constitutes a problem for readers.

At both Whitman College and The University of North Carolina at Charlotte, Soyinka's *Death and the King's Horseman* resurrects the American experience in the students. After all, every reader responds to a text based on prior experience. As I explained earlier, training in the Western critical canon makes my students compare Soyinka with Shakespeare. What I find most interesting is that many of my students who are black, Southern, and raised in an evangelical atmosphere compare Elesin to Christ and Martin Luther King, Jr. to understand the meaning of sacrifice.

Teaching Soyinka's *Death and the King's Horseman* especially here in the South, I have developed strategies and techniques that will alert my students to other dimensions of interpretation and understanding from which their culture alone would have excluded them. Their inquisitive questions and exchanges with me and among themselves have also widened my perspectives of the book as an African literary classic. Directing the students' response to the text from what they are already familiar with helps them to comprehend it fully. While my personal background as a Nigerian would help, I do not recommend an essentialist approach, but feel any teacher with some effort can make the play an enjoyable learning experience for students.

MARTIN ROHMER

Wole Soyinka's 'Death and the King's Horseman,' Royal Exchange Theatre, Manchester†

On 22 November 1990, the Royal Exchange Theatre (RET) in Manchester was the scene for the second British production of Wole Soyinka's *Death and the King's Horseman*. Although written in 1973, the play had only once before been staged in Britain, in a production by Chris Kamlongera in July 1983 for the Drama Department of the University of Hull. And so far as the press were concerned, the RET production, directed by Phyllida Lloyd, was generally regarded as the British premiere.

For western directors the staging of the play causes problems on a formal as well as thematic level, the main obstacle being the dramaturgical importance of music and dance as the two other basic means, apart from verbal dialogue, of communication in African culture. These three elements in fact constitute the fundamental pattern of communication throughout the play, and its success or failure in production will mainly depend on how the interrelation of each of these stylistic devices to one another is established.

The basic question is thus to what extent the unfolding of the tragic action leads to a shift within the different levels of expression —or, to put it another way, in what ways does a change within the patterns of communication reflect the development of the characters? This paper tries to outline this interrelation, the way it was realized on one of Britain's leading stages and the dramaturgical implications for the cast and the audience.

By her own admission, Phyllida Lloyd had little experience with African theatre in general or Yoruba culture in particular: but she was encouraged by Peter Badejo, who agreed to participate by acting as Nigerian cultural advisor as well as playing the Praise-Singer. He was in charge of the choreography, while Muraina Oyelami was 'Musical Director and Composer'. One could call this an extended *mise-en-scène*.

A major factor in determining Phyllida Lloyd's decision to direct *Death and the King's Horseman* was the very architecture of the Royal Exchange Theatre:

> This is obviously a very particular theatre space, a particular design. I've been directing a lot of classical plays in the last

† From *New Theatre Quarterly* 10, no. 37 (February 1994): 57–69. Copyright © *New Theatre Quarterly*. Reprinted by permission of the author.

couple of years, and I was looking for a modern play that had something important to say and also did it in a way that would do justice to the physical life here. And the fact that part of this play is set in a market place, and this theatre is built in a nineteenth-century market just seemed somehow too good to be true.

The Meaning of Space

The significance of the space in which a performance takes place and the fact that it plays an important role in the conveyance of meaning is generally accepted. Yet as Lloyd has pointed out, it is of special interest for her production. Moreover it is widely known that Soyinka, not only as the author but as an experienced theatre practitioner, has clear ideas about spatial issues in the staging of his plays, as I will discuss below. The architectural peculiarity of the RET is as a 'building within a building'—for the theatre is constructed inside the huge Victorian hall that was once the city's famous and busy Cotton Exchange. To avoid the colossal echo-effect the stage has a separate acoustic entity.

An examination of the Victorian building reveals its function as a conveyor of meaning on various levels: on the level of urban development, with its central situation close to the market and in the heart of the inner city, accessible from St. Ann's Square and Cross Street; on the optical level, with its visual appearance emblematic of strength and prosperity; and on the historical level, thanks to its age, the tradition of the Cotton Exchange being as a busy market and distribution centre for goods from the colonies, at a time when Manchester was one of the wealthiest communities in Britain or even the old Empire. As Phyllida Lloyd points out, this historical aspect made the RET an ironically apt venue for the play.

A main RET strategy is, however, to attract people by using the huge foyer for non-theatrical events. Through architectural and programmatic channels the RET tries to create an 'everyday space' by organizing exhibitions, concerts, lectures, children's shows, etc., and through the craft centre in the foyer.[1] According to its own estimate of 15,000 people passing through the foyer each week, one has to admit that the RET's purpose of maintaining its function as a magnet for the citizens has been fully successful: there is hardly a local person who is not familiar with the place's interior.[2]

1. Hanna Scolnicov, "Theatre Space, Theatrical Space, and the Theatrical Space Without," in *Themes in Drama*, vol. IX: *The Theatrical Space*, ed. James Redmond (Cambridge: Cambridge University Press, 1987), p. 22 [adapted from author's note].
2. See D. Fraser, ed., *The Royal Exchange Theatre Company: An Illustrated Record* (Manchester: Manchester University Press, 1988), p. 22 [adapted from author's note].

The modern glass building that forms the inner theatre space is constructed as a theatre in the round, and this corresponds to Soyinka's intentions for his play. A director with experience of both picture frame and arena staging, Soyinka leaves no doubt about his preference: 'As a decidedly anti-proscenium stage artist, I hope to see fewer and fewer of those mind-constructors left in the world.'[3]

Concerning *Death and the King's Horseman*, the communicative advantages of the arena stage match both the metaphysical concept of what Soyinka defines as 'ritual drama', and more particularly the notion of what he terms the audience's choric function:

> The so-called audience is itself an integral part of that arena of conflict; it contributes spiritual strength to the protagonist through its choric reality which must first be conjured up and established, defining and investing the arena through offerings and incantations.[4]

In Soyinka's plays with metaphysical implications (as opposed to his satiric comedies), the arena's function as a magic microcosm cannot be overestimated. During the performance it is turned into a spiritually energetic space where the actors may re-enact the basic conflicts of Yoruba mythology to regain cosmic harmony and to bridge the gap between the gods and man.

The conditions of a theatre in the round and the spatial integration of the foyer avoid the conventional and paralyzing illusionism which is so easily created by the proscenium arch form. Another dramaturgical advantage of the arena stage is its flexibility concerning the setting, whereby Soyinka's demand for rapid scene changes can be fully realized.[5]

The spatial conditions of the RET thus perfectly match Soyinka's aesthetic concept in relation to its tradition as an Exchange, or market, with a colonial history which correlates ironically with part of the play's setting; and owing to the building's roots in the city's community, the functioning of its stage as a 'magic microcosm' which positions the protagonist in the centre, surrounded by the choric circle of the audience, and through its huge foyer, which allows a spatial extension of the play's action and so intensifies its dynamics.

3. Wole Soyinka, "Who's Afraid of Elesin Oba?" in *Art, Dialogue, and Outrage: Essays on Literature and Culture*, ed. Biodun Jeyifo (Ibadan: New Horn Press, 1988), p. 116 [adapted from author's note].
4. Ibid., p. 39.
5. Wole Soyinka, *Death and the King's Horseman*, in *Six Plays* (London: Methuen, 1984), p. 146. All further quotations and the page numbers indicated in the text are taken from this edition.

A Personal or Communal Tragedy?

Of the five scenes in which Soyinka has constructed his play, the first, third, and fifth take place in a 'Yoruba setting', while the second and fourth are a reflection of the isolated life of Europeans in Nigeria. The play starts with a celebration on the market place: Elesin, the protagonist and chief horseman of the king—one of the highest positions in the community—enters with his drummers and praise-singers, and soon the place is filled with market women and others who join in the festive atmosphere. It is only after a while that the audience begin to suspect the reason behind these celebrations—which becomes completely clear in the second scene, when Simon Pilkings, the District Officer in his bungalow, urges his native Sergeant Amusa and his house-boy Joseph to tell him the true meaning of the unusual drum rhythms which are audible, and which gradually start worrying him.

Their response finally makes not only Pilkings but the audience aware that this merry atmosphere is nothing less than a preparation for death—since, according to custom, the horseman has to follow the king, who has died shortly before, by committing ritual suicide. The play tells the story of a failure—Elesin's failure to fulfil the demands of this ritual, due to a combination of external and personal factors.

In the RET production the Yoruba scenes were symbolized by a yellow circle (the intention, however, was 'earth colour') of stage size, marked on the floor, with two arrows leading through opposite doors. The basic idea behind this was, according to the director, the interpretation of the action as Elesin's spiritual journey, which should have led him through the door (A) to the centre point, where he is supposed to die. The correct path of his spirit to the ancestors would have been straight through door (B), but the Horseman is distracted, diverted by following his egoistic motives: seeing a beautiful young girl among the market women, he proposes to marry her before his death, and as it is his last day on earth the market women—although annoyed by this behaviour—don't dare deny him this last request.

However, Iyaloja, the leader of the market women, warns him not to cling to life and so unbalance the communal welfare by not following the ritual—a classical dramaturgic convention of Soyinka's, preparing the audience to expect what is being warned against. The importance of Elesin's egoism, clearly visualized in Manchester, gave a theatrical hint of this outcome: the bridal chamber was in the wrong direction. As Phyllida Lloyd commented: 'It's like a kind of pit-stop and possibly one of the contributory factors of his downfall.'

The production starts with an entry dance of Elesin and his friends through the foyer and around the theatre—some of the spectators joining in, and extending the dance to a procession, while others have already taken their seats inside. Indeed Elesin enters the stage after one circulation through door (A), while the first scene takes place in the centre.

By the end of Scene i, lengths of indigo cloth for the wedding have been rolled out from the side, visualizing Elesin's diversion. And no action could make Elesin's failure clearer than his re-entry in the fourth scene, when he is brutally pushed through door (B) by Simon Pilkings, who has arrested the horseman to prevent him from carrying out what he considers a barbaric custom. But this time Elesin is pushed in the opposite direction—back into the circle, back into the life that he now hates so desperately.

Even more clearly than by means of spatial indicators, Elesin's downfall is represented by a change in his personality. The crucial shift from the beginning to the end, which is already clear in Soyinka's script, was significantly transmitted in Lloyd's production through the depiction of the tragedy of the protagonist. Elesin's dramatic decline during the action could thus be followed in three steps. In the beginning, when the celebrants enter the arena, Elesin is carried in triumphantly on a friend's shoulders. As the market women are kneeling around him, the effect of his raising is even further intensified. And later we see him standing in his (alari) clothes of honour, arrogantly claiming the bride. In the end it is Elesin himself who is kneeling before Iyaloja, covered with shame. The configuration has been inverted.

A threefold downward trend in the choreography of the chief actor may thus be perceived—a dramatic diminution on a vertical and horizontal level. The first step shows much individual freedom of movement on the horizontal level, with the totality of the foyer's spatial facilities being employed. Carried shoulder-high, Elesin towers above all the others, the highest position that is possible on the vertical level. In the second stage his arrogance is making him stand stiff and static—preparing the ground for his ensuing destruction and humiliation, completed in the final scene when, kneeling, he is unable to move, weighed down by heavy chains—on both the horizontal and vertical level the lowest position possible.

Two stage directions at the beginning of the script illustrate Elesin's personality, the first being the introductory description:

> Elesin Oba enters along a passage before the market, pursued by his drummers and praise-singers. He is a man of enormous vitality, speaks, dances, and sings with that infectious enjoyment of life which accompanies all his action. (p. 147)

This stage direction emphasizes the chief actor's expressive versatility, gained through the traditional education which he is likely to have enjoyed, which has taught him to employ the power not only of the word but of music and dance as well to represent himself. The term has to be seen in an African semantic context. While the European might take the word 'vitality' as a broad state of being, the African associates it with an aesthetic concept.[6]

The versatility and expressive strength of Elesin's body language are stressed in another stage direction, where Soyinka focuses attention on the perfect interaction between the various expressive forms by describing the way the drummer takes over the Horseman's dance steps and integrates them in his own, improvised rhythm: 'He performs like a born raconteur' (p. 149).

Expressing the Community's Wholeness

But it is not only the protagonist himself who is depicted as versatile and vital: the Yoruba community is portrayed as an organic whole. Soyinka thus requires that the market women should sing and dance around Elesin. In West Africa the circle is an important element for any kind of theatrical action—a microcosm, symbolizing harmony, unity, and communal experience:[7]

> South of the Sahara, solo-and-circle, or solo-and-line, or solo-and-solo forms of dancing mirror melodic call-and-response. . . . Persons singing the chorus frequently double as the circling group who surround or are led by the master singer.[8]

The patterns of call-and-response and solo-and-circle could be observed quite often in Manchester. Frequently the market women created a choric circle around the chief actor Elesin, either dancing or—as, for instance, in the Not-I bird episode, which is based on oral tradition with Elesin as the story-teller—sitting. The system of call-and-response is not confined to solo-and-circle, but may be employed by two single actors or two groups. In any situation, however, it indicates an undisturbed natural state between the communicants.

6. According to R. F. Thompson, "vital aliveness" and "vitality" are basic aesthetic categories of African dance. See his *African Art in Motion: Icon and Act* (Berkeley: University of California Press, 1974), pp. 7 and 9 [adapted from author's note].
7. See, for example, J. N. Amankulor, "Ekpe Festival as Religious Ritual and Dance Drama," in *Drama and Theatre in Nigeria,* ed. Yemi Ogunbiyi (Lagos: Federal Department of Culture, 1981), pp. 113–29. Amankulor's depiction of this festival reveals remarkable parallels to the Manchester production concerning spatial structure, the importance of the circle, movement, direction, and content (the importance of a ritual sacrifice for the welfare of the community) [adapted from author's note].
8. Thompson, p. 27 [adapted from author's note].

Top: Elesin arrogantly claims his bride in his clothes of honour. *Bottom*: the shamed Elesin kneeling before Iyaloja. Photos: Jan Woollams.

In the production the cyclic structure was broken when harmony became threatened. Elesin's claim to the bride, surprising and unforeseen, is an affront to the others. It is significant that, as a consequence of his behaviour, the women gather around Iyaloja, while the Horseman sees himself in an isolated position: the circle has been changed to a two-block structure, which does not reflect a common, harmonious action of one group but a conflict of two in opposition.

It is thus noteworthy that shortly before his frank and proud claim Elesin shows his first signs of indifference and lack of will to communicate by not responding to the honours of the women who are dancing around him. Instead his eyes lustfully follow the bride dancing around him with the other market women—a serious neglect of conventions between chief actor and choric group, a departure from the ideal communicative pattern. Yet these two situations cannot destroy the basically harmonious atmosphere among the Yoruba characters: the irritations are soon reconciled, and the market women, once having blessed Elesin's marriage with the bride, commence the wedding preparations.

The *mise-en-scène* tried to prompt the audience's awareness of a basically positive communication among the Yoruba community in the first part of the play by other dramaturgic means. Firstly, expressive forms were combined and thereby given an emphatic function. Thus Elesin's words 'my rein is loosened' were supported by the chorus's imitations of riders—a highly stylized movement without any intention of creating theatrical illusion. In a similar way the storytelling episodes of the first scene employed this technique of doubling expressive forms.

Secondly, the relationship between Elesin as the patron and his drummers[9] is characterized in the play by mutual dependence and friendship. While the accompaniments are basically rhythmic, it is the lead-drummer who speaks with his instrument (hence the 'talking drum'). In Manchester he was therefore not confined to his role as a musician, but participated in the action on stage as both actor (although he never spoke a single word) and musician.

Thirdly—and the most obvious structural embodiment of call-and-response as a pattern of an harmonic communication—antiphonal singing was employed at the beginning of Scene iii, when two groups of market women came in through opposite doors.

9. These are not to be mistaken with the drummers in the secret place 'Osugbo'. The drummers on stage (i.e., the 'market drummers') are hired by Elesin and play mainly for the celebration itself, while the osugbo-players are in charge for the correct timing of the ritual.

The Community Paralyzed

In the fifth scene of the play the audience is confronted with a paralyzed community and two deaths—those of the protagonist, who has failed, and his son, who has tried to retain his family's honour by committing suicide in his father's place. It should be noted that Elesin is not merely silenced (metaphorically and literally), but that all the modes of expression which were multifaceted in the beginning have been reduced to the one that dominates and creates the tragic atmosphere—the dirge of the chorus, which 'rises and falls' as prescribed in several stage directions in the final act. Not only has Elesin's power of language been broken, neither is he able to move: his expressive versatility has been destroyed.

The question arises, whether Elesin's destruction influences the Yoruba community and, if so, to what extent it is able to make good this serious disruption. In a speech in the fifth scene accusing Elesin of weakness and of betraying the entire community, Iyaloja reveals the language and the world Elesin has lost—as David Richards has rightly observed, a world usually praised through proverb and metaphor.[1]

Yet neither she herself, her fellow market women, nor the entire community can ever be the same. All dancing has stopped, as there are no drums any more to provide the rhythms: 'The PRAISE SINGER and DRUMMER stand on the inside of the semi-circle but the drum is not used at all. The DRUMMER intones under the PRAISE SINGER'S invocations' (p. 216).

The reason for the drums' silence is simple: Elesin has undermined the osugbo drums' function by not following their instructions concerning his death. They have determined the action and the exact carrying out of the ritual for generations, and it was unthinkable that Elesin would now disobey. Neither the osugbo drummers nor Olunde (who is—erroneously—convinced of his father's death by the correct interpretation of the drums' message) can be expected to reckon with his failure, since this is a new experience for the whole community.

It is logical for Soyinka to emphasize the silence of the osugbo drummers in his stage direction. The talking drum's main task is, as its name indicates, to speak, to transmit messages, to communicate. But Elesin's behaviour has deprived the drums of this function, and they have become useless. The last scene is thus a theatrically brilliant documentation of the breakdown of a formerly harmonious communicative pattern.

1. David Richards, "Owe l'esin oro, Proverbs Like Horses: Wole Soyinka's *Death and the King's Horseman*," *Journal of Commonwealth Literature* 19, no. 1 (1984): 95 [adapted from author's note]. Parts of this essay are reprinted in this Norton Critical Edition.

In Manchester the envisaged *mise-en-scène* was modified in some crucial, musical respects. Thus, in the last scene the master drummer even advances to the leader of the chorus, slowly approaching through the foyer into the arena with the corpse of Olunde. The script requires no drumming at this point: however, in the RET production Muraina Oyelami plays the melody of the dirge that is chanted by the women. But although he drums the words 'Ale le le', he does not communicate with his instrument in the same sense as before.

Likewise the drum is employed in two crucial moments of the last act contrary to the author's stage direction: at the moment of the throwing back of the cloth over Olunde's corpse, and after Elesin's suicide. In these two situations the emotional and dramatic effect of the drumming was seen by the director as more important than its communicative aspect, this latter having been shattered by the dramatic action. Phyllida Lloyd: 'We actually use music as a sort of action itself. I'm trying to think of an example: the moment where Iyaloja throws back the cloth over Olunde, and the drum really goes into "batata".'

Through this alteration of the play's ending, which reduces the acoustic contrast with its beginning as suggested in Soyinka's script, the production was deprived of a definite interpretation of the community's future fate. Soyinka's powerful dramaturgic sense of the dichotomy between silence and dirge in the end was to some extent lost in the production—arguably one of its weaker aspects, though it could also be understood as a more optimistic interpretation, since Elesin's failure does not seem to paralyze the others in the way suggested by the author. This would make the play basically a tragedy of Elesin as an individual. If the drums, as the script indicates, were silenced, the whole community would appear to be weakened. Phyllida Lloyd comments:

> I think that there is hope at the end of the play. There is hope in the future of the unborn child, undoubtedly. In that sense the play is quite Shakespearean. It's a little bit like the end of *King Lear*, where you feel complete devastation around you, but that one of the forces for good, as it were, remains, to say, 'those of us who stay behind will never see such events again', and you see those people go off into the night and you know that somehow the circle, the wheel will turn and the world will be reborn in some way and will be perhaps wiser. It's kind of carthartic.

Communicating with the Supernatural

While Elesin's lust for the bride at the beginning of the play prepares the ground for the oncoming disastrous events, its turning point or peripeteia happens off-stage, some time after the end of Scene iii or in Scene iv. A closer look at the trance scene may shed some light on how the peripeteia is prepared by the foregoing expressive patterns.

The metaphysical aspect of the non-verbal forms of expression is important. Music as the 'intensive language of transition' and dance as 'the movement of transition' play an essential role within Soyinka's holistic world-view, as the basic means of reaching this transitional state of Elesin's consciousness.[2] The non-verbal forms of expression bring about Elesin's trance and make him dance into Orun, the otherworld.

In the Manchester production, Elesin and the Praise-Singer stand face to face, surrounded by the kneeling market women who perform a vague swaying movement with the upper part of their bodies and their arms, then start chanting the dirge. This choreography is the translation of the 'threnodic essence' in a language of movement, reminding one of an image employed by the author:

> In cult funerals, the circle of initiate mourners, an ageless swaying grove of dark pines, raises a chant around a mortar of fire, and words are taken back to their roots, to their original poetic sources when fusion was total and the movement of words was the very passage of music and the dance of images.[3]

The master drummer detaches himself from the musicians, running around Elesin, continuously drumming, forcing dynamics and speed. Here are Muraina Oyelami's comments on this situation:

> There was a point when I also joined the crowd and ran around Elesin. All this is preparing him to really get the lift. I mean he was about to fly off, to go to the world beyond. . . . Even in a real situation it's the drummer that makes the dancer become possessed—even the priestess or the priest to that possession. . . . And it will reach a climax where he will just let go.

In the background the audience can hear the osugbo drums. The Horseman and his Praise-Singer start jumping on the spot, panting heavily. That was the most evident divergence from the stage direction, which sees Elesin's dance as one 'of solemn regal motions,

---

2. Wole Soyinka, *Myth, Literature, and the African World* (Cambridge: Cambridge University Press, 1976), p. 36; Obi Maduakor, *Wole Soyinka: An Introduction to His Writing* (New York: Garland, 1986), p. 269 [adapted from author's notes].

3. Wole Soyinka, "The Fourth Stage," in *Myth, Literature, and the African World*, op. cit., p. 147.

each gesture of the body . . . made with solemn finality' (p. 182), though it seems clear that there is no definite way for a trance to 'look'. During this sequence of movement the dialogue starts, and the Praise-Singer changes his identity, at times entranced himself: then he speaks as the dead king.

In trying clearly to outline this change of identity, Phyllida Lloyd fell back on a theatrical trick. As a medium, Badejo spoke in Yoruba and with a guttural voice,[4] while as the Praise-Singer he used his normal voice and the English language. The effect is described by the director:

> To an English audience it sounds like a voice from beyond, a voice from another world. It's like a trick in a way. What we are losing is that textual clarity, but I think we're compensating by creating a sense of otherness: We are making contact to the other side, and we're using the Yoruba language as a way of doing that.

When Elesin has fallen completely in trance, he stands motionless. The Praise-Singer, who had mediated verbally a few moments before, now connects the world of the living with the world of the dead by means of gesture: looking at and speaking to his friend, he spreads his arms, the left turned to Elesin, the right pointing to the distant upper world.

Neither in the playscript nor in the production is there any sign of what is about to happen at the next moment. All seem to be prepared for the sacrifice, including the obviously deeply entranced protagonist. This makes the shock for the audience in the following scene even greater, when Elesin's 'animal bellow' from off is heard: 'Leave me alone!' (p. 201). Then he is himself pushed in by Simon Pilkings, who takes the horseman into custody.

Although most European spectators are unlikely to accept the ritual suicide as a communal necessity, the audience feels with Olunde, the son who 'stands frozen to the spot' (p. 201).

Harmonies and Juxtapositions

The reason for this identification lies in Soyinka's perfect preparation in the trance scene: here, with no hint of the final outcome, the situation is harmonious, the communication on a level of perfect interaction. Iyaloja's warnings in the opening scene, that Elesin should be aware of the possibility of being too earthbound with his final erotic adventure, have by this time been forgotten. The trance

---

4. A guttural voice as indicating a supernatural being is a common phenomenon in African ritual. See, for instance, Edward Lifschitz, "Hearing is Believing: Acoustic Aspects of Masking in Africa," in *West African Masks and Cultural Systems*, ed. S. L. Kasfir (Tervuren: Musée royal de l'Afrique centrale, 1988), pp. 221–29 [adapted from author's note].

sequence, with its depiction of communal and expressive harmony, has made the spectator feel safe and by that means induces the tragic awareness in the following action.

If we note that the communication of the Yoruba community is—at least in its unspoilt state—basically harmonious, complex, and technically elaborate, the opposite is true for the Europeans. First of all, music and dance in the second and fourth scenes have no aspects of communication but are reduced to status symbols or representation. Secondly the quality of the rendition of these art forms is obviously poor. Thirdly the Europeans are unable to decode the 'native' communication, as Pilkings's helplessness in Scene ii makes apparent.

The contrast is further intensified by the immediacy of the transition. Scene ii opens with music and dance, but the difference between this and what has gone before is only too obvious and reveals its satirical intention. The Pilkingses dance a tango, dressed in sacred Egungun costumes. The music is not rendered live, but comes from an old, hand-cranked gramophone, with its very restricted acoustic qualities. Moreover, the machine doesn't create but merely reproduces the music. The dancers are European, the Tango comes from Argentina, while the costumes are genuinely West African (and, more important, taboo). The contrast between the third and fourth scenes is constructed in a parallel way, and here Soyinka's characterization, scarcely the depiction of a healthy multicultural experiment, makes a satirical comment on colonialist attitudes and the alienation of western culture.

Phyllida Lloyd's *mise-en-scène* took such character contrasts to the verge of absurdism. In the second scene a *rectangular* green carpet is rolled out and covers the yellow circle—'a kind of rape of the market', as she describes it. The different position of Amusa and Joseph becomes clear in one detail: the houseboy, without fear, steps onto this symbol of European privacy, while the stubborn Sergeant desperately tries to remain standing outside the carpet during the dispute with his master. Yet he is alienated from his culture too: in this situation, as well as during the quarrel with the market women in Scene iii, he stands upright, in an exaggerated military manner. He has internalized the body language of the colonialists.

The contrasts were displayed in the other characters as well—cool but controlled agility, elasticity, and *joie de vivre* for the Yoruba figures, stiff, jerky, and clumsy movements for the Europeans. In the fourth scene a red carpet is rolled out that splits the yellow circle in two halves. A military drum-roll is heard that causes the dancing couples to deploy in one long row to honour the Prince of Wales, who is parading by. All movements are equal, the subjects have become automated: there is no space for any individualism. Phyllida Lloyd comments:

> It's like a contrast to Elesin Oba at the beginning with his Praise-Singers. And it was all free and joyful and alive. And then we had our Prince coming in, all stiff and absurd.

The choreography of the Yoruba movements reveals the very opposite—each actor being free to add a personal note to a certain movement that was distinct from the others and mirrors his or her individuality. Yet the audience was aware of the fundamental unity within the group. There was a basic movement pattern, but never a drilled symmetry.

Audience and Reception

For acoustic and logistic reasons, the dialogue that was spoken during the procession around the foyer at the beginning couldn't be understood. Part of the audience had already taken their seats inside, while those spectators who joined the procession could hardly follow the words because of the generalized 'noise'. Inside the arena, the market women obviously gossiped with each other in Yoruba and Pidgin respectively. While the Yoruba language in the trance sequence was used as a way of characterizing the communication between the entranced Praise-Singer and the dead King, the director's intention in this scene didn't focus on language as a tool for developing the plot, but to give a photograph-like impression of an alien culture. In Peter Badejo's words: 'What the audience need to know is to see this life rather than concentrate on what they're saying.' Or as Phyllida Lloyd put it:

> I think the reason that they're talking in Yoruba at the beginning when the audience come in is not an attempt to alienate the audience or to confuse them. It's simply trying to create a little bit of a 'fly on a wall' experience for them, so that they're coming into something that really is happening. Those women really are talking in their indigenous languages and relating to each other as characters. And the audience might feel they're part of some real experience. It's not a play—it's actually a slice of life.

The first scene reveals a language that is characterized by its highly poetic style and which is difficult to decode even for people familiar with the English language. Soyinka skilfully gives a theatrical translation in the second scene by showing the Pilkingses, who are not able to interpret the drum messages and thus depend on the information of Amusa and Joseph. It was this theatrical translation that made the director think of an unconventional *mise-en-scène*:

> If I'd had any time with Soyinka beforehand, I would have said, 'Why don't we perform that whole opening scene in Yoruba?'

The exaggerated military stance of the Sergeant, alienated from his own culture, during the quarrel with the market women in Scene iii.

> Because then the audience will stop trying to decode it. And they will relax as they would if they were watching an opera. Or if they went to Nigeria and were watching a procession go past. They would be thinking, they would be trying to read it, and they'd be saying, 'Oh, it's a celebration of something.' And: 'This man is getting married.' And then in the second scene it becomes clearer what is happening.

Bearing in mind the never-ending debate about the use of European languages in African drama, it appears almost paradoxical that a European director should consider translating a whole scene back from English into Yoruba. But bilingualism as it was employed in the trance scene was dramatically very effective, and Phyllida Lloyd surely correct in her claim that the main information of the first scene—the festival atmosphere and the marriage of Elesin—would be conveyed even if played in Yoruba. Yet it's likely that Soyinka's intention was precisely to show the richness of the language, the multitude of variations, the proverbs, the flamboyant images, rather than to develop the plot.

Lloyd's reference to the 'fly on the wall experience' implies, with respect to the audience, a realistic but distanced intention. For African theatre, African life and thinking, are still too alien for participation: first, one cannot do more than observe. And even that can be shocking, as Peter Badejo recalls in a wry recollection of the beginning of the show:

> It's new to them! The first day, the moment they heard drums, people started running helter-skelter for their seats! But as time goes on, some of them are beginning to relax and just enjoy it outside before they go in. But again, it might be the first time in their life they will have seen this kind of theatre, starting that way.

Problems of an 'Extended Mise-en-Scène'

The dirge in the play is a musical detail that caused some misunderstanding within the company. Badejo hinted at the fact that some of the (European) actors interpreted the dirge as a sad melody, akin to the conventions of European church music—composed in a minor key. The dirge in Manchester, however, revealed a melody basing on a major triad. Although the melody goes down, it doesn't sound like a motif of a requiem. As Gerhard Kubik has shown, it is unusual in African music to express feelings by harmonic patterns.[5] In his words, most indigenous African music is described as 'emotionally neutral'.

Phyllida Lloyd and Muraina Oyelami stressed the concessions made in the production to European acoustic habits. As the verbal nature of the talking drum cannot be perceived by a western audience (or even by some of the actors involved), the verbal stimulus has to be transformed into a musical stimulus to be acknowledged by the spectators as a hint to a certain action. Phyllida Lloyd gives an example from the first scene:

> Sometimes we have bridged the gap between the talking drum and western understanding. . . . And I might have said, 'You know, that sound needs to be much more important. It needs to draw the attention much more.' Whether that means it needs to be louder or it needs to be longer or have more contrast with what's just come before, I don't legislate on that. But what I just said is, that as a punctuation mark it's not drawing my attention. There is a moment where Elesin sees the bride the first time, and they all go 'ahhh', and the talking drum comments on that. We worked quite hard to try and give that its full value. At first nobody even noticed her. It just wasn't enough. And now, we've actually the whole company looking to her.

5. Gerhard Kubik, "Verstehen in afrikanischen Musikkulturen," in *Musik in Afrika*, ed. Artur Simon (Berlin: Museum für Völkerkunde, 1983), pp. 322–23 [adapted from author's note].

As can be seen, to achieve the intended effect on the audience the lack of intercultural understanding has to be compensated for by the quality of the acoustic stimulus. This wasn't the only compromise of the production: as I mentioned earlier, music was in some parts used as an emotional or dramatic booster. Yet the production could in no ways be regarded as a display of unreflected exotism.

The biggest challenge for the *mise-en-scène* was to create a homogenous work from a heterogenous team that had never worked together before. Soyinka's plays not only demand technically well-trained and highly specialized artists as musicians, dancers, drummers, etc., but need to be understood in their metaphysical dimension. The task of the director therefore is to integrate the various levels of expression in the play as well as the different personal backgrounds of the artists.

According to Phyllida Lloyd, a basic problem in Manchester was that the actors were unequally experienced in the language and metaphysics of the play. Peter Badejo is a brilliant dancer and choreographer, familiar with the Yoruba metaphysics—but he lacked the actors' training and experience, and had to struggle with the complex English language, while the other participants had the opposite problem.

Although Phyllida Lloyd expressed her difficulties mainly as concerned with the dualism of dialogue and metaphysics, these existed on other levels. The dance and music of the Yoruba culture were as alien to her as they were to the other actors of the ensemble, and this was likely to have an effect on her role as a co-ordinator of the various levels. Although thanks to Badejo and Oyelami she could rely on specialist help, her ability to control the correctness of the communicative pattern in its totality was limited, since she herself was only partly familiar with Soyinka's theatrical language. She agreed that in some crucial cases she was uncertain about what the drum was actually saying.

The lack of co-ordination between the different expressive levels as a consequence of intercultural misunderstanding became obvious in one detail, which accidentally emerged during my interviews. When Joseph is asked for a translation of the drums' message by Pilkings in Scene ii, David Webber, who played the Houseboy and is not himself a Yoruba, reacted with a gesture of obviously trying to listen to the direction of the drums. Yet Joseph's answer concerning the ambiguity of the drums' message was a contradiction to his own gesture of listening, as of Oyelami's drumming in this moment, since the latter was beating a completely regular and unambiguous rhythm (for Yoruba speakers). This detail, unimportant though it may seem, reveals the complicated structures of multicultural communication and the consequences which may follow in the staging of a play where this needs to be conveyed.

Patterns of Communication

In *Death and the King's Horseman*, Wole Soyinka sets up a pattern of communication that consists of three elements: words, music, and dance. In production, the ideal would be a well-balanced equality, a system where each of the Yoruba communicants is able to speak and understand on different levels, by contrast with the static expressive nature of the European representatives—for whom music and dance are either 'noise' or luxury, but never a tool for communication.

The Europeans thus become the dramaturgical vehicles for creating comic relief. By showing this contrasting communicative pattern, Soyinka develops and displays the tragic action, through which the breakdown of the protagonist has its cruel impact on his community, where it is mirrored by the loss of some of the expressive levels. The relation of each of these expressive levels to one another provides, then, the motor of the dramatic conflict.

Every non-Yoruba audience will necessarily realize that they can understand only a part of the overall structure of communication. What is crucial is not a complete understanding but a perception of the relation between the communicative elements and its shifts. This is even possible for people unfamiliar with the Yoruba culture.

The basic difficulty for a western theatre is to find the specialists necessary for a successful staging of *Death and the King's Horseman*. It is not sufficient to have actors 'playing' dancers or musicians: they have to *be* dancers or musicians, knowing the aesthetics of such African communicative patterns as 'call-and-response' or 'vital aliveness', and they have finally to reject the notion that communication is primarily a matter of speech.

If a theatre is lucky enough to find the specialists, it is the task of the *mise-en-scène* to develop the various expressive elements in such a way that the multiple dialogue becomes the basic structure of the dramatic action. The RET production in fact succeeded in realizing the concept described by Peter Badejo: Every Yoruba man or African believes in the total utility of the medium of communication. And that's the easiest way I can put it: total utility of the medium of communication.

CRITICISM

D. S. IZEVBAYE

Mediation in Soyinka:
The Case of the King's Horseman†

In this essay I intend to argue that the principle of mediation is fundamental to Soyinka's dramatic art, especially his dramatization of the tragic experience. I shall propose as the key figure in the pattern of mediation developed in *Death and the King's Horseman* not the familiar mythic figures in Soyinka's works, like Ogun, the candidate proposed in "The Fourth Stage" as the Yoruba tragic protagonist, or Sango, the rival god of lightning whose fiery temperament disqualifies him for the tragic role, but *Esu Elegba*, the principle of uncertainty, fertility and change, and the one god who makes possible the reconciliation of opposites which we associate with mediation.

In "The Fourth Stage" Soyinka describes Ogun as *the* tragic actor because he alone among the gods fulfils the Nietzschean requirement for the superman who has will enough to cross the abyss.[1] The primitive irrationality of Ogun is opposed to the sanity and serenity of Obatala, as Nietzsche's Dionysos to his Apollo. Ogun is a mediator between two states of being. There are other forms of mediation to which his qualities do not apply, but it will first be necessary to show why mediation is so central to Yoruba cosmology and consequently to the style of Soyinka's art.

The three-part structure which is often implicit in the cosmology of Soyinka's work reflects the three-part organization of Yoruba political and religious systems: the judicial, the religious and the executive arms of government; the world of the unborn, the world of the living and the world of the dead in religion.[2] Soyinka turns to this cosmology to explain his intentions in *The Road*, and he ends his most recent play, *Death and the King's Horseman*, with a similar allusion to "the dead . . . the living . . . the unborn".[3] Twice, before

† From *Critical Perspectives on Wole Soyinka*, ed. James Gibbs (London: Heinemann, 1980). Copyright © Three Continents Press/Heinemann. Reprinted by permission of the author. Unless otherwise indicated, the notes are adapted from the author's notes.
1. Wole Soyinka, "The Fourth Stage: Through the Mysteries of Ogun to the Origin of Yoruba Tragedy," in *The Morality of Art*, ed. D. W. Jefferson (London: Routledge, 1969), pp. 119–131.
2. Peter Morton-Williams, "The Yoruba Kingdom of Oyo," in *West African Kingdoms in the Nineteenth Century*, ed. Daryll Forde and P. M. Kaberry (London: Oxford University Press, 1967), pp. 36–69.
3. Wole Soyinka, "Drama and the Revolutionary Ideal" and three interviews, in *In Person: Achebe, Awoonor and Soyinka*, ed. Karen L. Morell (Washington: University of Seattle Press, 1975), p. 117.

the publication of this play, Soyinka had attempted an explication of what remains implicit in Yoruba ritual and philosophy, that there is a "fourth area—the area of transition . . . the area of the really dark forces . . . the area of stress of the human will."[4]

It is Ogun's ability to dare this region that qualifies him for tragic stature. But he is not the only figure who mediates between the other areas of existence. Other beings listed by Soyinka include cripples and albinos who are held in holy awe for their physical deformities, and wandering spirits like Abiku. Soyinka is here merely articulating a widely held belief: the women Cassandra, Clark's Orukorere and Armah's Naana are gifted with second sight; and an abnormal looking child pictured in Verger's book qualifies to be considered "a supernatural being" because he has chameleon eyes starting from their sockets, a hanging lower lip and a pyramidal forehead.[5] These beings are thus either in constant motion between the different realms or they permanently inhabit the area of transition and are in a constant state of passage. Iyaloja says of the proposed union between Elesin, who stands at the threshold of death, and the mystery market girl, that "the fruit of such a union will be neither of this world nor of the next. Nor of the one behind us . . . [but an] elusive being of passage."

But mediation is not only this kind of link between planes of existence as in *The Road*. It is also a reconciliation of opposites through either a finding of correspondences, as in the human-divine matching in *The Interpreters*, or the comparable political methods of Kongi and Danlola. The mediator can be a person, (a carrier or a trickster), an act (the dance in *The Road*) or a structure (the relationship between audience and performer, or the arrangement of Ifa divination furniture in which Esu is an essential companion of his opposite, Orunmila). Thus, although Soyinka does not actually use the word mediation or mediator in his writing, the presence and operation of the principle is implied in his description of the different forms of this device; the dance is "the movement of transition" in *The Road*, theatre is a "technique of interaction," and many of his protagonists are "twilight creatures," beings who have to "breach or cross this gulf over and over again," thus illustrating the phenomenon described as "human will under stress."[6] As a re-

---

4. Ibid., pp. 117–18.
5. In Greek myth and tragedy, Cassandra was cursed by Apollo so that her prophesies would never be believed; Orukorere and Naana are similar figures in J. P. Clark's *Song of a Goat* and Ayi Kwei Armah's *Two Thousand Seasons*. See also Pierre Verger, *Notes sur le culte des Orisa et Vodun: A Bahia, la Baie de tous les Saints, au Brésil et à l'ancienne Côte des esclaves en Afrique* (Dakar: IFAN, 1957) [editor's note].
6. Soyinka, "Drama and the Revolutionary Ideal," p. 65.

sult of this view his key characters are usually intermediaries: Lazarus, Murano, Aroni, the Kadiye, Eman, the Organizing Secretary, Si Bero and Elesin.

The device leaves its mark on Soyinka's language too, for it owes its vibrant quality partly to this feature. It is present in the love of paradoxes, punning, *double entendre*, and also the transposed attributes in this quotation from *The Interpreters*: "the *logic* of nature's growth was bettered by the *cabalistic* equations of the *sprouting* derrick." Mediation is thus useful as a principle of balance and moral judgement, even in his use of language. Such paradox is present in the traditional religious order, especially in the ordering of Ifa divination furniture. In the hymn to the creation of the gods in *The Interpreters*, Kola's canvas celebrates "the eternal war of the first procedure with the long sickle head of chance, eternally mocking the pretensions of the bowl of plan, mocking lines of order in the ring of chaos." In this description of the divination board and the sculpture of Esu the circles and the lines become the mediators between the certainty of Orunmila and the disorder of Esu, so that neither god enjoys complete control of the Yoruba cosmos. The result of this balance of forces is not disruption but a cosmic dance.

It is this same principle which gives *A Dance of the Forests* its title. In this play Soyinka treats drama as an art of mediation. It borrows its language and form from the procedure of the judiciary, its medium from the dance. The main questions that may be asked at a first reading of *A Dance of the Forests* is at what point in the play did this "dance" actually take place? The abortive festival planned by the Town Dwellers never takes place, so the "dance" is both the penitential progress of the three humans (a progress which makes the character grouping somewhat reminiscent of that of *The Tempest* in that Prospero/Forest Father leads the three men of sin to redemption and self-knowledge through the agency of Ariel/ Aroni). The central dramatic episode is "the trial" of humanity, in which the forests (the spirits of the palm, the pachyderms, the ants, rivers and volcanos) give testimony against the humans. It is after this that the triplets, the figure in red, the Interpreter, and the half-child "dance" for the humans. This play within the play has the structure of a judicial procedure in the employment of advocates, a prosecutor and witnesses, as well as the use of Oro, the punitive agent in traditional Yoruba society. A hint in this direction has been given when the first scene opens with a legal phrase, "Will you take my case, sir?" The dance is the mediator for linking the three aspects of the play, the legal idiom, the political occasion for the play and the religious interpretation of its action. The relationship of dance and religion is made obvious not only by the important place of dance in religious ritual but by the fact that it is the means of moving between planes of existence in *A Dance of the Forests*, as in *The Road*.

In the earlier play the link between the judicial and the religious aspects of the play is brought out by the interventions of Ogun and Eshuoro in the judicial procedure of the "dance" episode. Such interruptions occur frequently in the drum and dance incidents of later plays; they constitute the dramatic moment of these plays and signify the moment of truth for the characters. In *Kongi's Harvest* such a moment occurs when the Superintendent stops Danlola's drums and when Daodu "split/The gut of our make-believe". In *The Road* Murano's mask-dance is interrupted by Kotonu's accident and later by the indignant action of Say Tokyo Kid. Since the dance is described as "the movement of transition" in *The Road*, its interruption implies an arrest at the point where the dancer remains in transition.

This is the state of paralysis in *Death and the King's Horseman* where action is impossible and where fulfilment is frustrated for the protagonist who, unlike Soyinka's late father, cannot be celebrated for having "danced and joined the ancestors." That Elesin has arrived at the state of transition is suggested in the confusion in the mind of Joseph who cannot tell whether the chief is living or dead: the drumming "sounds like the death of a great chief and then, it sounds like the wedding of a great chief." The white man's intervention in the rites of passage is the historical stopping of the drums. It is presented off-stage to heighten its dramatic impact on both Olunde and the audience:

> OLUNDE: The drums. Can you hear the change? Listen. (The drums come over, still distinct. There is a change of rhythm, it rises to a crescendo and then, suddenly, it is cut off. After a silence, a new beat begins, slow and resonant.) There. It's all over . . . my father is dead. His will-power has always been enormous.

This is the main dramatic irony of the play, for at this point Elesin is neither dead nor has his will-power been proved to be enormous. This decline in the stature of Elesin comes in the Fourth Act of this classic Five Act play after we have witnessed the tragic, Ogun-like courage of Elesin in the climactic Third Act. The function of the fifth Act would be not only to bring about the usual resolution to tragic action but also to bring out the trickster side of the hero's personality—his quick tongue and failure of nerve. The five Acts alternate between the world of the white men and the world of the Africans, and dance is the mediator of both these worlds. Each of the first four Acts opens and closes with the action of dancing, thereby creating a basis for comparing and contrasting both worlds.

Death and the King's Horseman is thus an extended image. It dramatizes the interruption of the psychic and cultural harmony of traditional Oyo society. Its protagonist is an accomplished dancer and his entry involves drummers and praise-singers. When the play opens his dance is "no longer of this earth." The opening scene presents the Yoruba as a people who have had a vision of the void and whose values are an attempt to overcome it. The harmony of their world is imposed on their fear of chaos:

> If [our] world leaves its course and smashes on the boulders of the great void, whose world will give us shelter? . . . In your time we do not doubt the peace of farmland and home, the peace of road and hearth, we do not doubt the peace of the forest.

Part of this hope is expressed in the election and initiation of an "intercessor to the other world" whom they address as "you who now bestride the hidden gulf and pause to draw the right foot across." They thus seek a balance between the material world and the spiritual.

When the stage lights come up on the opening scene of the play, they would fall, significantly, on

> a passage through the market in its closing stages . . . stalls are emptied, mats folded . . . bolts of cloth taken down . . . and piled on a tray.

The symbolism of this setting is as important as that of the dance which occupies such a central role in the play. The cultural importance of the Yoruba market has been discussed by more than one writer:

> In a close relationship with the *Afin* in sharing the centre of the town is the main market which was held in front of the *Afin*, where the Oba could watch from a reasonable distance the regular assembling of his people.[7]

The Yoruba market appears to have the symbolic value of a microcosm. This is suggested by two facts. First, while the major Oba are addressed as *Alaiyeluwa* (Owner of the world and of life), the minor Oba who are founders of their towns have the title, *Oloja* (Owner of the market).[8] Second, there is the common Yoruba saying, *Oja L'aiye, Orun n'ile* (the world is a market, heaven is home). This attitude is reflected in Elesin's flippant boast, "this market . . . is

---

7. G. F. Afolabi Ojo, *Yoruba Culture* (Ife and London: University of Ife Press/University of London Press, 1971), p. 205.
8. N. A. Fadipe, *The Sociology of the Yoruba* (Ibadan: University of Ibadan Press, 1970), p. 160.

my roost . . . where I have known love and laughter away from the
palace," as well as the earnest song of the market women, "We shall
all meet at the great market", and the description of Iyaloja as
"mother of multitudes in the teeming market of the world."

The rich and colorful cloths in the market—damask, *alari*, *sanyan*
and cloth of indigo—are the material equivalent of the honor and
glory awaiting the people's emissary to the other world. The rich
cloths and sexual favors generously offered to Elesin are meant to
honor him for daring to bridge the gulf. The spiritual world is thus
spoken of in material terms: honor is not an abstract idea, but is
represented in concrete terms by the advance of rich food and
cloths, since the Yoruba like "man in any environment must eat
before he can philosophise".[9] Dishonor has its material expression
also. Elesin's disgrace is felt to be tragic because it is couched in
language which makes us feel it as a physical experience. When he
fails in honorable deeds the imagery of sweetmeats and rich cloths
with which he has been honored changes into a picture of the elder
who "has no more holes in [his] rag of shame" stepping "in the
vomit of cats and the droppings of mice" [to] fight them for the
left-overs of the world." A similar image is used in *Oba Waja* where
the Oyo people ask, "shall the commander of the horse/Remain
behind to eat earthworms and centipedes?"[1] Honor comes too late
restored to Elesin, and the final vision of him among the ancestors
which we are given is actually a dreadful curse:

> His son will feast on the meat and throw him bones. The pas-
> sage is clogged with droppings from the King's stallion; he will
> arrive all stained in dung.

The key to Elesin's failure would be found in his excessive love
of the material world symbolized by clothes and sex. It is significant
that in the crucial third Act when Elesin is being put through his
paces by the Praise-Singer, who is both the voice of tradition and
the spirit medium for the late Alaafin, it is the reminder of his vows
as well as the good life which Elesin has enjoyed (good food, fine
clothes), which prefaces the ritual test of his preparedness for his
spiritual role:

> PRAISE-SINGER: . . . . . . if there is
>   Weight on the loose end of your sash . . .
>   . . . if your sash is earthed

9. Ojo, *Yoruba Culture*, p. 205.
1. Duro Ladipo, *Oba-Waja*, in *Three Yoruba Plays*, trans. Ulli Beier (Ibadan: 1964). [It is
   reprinted in this Norton Critical Edition.]

> By evil minds who mean to part us
> at the last . . .

ELESIN: My sash is of the deep purple *alari*
It is no tethering-rope.

Having been assured that Elesin is not tied down by love of material things, the Praise-Singer drops the imagery of clothing and feasting from the ritual and gradually replaces it by that of pathfinding, of striving and endeavor: of horse and dog as guides, of finding one's way in the dark, of the elephant rushing into the forest and the albino making his way through the dark. Believing that Elesin has fulfilled his vows, the Praise-singer pronounces a song of praise: "How shall I tell what my eyes have seen . . . oh how shall I tell what my ears have heard?"

If Elesin's preparedness for his role seems assured by the end of Act Three, his failure in Act Four would seem to have been caused by the intervention of the white man, and the reproach of Olunde and Iyaloja in Act Five would seem a little harsh. But the first Act already shows Elesin's paralysis when he "enters along a passage before the market." He remains spiritually in this state till the end of the play when Iyaloja informs us that "he is gone at last into the passage." Between his first appearance at the market and his death he makes little progress. The white man's intervention in Act Four has been foreshadowed in the first Act by two minor interruptions of his dance. The first occurs when he halts the lyric grace of his dance by his surprising invocation of the "Not I" bird.

This break in the dance is part of his dramatic style, as he earlier stopped his dance to feign annoyance with the market women. But the dramatic irony of the "Not I" bird incident exposes his alienation from his world. Although Elesin explains that the "Not I" bird refers to the fear of death, it also ironically implies an anathema since it is the act of warding off evil by snapping the fingers round the head, as the farmer does in Elesin's tale, to ward of penalties for an unintended abomination. Elesin in a speech of dramatic irony "unrolled my welcome mat for him to see."

The other interruption of Elesin's dance is caused by his lust for an unknown girl glimpsed amidst the market stalls. She is his fatal Cleopatra. The encounter is actually a reversal of the one between the Complete Gentleman and the pretty girl, as the ominous phrasing of Iyaloja's warning suggests: "Elesin, even at the narrow end of passage I know you will look back and sigh a last regret for the flesh that flashed past your spirit in flight." This yearning for the girl is like the backward glance which turned Lot's wife into a pillar of salt. Soyinka detests all forms of womb-yearning. That is why, at the height of Elesin's strength, the Praise-singer finds it necessary to utter an incantation to ward off the danger of an infantile regression: "No arrow flies back to the string, the child does not return through the same passage that gave it birth."

If Elesin fails to attain the grandeur which makes Ogun the hero of "the Fourth Stage," his circumstances are close enough to that of Ogun for him to show a full awareness of his responsibilities as a being of transition. Nevertheless, in spite of the Nietzschean echo in his profoundly ambiguous excuse in the speech to his bride, its sexuality exposes a weak strain in his personality: "I needed you as the abyss across which my body must be drawn." So although Elesin functions well in his institutionalized role as a kind of scapegoat, when the time comes for him to confront his fate he lets himself be ruled by his trickster motives and blames his failure of nerve on "the alien hand [which] pollutes the sources of will."

An African historian has pointed out how widespread and popular this explanation of social change in Africa can be. When the Yoruba say "*Aiye Oyinbo at aiye baba wa*," they mean to divide their history into "the colonial period and that when power lay with our fathers."[2] Elesin adopts this interpretation of history. But his tragedy can also be explained in terms of the trickster trait in the personality of the nonconforming individual. Joan Wescott suggests that *Esu*, the Yoruba trickster-god, is a means of explaining the difficulties of conforming, and he serves as an agent of continual change and readjustment.[3] In Duro Ladipo's dramatization of the Elesin affair, the Oyo People assign the responsibility for change to *Esu*, the "confuser of men [and] the god of fate".

The concept of *Esu* as a folkloric explanation of uncertainty and the threat of individualism to social order must have been encouraged by the social pressures of the past. It has a mythical rather than contemporary reality. Johnson the Yoruba historian notes that at one time delay or reluctance on the part of chiefs who are expected to accompany a dead Alaafin had such grave moral implications that members of the offending official's lineage would rather strangle him than suffer the stain of ignominy. But he could add that by the end of the nineteenth century when he compiled his history "all the men now refuse to die and they are never forced to do so."[4] The Oyo period which provided the material for *Oba Waja* and *Death and the King's Horseman* had become less demanding on

2. J. A. Atanda, "The Changing Status of the Alaafin of Oyo Under Colonial Rule and Independence," in *West African Chiefs and Their Changing Status under Colonial Rule and Independence*, ed. Michael Crowder and Obaro Ikime (Ife: University of Ife Press, 1970), pp. 212–30.
3. Joan Wescott, "The Sculpture and Myths of Eshu Elegba, the Yoruba Trickster: Definition and Interpretation in Yoruba Iconography," *Africa* 32 (1962): 353.
4. Samuel Johnson, *The History of the Yoruba* (Lagos: CMS, 1921), p. 57.

her citizens than the plays emphasize. Voluntary suicide had become little more than an "act of love" by citizens.[5]

Factors making for change in Oyo after World War II included "the economic and social developments which accompanied colonial rule." It is worth noting that this factor is given its historical importance in Achebe's *Arrow of God* where the social disaster is as much a result of economic activity as of the stubbornness of the priest or the blundering of the white man.

The difference in the treatment of this theme is revealing especially since both protoganists, Elesin and Ezeulu, operate in identical circumstances, including the importance of their religious and political offices as mediators, the confusion in their minds at certain moments as to their relationship to the other world, their perception of the advantage of letting a son learn the wisdom of the enemy race, their dependence on the moon for their roles and the intervention of the white man who thus causes an eclipse in their fortunes. Ezeulu is ruined for insisting on what he considers right and honorable for himself and his god; Elesin, whose speech to the bride is a self-criticism that might be profitably applied to Ezeulu, suffers for being more attached to the material world than to his "peace of mind [and the] honour and veneration of his own people."

Soyinka and Duro Ladipo alter historical facts such as dates and the fate of the hero. Both seem to lean on oral traditions, especially the surviving conventions of myths and transition rituals, instead of strictly imitating the lines of the historical development of events as Achebe tries to do in his novels. As in myth, periodization seems less important to the dramatists than general historical significance. For example, 1946 is given as the date for the original historical event at Oyo. Soyinka takes his plot back to the War years. But the Alaafin under whom the Horseman in question would have served died in 1944, and was succeeded by another Alaafin in 1945, although Olunde, in Soyinka's play, says the action of the play occurs about a month after the King's death.

Soyinka's note informs us that some of his changes were made for "minor reasons of dramaturgy." Two points ought to be made from the point of view of the audience. First, the historical incident in which the *Olokun-esin* lives on would have been too untidy for tragic form, since it does not encourage the dramatist to focus and control the values of tragedy. Elesin's despair in the play is heightened by his almost futile suicide. But his suicide is partially restitutive—that is, he is not allowed to live on to feed on the corruption which he has created. In the second place, the four novels of Achebe have sought to demonstrate that the colonial intervention

---

5. Morton-Williams, p. 56; Atanda, p. 228.

in African societies provided an opportunity for abandoning the harsh ethical values of the past for more materialist values.

The situation which emerges from this interpretation of African history would make mimetic art unsatisfactory to a writer like So-yinka because such art upholds a decadent "ethic of reconciliation" to the existing situation. Soyinka accepts the view of drama as a communal art not in the sense of conforming to the values of its time, but in the sense that as "a revolutionary art form", the magic of the drama should be used to work the playwright's end upon the senses of his audience by "a conscious exploitation of the innate activity of man, play-making, in the service of the larger historic process".[6]

For Soyinka the kind of theatre which seeks to recreate the phys-ical conditions of traditional festival theatre is not the only medium favorable for audience participation. The proscenium barrier can be crossed if the playwright treats the modern theatre as "two fluctu-ating halves of the same unit both manipulated by a commonly shared dynamic." The dramatic action is thus a mediation between audience and performance, and "a direct operation of moral and sensual forces."[7] Soyinka gives a comically graphic but symbolic account of the bridging of the gulf between performers and audi-ence at a Cuban theatre during the revolution. A sudden panic in the theatre revived for him the problems of illusion and reality in the theatre and raised the issue whether the audience could have been distinguished from the revolutionary performers in the ensuing confusion.

Soyinka demonstrates this theory in *Death and the King's Horse-man* where the play-acting of the girls breaks down the barrier be-tween illusion and reality for Sergeant Amusa, and almost gets him to do their will by joining in the act. *Death and the King's Horseman* itself contains a more complex form of mediation between the play and its readers in the conduct of the debate between Mrs. Pilkings and Olunde on the cultural value of self-sacrifice. To clarify the true character of what Jane Pilkings describes as "a barbaric cus-tom," Olunde shows how the Prince of England's journey to the colonies at great personal risk helps to ensure "sanity in the midst of chaos" for Englishmen serving in the colonies. The story of the ship captain is used to provide a subtle justification for self-sacrifice in Oyo. The ship captain's sacrifice saved "the innocent people around the harbour" from "loaded ammunition [which] had caught fire" or "those lethal gases they've been experimenting on." In this Oyo state policy ensures that the cease of majesty dies not alone.

6. Soyinka, "Drama and the Revolutionary Ideal," p. 63.
7. Ibid., pp. 63–79 *passim.*

The general groan, sometimes intensified by palace plots and intestinal conflicts, had to be alleviated in the past by the voluntary suicide of the most favored of the king's officials, so that before the reign of Alaafin Atiba, even the Crown Prince had to pay his price.[8]

In this play Soyinka stresses the importance of honor for the well-being of man by pointing out the need for transcendence of material goals. Without this, there would be nothing left but a gulf of anguish which Elesin would have had to endure had he lived, or an emptiness represented by the figure of Pilkings capering at the Resident's fancy ball without recognizing his alienation from the costume he has borrowed and the culture from which it is borrowed.

An ethical code which would uphold death before dishonor is necessary if the tragic gesture of an Olunde is not to degenerate into the play-acting of a Pilkings. From the portrait of masquerades in *Things Fall Apart* and *A Man of the People* we know that such a change is possible when the younger generation of maskers begin to lose sight of the functions performed by some of the masks of their fathers as mediators between the material world and the spiritual.[9] The difference between the two generations is a difference between the ritual of the King's Horseman and the entertaining masque at the Residency.

ELDRED DUROSIMI JONES

Death and the King's Horseman†

The consciousness of an overwhelming public responsibility and a total commitment to it even when this involves death had been the theme of an earlier Soyinka play, *The Strong Breed*.[1] There are analogies between the call of blood in that play and the fatal call of duty in *Death and the King's Horseman*.[2] When Eman in the earlier play seeks to evade the call of his destiny, his father predicts: 'Your own blood will betray you, son, because you cannot hold it back. If you make it do less than this, it will rush to your head and burst it open.'[3] In spite of the call of blood, the play goes on to show how,

8. Morton-Williams, p. 61.
9. A reference to two of Chinua Achebe's novels [editor's note].
† From *The Writing of Wole Soyinka*, Third Edition. Copyright © 1988 by Eldred Durosimi Jones. Published in the United States by Heinemann, a division of Reed Elsevier Inc., Portsmouth, NH. Reprinted by permission of the publisher. Unless otherwise indicated, the notes are adapted from the author's notes.
1. Wole Soyinka, *The Strong Breed*, in *Collected Plays*, vol. 1 (London: Oxford University Press, 1973) [editor's note].
2. Wole Soyinka, *Death and the King's Horseman* (London: Eyre Methuen, 1975), pp. 60–67.
3. Soyinka, *The Strong Breed*, p. 134.

when confronted with the ultimate sacrifice, the human will is apt to flinch, and that the act of self sacrifice is no mere mechanical ritual. In *Death and the King's Horseman* the Elesin Oba's destiny, his 'blood', has similarly destined him for the ultimate sacrifice: 'It is not he who calls himself Elesin Oba, it is his blood that says it. As it called out to his father before him and will to his son after him. . . .' (p. 35) The play examines the Elesin's response when the actual call for which his whole life has been a preparation, and on which the future of his people depend, sounds in his ears.

His response, the play makes clear, has cosmic significance. The Praise Singer, himself a custodian of values, is fully aware of the consequences of a failure to maintain the integrity of a civilization at a crucial point in history: 'There is only one home to the life of a river-mussel; there is only one home to the life of a tortoise; there is only one shell to the soul of man; there is only one world to the spirit of our race. If that world leaves its course and smashes on boulders of the great void, whose world will give us shelter?' (p. 11) The responsibility for keeping the world on course rests on the Elesin; and there are ominous signs of a wavering of his will in the face of the enormous task.

A demand for richer cloths first stuns the market women under their leader Iyaloja, and their relief that this trivial request is all that has seemed to threaten a cosmic disaster is tinged with embarrassment. Iyaloja, as 'Mother of the market', has a representative role, and, like the Praise Singer, speaks for the people and for tradition.[4] She voices the anxiety of the whole community when the Elesin's demands grow and he asks for the hand of a young girl— who is betrothed to Iyaloja's own son. Nothing must be withheld from one who has such a great mission, however, and the request is granted. But after such demands—in themselves unworthy at this time—a failure to live up to the expected level of honour would be little short of pollution, and the anxious reminders of his role are never far from Iyaloja's thoughts. 'The living must eat and drink. When the moment comes, don't turn the food to rodents' droppings in their mouth' (p. 22). By the end of the first section of the play the Elesin's involvement with things of this world and his evident irritation at being reminded of his coming death have sown doubts about the firmness of his will.

This first section also introduces us to the heart of a culture. Its privileges and its responsibilities are understood by all, so that they are accepted, faced or shirked knowingly. What the portrait of the

---

4. In his essay "Mediation in Soyinka: The Case of the King's Horseman", in James Gibbs, ed., *Critical Perspectives on Wole Soyinka* (Washington, D.C.: Three Continents Press, 1980), Dan Izevbaye discusses, with interesting references, the representative role of markets in Yoruba society. [This essay is reprinted in this Norton Critical Edition.]

District Officer and his wife, Simon and Jane Pilkings, dancing the tango dressed in the captured regalia of an *egungun* masque presents to us is a trifling travesty of that same culture, which shocks even the converted Christian Sergeant Amusa. The Pilkings' act is *prima facie* one of desecration, but it is even more significant as a demonstration of their essential irrelevance, and that of the imperium the husband represents in the spiritual environment. There is irony, however, in the fact that through no special virtue, he represents great physical power. Pilkings is portrayed as a nervous, unimaginative, totally ungifted administrator. Soyinka is at pains to emphasize in a prefatory author's note that the District Officer is not the victim of a cruel dilemma. His lengthy pauses for thought are only to resolve such weighty problems as to what extent his actions are likely to disturb the sleep of His Visiting Highness. When the level of thought and action, coupled as it is with military power, is put beside the gravity of the trauma facing the people of Oyo, the cruel irony of the portrayal becomes glaring. To Pilkings the Elesin's sacrifice is a meaningless suicide which it is his duty to prevent. Pilkings's intervention does not start the weakening of the Elesin's will and is ignored by Iyaloja as a major factor in the Elesin's failure. For her, Pilkings is a 'child' and she addresses him persistently as such. She is, by contrast, unrelenting in her censure of the Elesin—fittingly so because of her representative position of 'Mother of the market' and also as the one who has been called to sacrifice her son's betrothed bride to the Elesin's untimely surge of lust. He has ignored her warning and has not only blurred his own vision but also, by fathering a child in those circumstances, has threatened even the unborn. She is as unsparing of her contempt as she was generous and accommodating when she thought the Elesin deserved indulgence:

> You have betrayed us. We fed your sweetness such as we hoped awaited you on the other side. But you said No, I must eat the world's left-overs. We said you were the hunter who brought the quarry down; to you belonged the vital portions of the game. No, you said, I am the hunter's dog and I shall eat the entrails of the game and the faeces of the hunter. We said you were the hunter returning home in triumph, a slain buffalo pressing down on his neck; you said wait, I first must turn up this cricket hole with my toes.   (p. 68)

In the face of her unrelenting prosecution of him, the Elesin asks not for pity but for understanding—'Even I need to understand'— and in this attempt to understand he suggests the nature and extent of Pilkings' role. The Elesin might have overcome even the late pull of the flesh ('even that, even if it overwhelmed one with a thousandfold temptations to linger awhile, a man could overcome it'); but the unexpected appearance of 'an alien hand' encouraged the belief that this was indeed the hand of the gods, a blasphemous thought which finally eroded the lingering vestiges of will and duty: 'I had committed this blasphemy of thought—that there might be the hand of the gods in a stranger's intervention' (p. 69).

Iyaloja brushes this and all other explanations aside. The reasons for the Elesin's failure are relevant to his personal peace of mind, but by now more than this is involved. The Elesin has betrayed history; he has pushed the world from its moorings. The son has now had to assume the role of his father and become—before his time—the bearer of the traditional responsibility of accompanying the dead king on his journey.

This loss of honour and the sacrifice of his son make up the Elesin's real tragedy. His suicide—Pilkings' judicial term would now be applicable—is now merely a matter of personal relief, mercifully executed with speed. The tragedy is that of a man faced with responsibilities which tax his human powers to their limit and collapsing under the weight. Does this also represent the erosion of a people's will?

The 'Mother of the market' has not flinched. True, both the old plantain and its young sapling are dead, but in his final day, the Elesin has left a seed. The young bride ceremonially seals the eyes of her dead husband and prepares to face the future under the guidance of Iyaloja: 'Now forget the dead. Forget even the living. Turn your mind only to the unborn' (p. 76). In this third part of the Yoruba cosmology, with all its uncertainty, lies the hope of the community. There is also some indication of the strength of the community in the voluntary return of Olunde to assume his traditional responsibility on the death of his father, but even more in his readiness to take his father's place in death when the latter's will crumbles. In this willing acceptance of his role, and in the promise latent in the unborn child, lie the society's hope of regeneration and of continuity.

HENRY LOUIS GATES, JR.

Being, the Will, and the Semantics of Death†

* * *

In response to the adage of Nietzsche's sage, Silenus, that it is an act of hubris to be born, Soyinka responds that "the answer of the Yoruba to this is just as clear: it is no less an act of hubris to die."[1] Not surprisingly, Soyinka's muse is his patron god Ogun, god of creativity and the Yoruba "proto-agonist," he who dared to cross the abyss of transition that separates the world of men from the world of the gods in the primal enactment of individual will.

I first confronted *Death and the King's Horseman* in 1973, two years before it was published. Soyinka, who was supervising my graduate work in English at the University of Cambridge, invited me to listen to the first reading of his new play. For three hours we listened as Oxford accents struggled to bring the metaphorical and lyrical Yoruba text to life. Although by now I had become accustomed to this densely figurative language of Soyinka's plays—indeed had begun to hear its peculiar music—I was stunned by the action of the play. That the plot was an adaptation of an actual historical event was even more stunning. And if the play's structure was classically Greek, the adaptation of a historical action at a royal court was compellingly Shakespearean. This, I thought, was a great tragedy.

Perhaps I should describe in outline the historical events before I recount the plot. In December 1944, Oba Siyenbola Oladigbolu, the Alaafin, or King of Oyo, an ancient Yoruba city in Nigeria, died. He was buried that night. As was the Yoruba tradition, the Horseman of the King, Olokun Esin Jinadu, was to commit ritual suicide and lead his Alaafin's favorite horse and dog through the transitional passage to the world of the ancestors. However, the British Colonial District Officer, Captain J. A. MacKenzie, decided that the custom was savage and intervened in January 1945 to prevent Olokun Esin Jinadu from completing his ritual act, the act for which his entire life had been lived. Faced with the anarchy this unconsummated ritual would work upon the order of the Yoruba world, Olokun Esin Jinadu's last born son, Mutana, in an unprec-

---

† From *Harvard Educational Review* 51, no. 1 (February 1981): 163–73. Copyright © 1981 by the President and Fellows of Harvard College. All rights reserved. Reprinted by permission of the author and the publisher. Unless otherwise indicated, the notes are adapted from the author's notes.
1. Wole Soyinka, "The Fourth Stage: Through the Mysteries of Ogun to the Origin of Yoruba Tragedy," in *Myth, Literature and the African World* (Cambridge, Eng.: Cambridge University Press, 1976), p. 158.

edented act, assumed his hereditary title of Olokun Esin, stood as surrogate for this father, and sacrificed his own life. The incident, Soyinka told us following the reading, had intrigued him ever since he had first heard of it. It had, he continued, already inspired a play in Yoruba by Duro Lapido called *Oba Waja*.[2]

Soyinka adapted the historical event rather liberally in order to emphasize the metaphorical and mythical dimensions, outside of time, again reflecting implicitly the idea that an event is a sign and that a sign adumbrates something other than itself by contiguity as well as by semblance. The relation that a fiction bears to reality is fundamentally related to the means by which that relation and that fiction are represented. For Soyinka, a text mediates the distance between art and life, but in a profoundly ambiguous and metaphorical manner. In that space between the structure of the historical event and the literary event, that is to say, the somehow necessary or probable event, one begins to understand Soyinka's idea of tragedy. The plot of a play, certainly, can indicate what may happen as well as what did happen, and this concern with what a protagonist will probably or necessarily do, rather than what he did do, distinguishes Soyinka's universal and poetic art from particular and prosaic Yoruba history. It is this central concern with the philosophical import of human and black experience which so clearly makes him unlike many other black writers. A summary of the play's plot suggests this relation.

The Alaafin of Oyo is dead. To guide the Alaafin's horse through the narrow passage of transition, as tradition demands, the Horseman of the King, Elesin Oba, must on the night of his King's burial, commit ritual suicide through the sublime agency of the will. The action of the play occurs on the day of this death. Death for Elesin is not a final contract: it is rather the rite of passage to the larger world of the ancestors, a world linked in the continuous bond of Yoruba metaphysics to that of the living and the unborn. It is a death which the Elesin seems willingly to embrace—but not before he possesses a beautiful market girl, a betrothed virgin whom he encounters as he dances his farewell greeting before the ritual marketplace. Though Iyaloja, the "mother" of the market, protests the Horseman's paradoxical selection, she consents to and arranges this ritualistic union of life with death.

Revolted by the "barbarity" of the custom, a British Colonial Officer, Pilkings, intervenes to prevent the death at the precise moment of the Horseman's intended transition. Notified by his family, Olunde, the Horseman's eldest heir, has returned from medical

---

2. Duro Ladipo, *Oba Waja*, in *Three Nigerian Plays*, ed. and trans. Ulli Beier (London: Longmans, 1967). Beier's translation captures almost nothing of the lyricism of the Yoruba. [This play is reprinted in this Norton Critical Edition.]

school in England intending to bury his father. Confronted with his father's failure of will, the son assumes this hereditary title only to become his surrogate in death to complete the cosmic restoration of order. In a splendidly poignant climax to the action, the women of the market, led by Iyaloja, unmask the veiled corpse of the son and watch placidly as the Horseman of the King breaks his neck with his chains, fulfilling his covenant with tradition and the communal will, alas, too late. Two men have died rather than one.

As adapted by Soyinka, this is no mere drama of individual vacillation. Communal order and communal will are inextricable elements in the Elesin's tragedy, which not only reflect but amplify his own failure of will. In this sense, Soyinka's drama suggests Greek tragedy much more readily than Elizabethan tragedy, and is akin to the mythopoeic tragedies of Synge and Brecht and to Lorca's *Blood Wedding*. Nor is this merely a fable of the evils of colonialism or of white unblinking racism. *Death and the King's Horseman* is a classical tragedy, in which structure and metaphysics are inextricably intertwined.

Structurally, the play is divided into five acts and occurs almost exactly over twenty-four hours. Its basis is communal and ritualistic; its medium is richly metaphorical poetry which, accompanied continuously by music and dance and mime, creates an air of mystery and wonder. The cumulative effect defines a cosmos comprised at once of nature, of human society, and of the divine. The protagonist's bewilderment and vacillation, his courage and inevitable defeat, signify a crisis, confrontation, and transformation of values, transfixed in a time that oscillates perpetually in an antiphonal moment. Finally, the reversal of the *peripeteia* ("situation") and the *anagnorisis* ("recognition") occur at the same time, as they do in *Oedipus Rex*.

The characterization of Elesin, the protagonist, is also classically Greek. The play records the reciprocal relationship between his character and his fate. Elesin's grand flaw does not stem from vice or depravity, but from *hamartia* ("an error of judgment"), a sign of his weakness of will. Although not eminently good or just, he is loved. His will and his character are neither wholly determined nor wholly free. His character is at once noble and prone to error. The nine-member chorus again and again speaks against Elesin's special hubris, his unregenerate will. His, finally, is the great defeat, but suffered only after the great attempt. The play's action is timeless, as timeless as the child conceived by Elesin on the day of his death. Its plot unfolds in "the seething cauldron of the dark world will and psyche,"[3] where ambiguity and vacillation wreak havoc upon the individual.

---

3. Soyinka, "The Fourth Stage," p. 142.

Although self-sacrifice is a familiar motif in Soyinka's tragedies, Elesin's intended sacrifice is not meant to suggest the obliteration of an individual soul, but rather is an implicit confirmation of an order in which the self exists with all of its integrity but only as one small part of a larger whole. Elesin Oba, after all, is a conferred title, the importance of which derives from its context within the community and from its ritual function. The Elesin's character is determined in the play, not by any obvious material relationships, however, but rather by the plot itself, as the formal dramatic elements of any tragedy are determined by a silent structuring principle. Great tragic plots always determine the tragic character of their protagonists. To paraphrase Pilkings's servant, Joseph, the Elesin exists simply to die; he has no choice in the matter, despite the play's repeated reference to the ambiguity inherent in his role. And Pilkings's intervention, a kind of self-defense, challenges fundamentally the communal defense of self which this ritual embodies.

Elesin's dilemma is both individual and collective, both social and psychic, all at once. In the same way that Faust's hubristic transgression occurs within his consciousness—occurs, indeed, because of his deification of mind and will—so too is Elesin's tragic dilemma enacted internally, here within his will. As he suggests ominously early in *Death and the King's Horseman,* "My will has outlept the conscious act" (p. 18). His hubris is symbolized by the taking of a bride on the morning of his death in a ritual in which the thanatotic embraces the erotic; he chooses the satisfactions of the self over the exactions of the will. This is his tragic flaw. Elesin's inevitable fall results from a convergence of forces at work within the will and without, which conspire to reinforce those subliminal fears that confront all tragic heroes.

Not only is the Westernized Olunde's suicide a rejection of the relief of the resolution afforded by the Western philosophical tradition; it is also the ritual slaying of the father at the crossroads. Olunde's death leaves his father entrapped, penned outside of the rite of passage, for the fleeting moment of transition has passed, making ironic even an act as final as death. Iyaloja, perhaps the most powerful characterization of a woman in African literature, expresses the paradox: "We said, the dew on earth's surface was for you to wash your feet along the slopes of honor. You said No, I shall step in the vomit of cats and the droppings of mice; I shall fight them for the left-overs of the world" (p. 68). In the face of his son's slaying, the Elesin is poignantly "left-over." There will be no more Elesins, for the unbroken order of this world has now been rent asunder. As Iyaloja remarks acidly, "He is gone at last into the passage but oh, how late it all is. His son will feast on the meat and throw him bones. The passage is clogged with droppings from the King's stallion; he will arrive all stained in dung" (p. 76). To paraphrase the praise singer, the world has finally tilted from its groove (p. 10).

The ritual passage of the Horseman had served for centuries to retrace an invisible cultural circle, thereby reaffirming the order of this Yoruba world. The ritual dress, the metaphorical language, the Praise-Singer's elegy, the Elesin's dance of death—these remain fundamentally unchanged as memory has recast them from generation to generation. The mixed symbols of semen and blood, implied in the hereditary relationship between succession and authority and reiterated in the deflowering of the virgin on the day of death, stand as signs of a deeper idea of transition and generation. But the role of the Horseman demands not only the acceptance of ambiguity, but also its embrace.

Although Elesin's is an individual dilemma and a failure of the human will, the dilemma is implicit in his role of the King's Horseman, a communal dilemma of preservation of order in the face of change. During the play, at a crucial moment, a traditional proverb is cited which reveals that doubt and ambiguity are not emotions uncharacteristic of the Elesin: "The elder grimly approaches heaven and you ask him to bear your greeting yonder; do you think he makes the journey willingly?" (p. 64). All myth, we know, reconciles two otherwise unreconcilable forces, or tensions, through the mediation of the mythic structure itself. The *Orestia* is a superb example of this. This trick of "structuration," as it were, is the most characteristic aspect of human mythology. Soyinka, in his "Director's Notes," in the *Playbill* of *Death and the King's Horseman* puts the matter this way: "At the heart of the lyric and the dance of transition in Yoruba tragic art, that core of ambivalence is always implanted. This is how society, even on its own, reveals and demonstrates its capacity for change."[4]

We do not need to know, as the Yoruba historian Samuel Johnson tells us, that at one time the reluctance of an Elesin to accompany a dead Alaafin engendered such disgrace that the Horseman's family often strangled him themselves, nor that the reluctance of the Elesins grew as contact with the British increased.[5] We do not need to know these historical facts simply because the Horseman's ambiguity over his choices is rendered apparent throughout Soyinka's text. And from *Hamlet* it is that sense of "conscience" as defined in the epigraph from Hamlet's soliloquy, implying self-consciousness and introspection, which is also the Horseman's fatal flaw—

4. Chicago, Goodman Theatre, 1979.
5. Samuel Johnson, *A History of the Yorubas: From the Earliest Times to the Beginning of the British Protectorate*, ed. O. Johnson (London: Routledge & Kegan Paul, 1969).

that which colors "the native hue of resolution . . . with the pale cast of thought."[6] As Elesin Oba puts it, in a splendid confession near the end of the play, he commits "the awful treachery of relief," and thinks "the unspeakable blasphemy of seeing the hand of the gods in this alien rupture of his world" (p. 69). This ambiguity of action, reflected in the ambiguity of figurative language and of mythic structure, allows this to remain a flexible metaphysical system. Formal and structured, it remains nonetheless fluid and malleable with a sophisticated and subtle internal logic.

Soyinka embodies perfectly the ambiguity of the Elesin's action in the ambiguity of the play's language. A play, among all the verbal arts, is most obviously an act of language. Soyinka allows the metaphorical and tonal Yoruba language to inform his use of English. Western metaphors for the nature of a metaphor, at least since I. A. Richards, are "vehicle" and "tenor," both of which suggest an action of meaning, a transfer through semantic space. The Yoruba, centuries before Richards, defined metaphor as the "horse" of words: "If a word is lost, a metaphor or proverb is used to find it."[7] As do tenor and vehicle, the horse metaphor implies a transfer or carriage of meaning, through intention and extension. It is just this aspect of the Yoruba language on which Soyinka relies. The extended use of such densely metaphorical utterances, searching for the lost or hidden meanings of words and events, serves to suggest music, dance, and myth, all aspects of *poeisis* long ago fragmented in Western tragic art.

In Soyinka's tragedies, languages and act mesh fundamentally. A superb example of this is the Praise-Singer's speech near the climax of the play, in which he denounces in the voice of his former King, the Elesin Oba:

> Elesin Oba! I call you by that name only this last time. Remember when I said, if you cannot come, tell my horse. What? I cannot hear you, I said, if you cannot come, whisper in the ears of my horse. Is your tongue severed from the roots Elesin? I can hear no response. I said, if there are boulders you cannot climb, mount my horse's back: this spotless black stallion, he'll bring you over them. Elesin Oba, once you had a path to me. My memory fails me but I think you replied: My feet have found the path, Alaafin. I said at the last, if evil hands hold you back, just tell my horse there is weight on the hem of your smock. I dare not wait too long. . . .
>
> . . . Oh my companion, if you had followed when you should, we would not say that the horse preceded its rider. If you had

6. William Shakespeare, *Hamlet*, Act III, Scene 1.
7. The Traditional Yoruba reads, "Owe l'esin oro, bi oro ba sonu owe ni a fi n wa a."

followed when it was time, he would not say the dog has raced beyond and left his master behind. If you had raised your will to cut the thread of life at the summons of the drums, we would not say your mere shadow fell across the gateway and took its owner's place at the banquet. But the hunter, laden with a slain buffalo, stayed to root in the cricket's hole with his toes. What now is left? If there is a dearth of bats, the pigeon must serve us for the offering. Speak the words over your shadow which must now serve in your place. (pp. 74–75)

In this stunning speech, the language of music and the music of language are one. In one sense, the music of the play gives it its force, the reciprocal displacement of the language of music with the music of language. The antiphonal structure of Greek tragedy is also perhaps the most fundamental African aesthetic value, and is used as the play's internal structuring mechanism. As in music, the use of repetition, such as the *voudoun* ("voodoo") phrase, "Tell my horse," serves to create a simultaneity of action. The transitional passage before which the Elesin falters is inherent in all black musical forms. Soyinka's dances are darkly lyrical, uniting with the music of the drums and songs of the chorus to usher the audience into a self-contained, hermetic world, an effected reality. Soyinka's greatest achievement is just this: the creation of a compelling world through language, in language, and of language. He has mastered the power of language to create a reality, and not merely to reflect reality. But his mastery of spoken language is necessarily reinforced by mastery of a second language of music, and a third of the dance. "Where it is possible to capture through movements what words are saying," he says, "then I will use the movement instead of the words."[8] To evoke these languages, and to evoke the threnodic celebration of the meanings of death and the reciprocity of passage among the past, the present, and that state of being to be, and to escape the naive myths of Africa which persist in this country, Soyinka insists upon directing his tragedies himself, as he did the production at Chicago.

As a critic of silent literary texts, I was struck by the dynamic nature of the Chicago production, ever shifting, ever adapting itself toward an unspoken ideal, in a manner which in short space and time parallels what happens to a text when studied by a critic, but only over a much longer period. Soyinka, of course, knows what he wants a performance to say, and knows what combination of textures will suggest his meaning to an alien audience. Confronting

8. Personal interview with Wole Soyinka by Henry Louis Gates, 5 Oct. 1979.

an American audience's usual unease with, or condescension toward, an African setting no doubt reinforced whatever tendencies
he had to adhere to a strict rendering of the play.

But is Soyinka's Yoruba world so very obscure? Is it any more
obscure than the tribal world of the ancient Greeks, than Joyce's
voices in *Ulysses* or the private linguistic circle of *Finnegans Wake*?
Footnotes to *The Waste Land*, topographies to Joyce, concordances
to Shakespeare: we presume a familiarity with these texts which is
made possible only by the academic industry of annotation. The
fact of Soyinka's Africanness only makes visible an estranged relation which always stands between any text and its audience. As
Shakespeare used Denmark, as Brecht used Chicago, Soyinka uses
the Yoruba world as a setting for cosmic conflict, and never as an
argument for the existence of African culture. Always in the language of his texts are ample clues for the decoding of his silent
signs, since the relationship among character, setting, and language
is always properly reinforcing. This is no mean achievement: it is
the successful invocation of a hermetic universe.

It is for this reason that Soyinka is often compared favorably to
his direct antecedents, Euripides and Shakespeare, Yeats and
Synge, Brecht and Lorca. Statements such as this sound necessarily
hyperbolic, no doubt. But it is impossible not to make such com-
parisons when one searches for a meaningful comparison of Soyinka's craft with Western writers. For so long, black Americans,
especially, have had to claim more for our traditions than tact, re-
straint, and honesty might warrant, precisely to redress those claims
that our traditions do not exist. But Soyinka's texts are superbly
realized, complex meditations between the European dramatic tradition and the equally splendid Yoruba dramatic tradition. This
form of verbal expression, uniquely his own, he uses to address the
profoundest matters of human moral order and cosmic will.

What does remain obscure, nevertheless, is something else, a set
of matters so much more subtle and profound than mere reference
can ever be. And these matters involve an understanding of tragedy
seemingly related to, yet fundamentally unlike, that notion of the
tragedy of the individual first defined by Aristotle and, in essence,
reiterated by Hegel, Nietzsche, and even Brecht. Set against the
hubris, hamartia, and violent obliteration of a noble individual is
Soyinka's evocation of a tragedy of the community, a tragic sense
which turns upon a dialectic between retributive and restorative
justice and order. The relation which the individual will bears to
this process, the always problematic relation between the order of
the community and the self-sacrifice of the protagonist, whose role
is defined by his own intuition and will to act, forms the center of
Soyinka's plays and of his conception of the role of the artist in

society. Soyinka's protagonists are protagonists for the community; they stand as embodiments of the communal will, invested in the protagonist of the community's choice. Even the moment of most distinct individuation must always be a communal moment. He summarizes his own conception of this relationship in his art:

> Morality for the Yoruba is that which creates harmony in the cosmos, and reparation for disjunction within the individual psyche cannot be seen as compensation for the individual accident to that personality. Thus it is that good and evil are not measured in terms of offences against the individual or even the physical community, for . . . offences even against nature may in fact be part of the exaction by deeper nature from humanity of acts which alone can open up the deeper springs of man and bring about a constant rejuvenation of the human spirit. Nature in turn benefits by such broken taboos, just as the cosmos by the demand made upon its will by man's cosmic affronts. Such acts of hubris compel the cosmos to delve deeper into its essence to meet the human challenge. Penance and retribution are not therefore aspects of punishment for crime but the first acts of a resumed awareness, an invocation of the principle of cosmic adjustment.[9]

It is this disintegration and subsequent retrieval of the protagonist's will which distinguishes Soyinka's tragic vision from its Western antecedents. His understanding of tragedy at long last gives some sense to what is meant by "the functional" and "the collective" in African aesthetics, two otherwise abused and misapprehended notions. Clearly, he reveals, these are relationships effected by the prototypic agonist, the acting individual will. Rightly, we look first to Soyinka's language to begin to understand his direct relation to Shakespeare's mastery of language. And Soyinka's language, always, is his own. Yet, it is this curious metaphysical structure of the tragic which most obviously remains unlike ideas of Western tragedy. Paradoxically, it is "African" certainly, but it is ultimately a Soyinka construct. Soyinka has invented a tragic form, and registered it in his own invented language, a fusion of English and Yoruba. Surely this is his greatest achievement. For, in the end, *Death and the King's Horseman* itself stands as a mythic structure, as a structure of reconciliation. As he concludes about the nature of tragedy:

> Great tragedy is a cleansing process for the health of the community. Tragic theatre is a literal development of ritual. It is necessary for balancing the aesthetic sensibilities of the com-

---

9. Wole Soyinka, "Drama and the Revolutionary Ideal," in *Person: Achebe, Awoonor, and Soyinka*, ed. Karen L. Morell (Seattle: Institute for Comparative and Foreign Area Studies, 1975), pp. 68–69.

munity. Tragedy is a community event. It is the acting out of
the neuroses, the recoveries, within a community. It does not
just involve a single individual.[1]

BIODUN JEYIFO

[Ideology and Tragedy]†

II

* * *

Soyinka's *Death and the King's Horseman*[1] is, to date, his only dramatisation of historical material, a remarkable fact for a playwright
who, by his own admission, has been largely concerned with the
meaning of history and historical experience.[2] But this is remarkable
only for those unfamiliar with Soyinka's 'mythopoeic' attitude to
history, his constant penchant for transforming experience into
metaphysical, transhistorical, mythic dimensions. Soyinka reveals
this attitude clearly when he says in his preface to *Death and the
King's Horseman*:

> The Colonial Factor is an incident, a catalytic incident merely.
> The confrontation in the play is largely metaphysical, con-
> tained in the human vehicle which is Elesin and the universe
> of the Yoruba mind—the world of the living, the dead and the
> unborn, and the numinous passage which links all: transition.
> *Death and the King's Horseman* can be fully realised only
> through an evocation of music from the abyss of transition.[3]

Moreover, of greater significance than this explicit prefatory
statement is Soyinka's considerable dramaturgical departures from
his historical material. The following segments of the play's action,
so crucial to Soyinka's purposes as to constitute the play's basic
dramaturgical supports, are entirely 'fabricated': Elesin Oba's marriage to the young maiden; the visit of H.R.H. the Prince; Olunde's

1. Personal interview with Wole Soyinka by Nancy Marder, July 1979.
† From *The Truthful Lie: Essays in a Sociology of African Drama* (London: New Beacon,
   1985). Reprinted by permission of the publisher. Unless otherwise indicated, the notes
   are adapted from the author's notes.
1. Wole Soyinka, *Death and the King's Horseman* (London: Eyre Methuen, 1975).
2. This is as much a prevalent critical reaction to Soyinka as his own pronouncement on
   history, as shown by the following quote from an interview with the present writer in
   Transition 42 (1973) 63: "It is because I believe that the forces of history may be confronted that I believe in social and political action. (On whose side was history in the
   last Nigerian war?)"
3. *Death and the King's Horseman.*

sojourn in, and timely return from Britain;[4] and above all, the suicide of Elesin. I have cited *only* these crucial segments of the play's
plot and action in order not to seem to be tying Soyinka to too
literal a notion of historical verisimilitude. For there are many more
minor details and points of departure from the historical material
which properly and unarguably belong in matters of dramatic structure and technical craftsmanship.

It is necessary to emphasize that Soyinka is not the first major
playwright to be more or less indifferent to historical exactitude in
a work which deals with an historical event. Apart from the eminent
authority of such practitioners of the attitude as Shakespeare, Shaw
and Brecht, there are many important theoretical rationalisations
which underpin it. Friedrich Schiller's contribution comes to mind
with special relevance:

> . . . I may say that tragedy is the poetic imitation of an action
> deserving of pity and therefore, tragic imitation is opposed to
> *historic* imitation. It would only be a historic imitation if it
> proposed a historic end, if its principal object were to teach or
> that a thing has taken place and how it took place. . . . It may
> thus be understood how much poetic truth may lose, in many
> cases, by a strict observance of historic truth, and reciprocally,
> how much it may gain by even a serious alteration of truth
> according to history. . . . It is, therefore, betraying very narrow
> ideas of tragic art, or rather poetry in general, to drag the tragic
> poet before the tribunal of history, and to require instruction
> from a man who by his very title is only bound to move and
> charm you.[5]

We shall see presently that unlike Schiller, Soyinka does not
counterpose 'historical truth' to 'poetic truth'. However, an important convergence of attitudes which derives from the Aristotelian
tradition must be noted: Soyinka's 'fabrications' in the plot of the
play, while retaining the main outlines of the historical confrontation, all but lift the action into the realm of imagined reality. Of
these 'fabrications' I want to point out for especial notice Elesin
Oba's suicide and the sojourn of his son Olunde in Britain and
consequent to this, the fact that Olunde is pressed into dramatic
service by the playwright as the mouthpiece for anathemas against

---

4. It is interesting to compare, on this note, Soyinka's play with Duro Ladipo's *Oba Waja*
(The King is Dead) on the same material. In Ladipo's play, Elesin's son is called Dawudu
and is away to Ghana trading, when the events take place. For an English adaptation of
this play see Ulli Beier, *Three Yoruba Plays* by Duro Ladipo (Ibadan: Mbari Publications,
1964). [It is reprinted in this Norton Critical Edition.]
5. Quoted in Bernard F. Dukore, *Dramatic Theory and Criticism: Greeks to Grotowski* (New
York: Holt Rinehart, 1974), p. 456.

the arrogance and the chauvinism of European civilisation. This point has a lot to do with the implicit ideological connotations of Soyinka's tragic historical issue in the play.

III

We may briefly summarize the storyline dramatised by Soyinka in *Death and the King's Horseman*:

The Alafin (King) of Oyo having died about a month prior to the action proper of the play, the important chief, Elesin Oba (Commander of the King's Stables), must, as custom and tradition demand, commit ritual suicide on the night of the King's burial. Elesin Oba is more than prepared for his destiny; he embraces it in a harmonious reconciliation of personal volition and cultural and metaphysical sanctions. The system which demands his ritual suicide constitutes the organic social, moral and metaphysical rationalisation of his life. Death is no negation, especially the kind of death which he will die: it is a crossing over to the world of the ancestors, one phase of the unbroken link between the world of the dead, the living and the yet to be born. As a consummation of this unbroken chain of being(s) Elesin takes a young wife on this night of his death: the product of their union—the old, ancestor-to-be and the young—will attest to that consummation. . . .

However, the Oyo kingdom is an enclave in the colonial territory of Nigeria; it is administered by a white Colonial District Officer named Pilkings. Pilkings learns of the impending suicide of Elesin and in a well-meant intervention (which, however, is not unmixed with racist disdain for 'barbaric customs') he arrests Elesin, to 'protect' him from himself and his culture. The tragic reversals then unfold in a swift manner. Olunde, Elesin Oba's first son and heir who, on receiving the news of the Alafin's death, had returned home to bury his father, himself now commits suicide, to save the family honour and to avert the spiritual disintegration which might arise from his father's collapse before Pilking's intervention. Elesin is stung by the death of his son and the negation of the moral and metaphysical foundations of his existence which Olunde's suicide signifies. He therefore strangles himself in his prison cell. Pilkings is traumatised by the reversals in the effects of his actions; the other major characters of the play—Iyaloja and the Praise-Singer—lament the destruction of a people's spirit by the infliction of a rupture between their existence and the vision of life which sustains it. This is the 'threnodic essence' of the play and Soyinka's exalted lyrical reaches in the play make good his prefatory promises, as shown by the following movement in the devolution of the play's action:

IYALOJA (moves forward and removes the covering): Your Courier Elesin, cast your eyes on the favoured companion of the
King.
(Rolled up in the mat, his head and feet showing at either
end is the body of OLUNDE.)
There lies the honour of your household and of our race.
Because he could not bear to let honour fly out of doors, he
stopped it with his life. The son has proved the father Elesin,
and there is nothing left in your mouth to gnash but infant
gums.

PRAISE-SINGER: Elesin, we placed the reins of the world in your
hands yet you watched it plunge over the edge of the bitter
precipice. You sat with folded arms while evil strangers tilted
the world from its course and crashed it beyond the edge of
emptiness—you muttered there is little that one can do, you
left us floundering in a blind future. Your heir has taken the
burden on himself. What the end will be, we are not gods
to tell. But this young shoot has poured its sap into the parent stalk and we know this is not the way of life. Our world
is tumbling in the void of strangers, Elesin.[6]

IV

What does one make of Soyinka's grand subject in *Death and the
King's Horseman*? Barely eight years after the episode which Soyinka dramatises and transmutes in the play, the Afro-American
writer, Richard Wright, visited Ghana (then the Gold Coast) and
seeing everywhere the absurd, pathetic products of the colonial enterprise, he made observations which seem to accord in particulars
and in spirit with Soyinka's tragic issue in the play:

> The gold can be replaced, the timber can grow again, but there
> is no power on earth that can rebuild the mental habits and
> restore that former vision of life that once gave significance to
> the lives of those people. Nothing can give back to them that
> pride in themselves, that capacity to make decisions, that or-
> ganic view of existence that made them want to live on this
> earth and derive from that living a sweet even if sad meaning.
> Today the ruins of their former culture, no matter how cruel
> or barbaric it may seem to us, are reflected in timidity, hesi-
> tance and bewilderment. Eroded personalities loom here for
> those who have psychological eyes to see.[7]

6. Soyinka, *Death and The King's Horseman*, p. 9.
7. Richard Wright, *Black Power: A Record of Reactions in a Land of Pathos* (New York: Harper & Brothers, 1954), p. 153.

The episode which Soyinka dramatises in *Death and the King's Horseman* took place in 1946; Richard Wright wrote the words quoted above in 1955; Soyinka wrote his play in 1975. Is Soyinka seeing, some twenty years after Richard Wright, the same vacant souls, the same bewildered victims of a fragmented world? I suppose that Soyinka himself would give both a negative and a positive response to this question. Yes: because contemporary Africa is still wracked by immense contradictions and negations, some of which are often expressed in psychological and spiritual forms. No: because Soyinka the man of the world and the self-avowed revolutionist of thought has recently and with increasing passion observed in his writings a positive act of collective 'self-retrieval' and 'self-apprehension' in contemporary Africa. These themes find their most complete statement in his published collection of essays titled *Myth, Literature, and the African World*.[8] By Soyinka's own lights one can therefore see in *Death and the King's Horseman* one aspect of a whole ideological programme in contemporary Africa. The play presents a moment of *negativity* when the contradictions in our societies, at the level of psychic and spiritual disjuncture, are revealed and probed. Soyinka's tragic issue in the play, the referential representativeness of his tragic hero, plus the ideological underpinnings of these structures, are all to be grasped at this level of the collective psyche and spirit of a whole continent.

That a tragedy and a tragic hero can express, symbolically, the basic myths and the psychic experience of a culture, has been amply demonstrated by great examples in Western literature. One thinks particularly of *Oedipus Rex* and *Hamlet*, in an extensive field which includes, apart from the great Greek classics, others such as Shakespeare's *Macbeth* and Brecht's *Galileo*. How can the personal disaster or tragic destiny of one character come to express the collective destiny of a people or a race? The question has never been wholly resolved. But, to refer back to our theoretical model, it seems that we are here at a point between Aristotle and Hegel. The actions and fate of a protagonist hero assume an *essentiality* and representativeness both by virtue of *his* nature and the potentiality of symbolic reverberations carried by his goals and aspirations—which of course are defeated in the course of the tragic action. In other words, both in his person and in the enterprise which he comes to assert and defend, a tragic hero of the kind we are discussing must embody the basic emotions and the collective will of a people.

8. Wole Soyinka, *Myth, Literature, and the African World* (Cambridge: Cambridge University Press, 1976).

In *Death and the King's Horseman* both Elesin Oba and other African characters of the play, excepting the native functionaries of the colonial machine, are made to express, consciously and with considerable lyrical force, the redemptive nature of Elesin Oba's intended ritual suicide. The lyrical and rhetorical aspect must be emphasized. The play never really *dramatises* either the force of Elesin Oba's personality or the inevitability of his actions. We are simply presented these matters as given realities and the playwright compels our acceptance of them by the lyrical brilliance of his dramatic language, perhaps unsurpassed by any of his plays. In the following dialogue, consider, for instance, the metaphorical language which expresses the relationship between Elesin Oba and the Praise Singer (one of the major characters of the play), a relationship that is much like that between Elesin and the other characters of the play:

> PRAISE-SINGER: Elesin o! Elesin Oba! Howu! What tryst is this the cockerel goes to keep with such haste that he must leave his tail behind?
> ELESIN (slows down a bit, laughing): A tryst where the cockerel needs no adornment.
> PRAISE-SINGER: O-oh, you hear that my companions? That's the way the world goes. Because the man approaches a brand-new bride he forgets the long faithful mother of his children.
> ELESIN: When the horse sniffs the stable does he not strain at the bridle? The market is the long-suffering home of my spirit and the women are packing up to go. That Esu-harrassed day slipped into the stewpot while we feasted. We ate it up with the rest of the meat. I have neglected my women.
> PRAISE-SINGER: We know all that. Still it's no reason for shedding your tail on this day of all days. I know the women will cover you in damask and *alari* but when the wind blows cold from behind, that's when the fowl knows his true friends.[9]

Elesin Oba is the flamboyant, zestful cockerel and his retinue and praise-singers are his adorning and protective tail: an ingenuous, disarming image but it nevertheless expresses a relationship crucial for the action of the play. However, we are not left without a more telling, more passionate expression of the stature of our tragic hero or the essentiality of his action. The following altercation between Amusa, the police sergeant, and the market women who block his attempts to arrest Elesin and who mercilessly satirise Amusa's servitude to the white colonial administrator, illustrates this point well:

---

9. Soyinka, *Death and the King's Horseman*, p. 9.

AMUSA (shouting above the laughter): For the last time I warn
you women to clear this road.

WOMAN: To where?

AMUSA: To that hut. I know he dey dere.

WOMAN: Who?

AMUSA: That chief who calls himself Elesin Oba.

WOMAN: You ignorant man. It is not he who calls himself Elesin
Oba, it is his blood that says it. As it called out to his father
before him and will to his son after him. And that is in spite
of everything your white man can do.

WOMAN: Is it not the same ocean that washes this land and the
white man's land? Tell your white man that he can hide our
son away as long as he likes. When the time comes for him,
the same ocean will bring him back.

AMUSA: The government say dat kin' ting must stop.

WOMAN: Who will stop it? Tonight our husband and father will
prove himself greater than the laws of strangers.[1]

In *Death and the King's Horseman* Soyinka polarises the conflict
between a traditional African, organic vision of life and an alien
system of discrete laws and social polity, with tragic results for the
indigenous system. In other words, it is a confrontation at the level
of categorical super-structures wrested from their economic and
social foundations. Thus, Soyinka can totalize the conflict such that
a man like Amusa, otherwise a zealous servant of the colonial regime, is, in his mental universe, as resolutely opposed to the foreign
cultural penetration (or aggression) as either Olunde or Elesin himself. This is perhaps why Soyinka is anxious, in his prefatory notes,
to tell us that 'The Colonial Factor is an incident, a catalytic incident merely. The confrontation in the play is largely metaphysical . . .' .

Elesin Oba's *honour*—and the honour of the 'race'—in the play
hangs on his performance of the ritual suicide. However, as the
sections of the altercation between Amusa and the women quoted
above indicate, the notion of honour (and integrity and dignity) for
which Soyinka in the play provides a metaphysical rationalisation
rests on the patriarchal, feudalist code of the ancient Oyo Kingdom,
a code built on class entrenchment and class consolidation. The
superstructures can never totally free themselves of their material
foundations. Elesin Oba is lauded, feted and celebrated by his retinue and the women, and all this is presented by Soyinka as *naturally* due to a man on whose personal destiny rests the integrity and
maintenance of a vision of life which holds society together. But
that vision is not a natural outgrowth, like trees and leaves, not an

---

1. Soyinka, *Death and the King's Horseman*, pp. 35–36.

[handwritten margin note: but what is natural, in a sense, is followers this]

effusion of metaphysics, but an elaborated system of human social relationships in a precise form of society. It is useful to recall here Hegel's description of the use, in tragic writing, of the notion of honour deployed by Soyinka in *Death and the King's Horseman*, a notion of honour based on rank, or 'blood', or nature:

> The difference of rank is, from the nature of the case, something necessary and predetermined. If now, secular life has not yet been regenerated, through the infinite comprehension of true freedom, in virtue of which the individual can himself choose his condition and determine his vocation, it is, on the one hand, and in greater or lesser degree, nature, birth, which assigns man to his permanent position; on the other hand, the dimensions which thus appear are also, through honour . . . held fast as absolute and infinite.[2]

In the process of polarising the conflict of *Death and the King's Horseman* between an alien, and an indigenous African world view, Soyinka has suppressed the real, objective differences between conflicting groups and classes within the indigenous system. It is illustrative of the gaps and dents in Soyinka's present ideological armour that he selected *this* particular metaphysical and philosophical order to symbolize pre-colonial African civilization and NOT other more egalitarian African cosmogonic and metaphysical systems, the erosion of which ideological and political progressives can, with greater reason, regret. A metaphysics which idealizes and effaces the conflicts and contradictions in African societies, which rationalizes the rule of the dazzling FEW (such as Elesin) over the deceived MANY (the women, the retinue, Amusa, etc.) is an extension, in the ideological sphere and in the realm of thought, of class rule in the economic and political spheres. Marx has demonstrated clearly the manner in which this extension takes place:

[handwritten margin note: isn't this a highly colonialist statement?]

> The ideas of the ruling class are in every epoch the ruling ideas, i.e., the class which is the ruling material force of society, is at the same time its ruling intellectual force. . . . The ruling ideas are nothing more than the ideal expression of the dominant material relationships, the dominant relationships grasped as ideas. . . . [3]

*　*　*

---

2. Quoted in Dukore, *Dramatic Theory and Criticism*, p. 530.
3. Karl Marx, *The German Ideology* (New York: International Publishers), 1970, p. 64.

172

WOLE SOYINKA

[Elesin Oba and the Critics]†

* * *

When art ceased to imitate life, it did not thereby aspire to imitate ideology: while criticism which fails to emulate life ends up as imitation of art.

In clarification of the above, 'emulate life' is used in the sense of making criticism subject to the interacting processes which we observe in life—in its totality, not hiding away from uncomfortable modes of realities or wishing them out of existence. In other words, not 'running away from life'. 'Imitate life' is of course the traditional objection to pallid reproductions, one-dimensional photographs. The danger is greater for criticism since Art confessedly elects its area of attention, its manageable scope for re-creation, while Criticism pretends to draw from the *entire* principles of life in order to penetrate the elective scope of Art. The most cursory reading of any of the schools of criticism, and most especially of Jeyifo's justly represented triad—Aristotle, Hegel, and Marx—confirms this.[1]

Criticism imitates art when it attempts to force all works of the imagination, including 'historic re-creation' into the laws of its own hermeticisation of the world. This may, of course, be a good or a bad thing—but let that fact first be recognised. The sociology of critics and/or criticism, therefore becomes doubly of interest and significance. As, for example, the original canons that form today's armoury of Marxist criticism, did they start out as part of the body of Party directives, becoming appropriated into 'objective' analyses of the relation of Art to society losing, along the way, important reservations by the formulators themselves on the Nature of Art? Vatic certitude, absolutism and comprehensiveness, adopted for action at a particular moment in history deliberately *suppress* uncomfortable deductions in over-all interest of a Cause. This we know as heavily documented historical fact. The questioning processes of the originals—Marx, Lenin, Engels and Trotsky—therefore offer greater illumination on the creative universe of the artist than the narrow schematism favoured by their followers. And this illumination comes, I find, not so much from the actual pronouncements,

---

† From *Art, Dialogue, and Outrage: Essays on Literature and Culture,* ed. Biodun Jeyifo (Ibadan: New Horn Press, 1988). Copyright © Wole Soyinka.

1. See Biodun Jeyifo, "Tragedy, History and Ideology: Notes towards a Query on Tragic Epistemology," Seminar Paper, University of Ife, now published in *The Truthful Lie* (London: New Beacon Books, 1985), pp. 23–45 [adapted from author's note]. [An excerpt from this essay is published in this Norton Critical Edition.]

as from their 'history' or, to use my own preferred expression, the *process*, for this last brings the distanced intelligence into the formulative picture, not as a passive receiver, but as a reconstructing strategist of *his* world. Thus, for the narrow-schema approach, it is enough to evoke the authority of Marx in the familiar quotation:

> The ideas of the ruling class are in every epoch the ruling ideas; i.e. the class which is the ruling material force of society, is at the same time its ruling intellectual force. . . . The ruling ideas are nothing more than the ideal expression of the dominant material relationships, the dominant relationships grasped as ideas. . . .

But suppose, in addition, we mediate this crucial analysis with the following (or a thousand equally valid examples):

> According to the materialist conception of history, the determining element in history is *ultimately* the production and reproduction in real life. More than this neither Marx nor I have ever asserted. If, therefore, somebody twists this into the statement that the economic element is the only determining one, he transforms it into a meaningless, abstract and absurd phrase. (Engels in a letter to Joseph Bloch, 1890)

The obvious mediation involves the critic in the *process*, which alone—not the literal application of one or the other elicited principle from material reality—can lead to a true understanding of the nature of Art and Ideas *in any given epoch.*

Concerning *Death and the King's Horseman,* the attempt to stretch its horizons beyond the demonstrable intent of the author only contracts its universe into the schema of the critic. The truly creative writer who is properly uninhibited by ideological winds, *chooses*—and of course we can speculate on the sociological factors involved in this choice ad infinitum—he *chooses* when to question accepted History—*A Dance of the Forests*; when to appropriate Ritual for ideological statements—*The Bacchae of Euripedes* and equally, when to 'epochalise' History for its mythopoeic resourcefulness—*Death and the King's Horseman.* In the last event, he deliberately eschews distractions from the mythopoeic intent, especially such as happen to be fashionable, reserves its innate intellectual muscularity for the deductive mechanism of the audience or else, locates it legitimately in the *dramatis personae* of the period and locality, in the 'probable' events of the period, the 'probable' courses of those events and sometimes, even in the 'probable' resolutions.

Biodun Jeyifo's concern with the historical emendations of the play belong in the same category of one of my professors at Leeds

University who, on reading *The Swamp Dwellers*, queried: But do your peasants think in such sophisticated terms? Jeyifo's approach is, of course, the obverse: why do not your 'peasants' (substitute 'exploited classes') speak, act, event-wise relate and generally conceptualise in a 'sophisticated' ideological idiom (substitute framework)? My answer to the former was: Yes, they do speak in such 'sophisticated' terms, they do conceptualise and give verbal expressions to the resulting concepts, but—they engage in this routine exercise in their own *language*. To the latter, I respond: No, they need not, for they already possess their own organic language of experiential and history-summative understanding. Inadequate? Of course, from the contemporary advance of human knowledge. But adequate at *their* level of world and self-apprehending. The artist or the ideologue is quite free to reconstruct History on the current ideological premises, and thereby prescribe for the future through lessons thus provoked. But to insist that the *personae* of History conceptualised experience anachronically is a presumption that offers no *exclusive* orientation to the creative mind when it confronts an unarguably timeless phenomenon. Such as Death. Valid or invalid though our reconstruct may be, it is of no consequence to society *in its particular epoch* confronted with the problems of ameliorating an eternally tyrannic negation of its will to being. The collective phenomenisation of death is one such ameliorating device. It is not only worthy of study or presentation within its own terms; it confronts the arrogance of ideated systems with the authority of the irreducible. A study of society, even of contemporary society reveals that Man resorts to the strangest devices for nullifying that unanswerable nullity of History, progress, materialist certitude, etc. *as experienced*, in the phenomenon of death. Now that is the ultimate, imponderable dialectic over which tragic poetry builds its symbolic edifice. It is better than nothing, and *nothing* is precisely what is offered even by the most radical and humanistic systems of world or self-apprehension, faced with this one definitive human experience, and of its surrogate relations in the 'tragic' fortunes of the individual in socio-political contexts.

In other words, the desire 'to put off Death', 'to come to terms with Death', to 'communalise' Death so as to make it more bearable for the individual, 'to humour Death' (a quasi-magical propitiation), these are all social and individual devices and of course they make for untidiness in 'scientific' systems, so they have to be wished away. Now the actual forms which such devices take can of course be translated in terms of property and productive relations, etc., the most direct expressions of which have been the slaughter of slaves and retainers, mummification, domestic animal cult, *egungun* and other court-originated cults, etc., etc. The poet, especially the mythopoet, is not entirely satisfied with that secondary level of forms of inventiveness or appropriation, however, and, while he deals in concrete manifestations, may choose not to further reduce the original primordial fear by new extra epochal analytical games. For that is to move away from the mythopoeic source—and for no discernible illuminating results for the specific poetic enterprise. Nobody, I hope, will tell us that the fear of—or at the very least, the *resentment of, sense of unpleasantness about,* etc.—Death is simply due to the failure of the individual or society to as yet exist within an egalitarian environment. My suspicion is that this need to communually contain Death will always be there. Whether indeed the desperation with which this primary (human) hostility to death is sublimated under historico-materialist incantations is not in itself a superstitious device for evading the end of the material self is a question that can only be resolved by a deep probing of the critic's deeper sub-conscious. Certainly it leads easily to a tendency towards 'vulgar Marxist criticism' or, in this context, superstitious Marxism.

To substantiate the above, the paper by O. Onoge and C. G. Darah: *The Retrospective State: Reflections on the Mythopoeic Stage at Ibadan* should be contrasted to Jeyifo's essay. The comparison is most telling. The former is deeply conscious of a creative universe, however scant the lip-service the authors pay directly to it, while Jeyifo remains locked exclusively within a system where all properties of art that do not fit into it become evidence of reaction or bourgeois art. This is something very disquieting about the attempt to import wholesale the Stalinist-Zhdanovian line into Marxist criticism here, with all the sterile dogmatism of the hideous machinery of Proletkult! To return to the central axis of my historical emendations, around which Jeyifo's principal strictures are constructed, here is an alternative reading of history as material of creative presentation:

The District Officer has not been invented for the purposes of this reconstruction—that much of course is easily proved. His sociology therefore, insofar as it informs his attitudes to the colonised society, has not been invented. The District Officer and his world, in short have *provoked* the argument of the drama. Furthermore, unless that District Officer is imbued by Jeyifo with a greater sociopolitical habit of analysis than *I* am prepared to credit him with, the motivating factor for his action, his interference is squarely and hermetically posed within the simple confrontation of 'civilised' values versus the 'barbaric'. Within those terms, the location of Olunde in War-time England, as opposed to Ghana (then the Gold Coast), is a legitimate device to equalise, *precisely within those terms and none other,* the claims of a 'civilisation' which, historically speaking, has persistently incorporated no less barbaric usages into its social organisation—the slave trade is one obvious, emotive example. My circumscription of the possible areas of 'argument', my rejection, for instance, of the option to make Olunde reject suicide because of 'overseas' enlightenment is a creative prerogative, logically exercised, since I have no wish to demonstrate that the colonial factor is ethically superior to the indigenous. Fastening onto the use of the concept 'honour' is an exaggeration which merely obscures the issue. The concept of 'honour' in that Oyo society is, for this dramatist, precisely on the same level of honour, mission duty, as revealed in the imperialist ethic that brought Europe into Africa in the first place. Yet even here, the historic personae will— probably again—pose an unexceptionable view:

> ELESIN: Even the honour of my people you have taken already; it is tied together with those papers of treachery which make you masters in this land.

When a mere word is used to do service for a number of differing concepts, acts, situations, etc. the exclusive attribution of one particular concept of it to the author is a fraudulent act by any critic. But does it merit such attention at all? A very possible reading is one of a portrayal of characters in a historical situation with differing and conflicting senses of 'honour', 'duty', etc. Perhaps such a reading is too prosaic since one side rhapsodises 'honour', while the other (Pilkings and wife) merely castigate it in plain prose and action. A society whose usage, even in 1977 is to lyricise *guguru* in the streets of the city now creates ideological problems because, in a ritualistic encounter with Death they reach into their deepest mythopoeic resources for an 'ultimate' experience. We must keep away from selective readings which lead to libellous assertions such as, 'the kind of *honour* which Soyinka deploys in *Death and the King's Horseman*', etc.

The actual language used in criticism is of course extremely revealing as a gauge of the critic's commitment to 'making a case' as opposed to objective commentary. 'It is illustrative of the gaps and dents in Soyinka's present ideological armour that he selected *this* particular metaphysical and philosophical order to symbolize African civilisation, etc. etc.' *Selected* is of course not a chance word, any more than 'symbolise'. This slice of Oyo history has floated in and out of my creative consciousness since 1960. Once or twice I had been on the verge of writing it but other more pressing themes intervened. As Femi Osofisan pointed out in his own critical observations, a year's Fellowship at Churchill College, Cambridge, 72/73 finally provided some uninterrupted leisure. The actual triggering event was a bust of Churchill on the stairs in the college named after him. The history came back; the play was written. So much for *selection*. Now for *symbolise*. If a world has been deliberately re-created with little or no recourse to actual history, the author may indeed be held suspect; here, the 'symbolic intent' requires proof. Without it, the charge remains a wild presumption of intent. I find it particularly ironic when I recall that Ulli Beier actually suggested to me that history of Oyo as a usable theme for the Independence Celebrations Drama Competition in 1960. I preferred instead to write *A Dance* which, as fabricated history, may be more truthfully held to indicate any deliberate attempt to symbolise African civilization. Even without benefit of that knowledge, the existence of *A Dance* should have curbed this and other generalisations of dubious accuracy. At the moment I feel no particular anxiety about the possible corruption of the African will to egalitarianism through an 'unmediated' play such as *Death*. If any school of thought accepts the opposite, I suggest that this is because they are living almost wholly on the pages of books and are divorced from the *totalist* reality of African political consciousness within its active history or underestimate the responsive intelligence of the general readership masses who are not locked within the reification realm of literature. For here we are once again back to that basic factor: the sociology of the critic.

Marx, Engels, Trotsky and Lenin were revolutionaries of the total society. I hope we do not need to spend any more time in libraries to have it accepted on all sides that, for every statement which can be used on behalf of the Stalinist-Zhadnovian school of literacy culture, an equally weighty number can be adopted for the view that the critic owes serious obligations to the creative universe of the artist at work. The artist will continue to speak in his own voice; hopefully someday, the critic will learn to do the same.

* * *

JOAN HEPBURN

[Ritual Closure in *Death and the King's Horseman*]†

* * *

Ritual closure is the central issue in Soyinka's *Death and the King's Horseman,* and Iyaloja mediates between the characters inimical to the ritual's progress in the Yoruba world depicted in the play. Rit-

† From *Black American Literature Forum* 22, no. 3, Wole Soyinka issue, pt. 2 (Autumn 1988): 577–614. Reprinted by permission of the author. Unless otherwise indicated, the notes are adapted from the author's notes.

uals figure in the European environment in the play as well, though these rites are not rites per se. Only the Yoruba rite of passage through which the protagonist Elesin goes involves the separation-initiation-reintegration paradigm described by Joseph Campbell in his *Hero with a Thousand Faces*.[1] Elesin separates from his known world among the living, enters the chthonic realm where he communicates with the dead, and attempts thereby to revitalize his universe.

In *Death and the King's Horseman*, * * * Soyinka integrates Western and Yoruba dramatic techniques to develop his theme of ritual closure. For example, the traditions of the *egungun* and the seventeenth-century European masque are used in this play. Even so, *Death and the King's Horseman* should be grouped, with *A Dance of the Forests* and *The Strong Breed*, as one of Soyinka's most African plays. In *Death and the King's Horseman*, Soyinka makes his best use of proverbs, music, mask, and dance. The lyrical language of Elesin, whose gestures while in the passage make him a spokesman for the dead, is especially moving. Also, the folk humor missing in some of Soyinka's political and ritualistic plays is present in *Death and the King's Horseman*.

Failure to complete the central ritual successfully in this play could destroy the Yoruba universe. The death of a king has occasioned the ritual through which the king's horseman, Elesin, must go. According to Yoruba tradition, a month after a king dies, his horseman must ritualistically will himself dead so as to join the king. If Elesin fails to join his king at the appointed time, the king is trapped alone in the pathway between the living and ancestor worlds. Thus trapped he would curse the living. As a result of this curse, humans would suffer unspeakable punishments; all of nature would be in a state of imbalance and chaos, the world tipped off its axis, a crisis state par excellence.

The difficulty in closing the ritual for the renewal of the Yoruba universe has been the subject of critical controversy. According to some critics (see the "Author's Note" to the play), Elesin is prevented from dying and joining his king by a white district officer who is a cultural chauvinist, bent on eradicating the savage customs of the Yoruba, but it is apparent that Pilkings' attempt to prevent the completion of Elesin's ritual merely complicates things. As in the case of Eman in *The Strong Breed*, Elesin plans to die by midnight at full moon, but Pilkings, thinking it his duty to save Elesin's life, interrupts his ritual. Pilkings captures Elesin and imprisons

---

1. Joseph Campbell, *The Hero with a Thousand Faces* (New York: Pantheon, [1949], 1961) [editor's note].

him in the old storehouse for slaves, now, ironically, a storeroom for broken furniture, in the annex of the Residency, which is the British imperialists' headquarters. Pilkings imagines that if he holds Elesin in a cell until dawn, he will prevent a barbaric act. He does not. Even before Elesin commits suicide, the mediator Iyaloja tells Pilkings as much. Pilkings' meddling merely deepens the tragedy, for to save his father's face with the king and to save his world, Elesin's son rushes into the passage before Elesin is shamed into entering it. Thus two die rather than one, and one of them prematurely. Significantly, Iyaloja tells Pilkings that she is not interested in his understanding or misunderstanding of her traditions.

Soyinka himself cautions against the superficial reading of his play which some reviewers have given it. In his author's note, he says:

> The Colonial Factor is an incident, a catalytic incident merely. The confrontation in the play is largely metaphysical, contained in the human vehicle which is Elesin and the universe of the Yoruba mind—the world of the living, the dead and the unborn, and the numinous passage which links all: transition. *Death and the King's Horseman* can be fully realised only through an evocation of music from the abyss of transition.[2]

In other words, the play is not simply about a clash of cultures. What the Praise-Singer says to Elesin about Yoruba history applies to Pilkings' efforts: "Our world was never wrenched from its true course."

Iyaloja forces the closure of the ritual that Elesin was to have performed according to set procedures. For the ritual to work, members of the secret society of *osugbo* would inform Elesin of the opening of the door of the pathway to the dead king and other ancestors, which would occur on the full moon. He would be accompanied by the king's couriers, evidently other chiefs who would ritually die to accompany Elesin into and through the passage. In the world of the living, there would be drumming and singing spectators/celebrants along "the pulse-centers of town," through which those who enter the passageway would pass. Once Elesin were dead, his wife would pour earth on his eyes, and his son prepare his body for burial in the prescribed way taught him by his father. The problem is that the father upsets the order of things.

Iyaloja's goading of Elesin into the passage is calculated to set the order of things right; that is, as right as possible. To this end,

---

2. Wole Soyinka, *Death and the King's Horseman* (London: Methuen, 1975). Page references are to this text [editor's note].

she visits the Residency, where a European ball is in progress and where Elesin is being held prisoner, and she ignores Pilkings to say angrily:

> I warned you, if you must leave a seed behind, be sure it is not tainted with the curses of the world. Who are you to open a new life when you dared not open the door to a new existence? I say who are you to make so bold? Oh you self-vaunted stem of the plantain, how hollow it all proves. The pith is gone in the parent stem, so how will it prove with the new shoot? How will it go with that earth that bears it? Who are you to bring this abomination on us? (68)

In this same brutal way, she continues until, at the climax, also the point of revelation for Elesin, the dramatic irony and dramatic reversal in the play, she does and says this:

> IYALOJA (moves forward and removes the covering): Your courier Elesin, cast your eyes on the favored companion of the king.
> (Rolled up in the mat, his head and feet showing at either end is the body of Olunde.)
> There lies the honour of your household and of our race. Because he could not bear to let honour fly out of doors, he stopped it with his life. The son has proved the father Elesin, and there is nothing left in your mouth to gnash but infant gums. (75)

Iyaloja's language is harsher than that of Jaguna and Aroni,[3] who are also concerned with the well-being of their nations, but with all three of these characters the harshness of speech and character is appropriate to the degree of threat to their universe, especially since a mere individual's selfish desires are the cause of their world's toppling. Again, in Soyinka's drama the individual will is subordinated to that of the collective. It is the community one seeks, at all costs, to save, not one person. Even Iyaloja's final lines, with which the play ends, focus on the communal urge to survive. She says to the pregnant Bride, "Now forget the dead, forget even the living. Turn your mind only to the unborn" (76). Still, Elesin is one of Soyinka's most engaging characters, a real individual.

The mediator Iyaloja intervenes in all the crucial events and decisions made in the play. Thus it is not surprising that she, along with her partner in the mediation of ritual closure, the Praise-Singer, warns Elesin many times not to "jeopardise the welfare of

---

3. A reference to characters in Soyinka's *The Strong Breed* and *A Dance of the Forest* [editor's note].

[his] people" (57). However, one of the most powerful and moving of these warnings is spoken by the dead king himself, through Elesin's Praise-Singer, his mouthpiece, as Elesin dances solemnly, regally, in a semi-hypnotic state into the chthonic passage. As Iyaloja later goads Elesin into this passage, it is worth examining the king's warning during which something of this passage is revealed:

> Is your memory sound Elesin?
> Shall my voice be a blade
> of grass and
> Tickle the armpit of the past? . . .
>
> If you cannot come Elesin, tell my dog.
> I cannot stay the keeper too long
> at the gate.
>
> I know the wickedness of men. If there is
> Weight on the loose end of your sash such weight
> As no man can shift; if your sash is earthed
> By evil minds who mean to part us at last . . . (42)

The significance of these lines extends beyond the fact of Elesin's warning to reveal something of the nature of the gulf, of the "state of possession," and of the sheer lyricism of the ancestors' speech; like Eman, Elesin crosses over to be with his ancestors when he dances prematurely partway into the passage. Besides, the music and dance of dirge during his passage enhance the trance-like quality of Elesin's state. The music of the drums, especially of the *gbedu*,[4] is heard on either side of the living world, in both the mundane and the great ancestral market place. Elesin is evidently moving in step with the invisible ancestors who surround him. Both the drums and dancers from the other world drown out Elesin's awareness of the world he is still in, so that he appears not to hear Iyaloja or his Praise-Singer when they speak in their own voices. Elesin's gestures grow weightier as he moves deeper into his trance and into the passage.

Several warnings from the mediator Iyaloja and the Praise-Singer draw out of Elesin a declaration of his responsibility to his king and to his universe. One of the richest metaphorical statements of his intention to fulfill his ritual responsibility is couched in his "Not-I Song." Because this song about his confronting Death reveals a good deal about the complexity and charm of Elesin's character

---

4. According to Oyin Ogunba, "The *gbedu* drums are a traditional symbol of royalty. In some places there are sixteen of these royal drums in a set, all pot-like and of different sizes, tones and pitches. They are to be beaten loud and joyously on state occasions." See *The Movement of Transition: A Study of the Plays of Wole Soyinka* (Ibadan: Ibadan University Press, 1974), p. 167.

—which gets him into trouble and demands the mediator's intervention—and about the language of riddles in which he as royalty speaks, I quote him at length:

> Death came calling.
> Who does not know his rasp of reeds?
> A twilight whisper in the leaves before
> The great araba falls? Did you hear it?
> Not I! swears the farmer. He snaps
> His fingers round his head, abandons
> A hard-worn harvest and begins
> A rapid dialogue with his legs.
>
> 'Not I,' shouts the fearless hunter, 'but
> It is getting dark, and this night-lamp
> Has leaked out all its oil. I think
> It's best to go home and resume my hunt
> Another day.' But now he pauses, suddenly
> Lets out a wail: 'Oh foolish mouth, calling
> Down a curse on your own head! Your lamp
> Has leaked out all its oil, has it?'
> Forwards or backwards now he dare not move.
> To search for leaves and make *etutu*
> On that spot? Or race home to the safety
> Of his hearth? Ten market-days have passed
> My friends, and still he's rooted there
> Rigid as the plinth of Orayan. . . .
>
> Why is the pupil crying?
> His hapless head was made to taste
> The knuckles of my friend the Mallam: . . .
>
> Ah, but I must not forget my evening
> Courier from the abundant palm, whose groan
> Became Not I, as he constipated down
> A wayside bush. He wonders if Elegbara
> Has tricked his buttocks to discharge
> Against a sacred grove. Hear him
> Mutter spells to ward off penalties
> For an abomination he did not intend. . . .
>
> There was fear in the forest too.
> Not-I was lately heard even in the lair
> Of beasts. The hyena cackled loud Not I,
> The civet twitched his fiery tail and glared:
> Not I. Not-I became the answering-name
> Of the restless bird, that little one
> Whom Death found nesting in the leaves
> When whisper of his coming ran

Before him on the wind. . . .
What a thing this is, that even those
We call immortal
Should fear to die. . . .

I, when that Not-I bird perched
Upon my roof, bade him seek his nest again,
Safe, without care or fear. I unrolled
My welcome mat for him to see. Not-I
Flew happily away, you'll hear his voice
No more in this lifetime—You all know
What I am. (11–14)

The animal figures remind one of Aesop's Fables and other tales. The point of this song which Elesin chants like a born raconteur as he dances energetically and humorously into the market place is that all living things may fear and resist Death, but he welcomes it. Elesin's catalog of living beings afraid of death includes a cross-section of Yoruba society—the farmer, the hunter, the courtesan, the pupil, the priest, the evening courier, the beasts of the forests, the ancestors, and the gods. His list includes all the Yoruba planes of existence, and his daring exceeds all of these; his boastful "Not-I" is his praise song to himself. Though Elesin mocks Death and claims that even the gods lack his courage to face Death, this song which Elesin sings at the pinnacle of his career contrasts markedly with Elesin's actual moment for encountering Death. The song helps to establish the height from which Elesin falls.

The style of the song has interest too. Clearly, Elesin speaks in an elevated style. In earlier plays Soyinka demonstrated his skill in handling lower forms of expression, such as those Shakespeare's Mechanicals might speak in *A Midsummer Night's Dream*. In *Death and the King's Horseman* Elesin's language is appropriately suited to his status as royalty, for he sings in proverbs and riddles, part of Yoruba folk tradition, and a sign of his wisdom and wit. The song both poses and answers a riddle. The details with which he develops his song, his images (e.g., of the courtesan and the courier), are graphic and, at times, sensual. The structure of the riddle explains the many queries in the song, which mark an active and analytical mind, despite the simple diction, peppered with Yoruba words, and the short sentences. The short sentences are appropriate for oral delivery, and the repetition of "Not-I" in the sixth quoted stanza speeds up the pace of the passage; in this stanza the rhythm builds to a climax. Iambic pentameter is the dominant meter, with the trochaic, then the spondaic foot being the most frequently substituted to suit the Elesin's energy, his oral literary style, and the music and dance with which he accompanies himself. While only twenty-five percent of the song is composed of verbs and verbals, Elesin's use of adverbial modifiers is colorful, as in his expression "consti-pated down a wayside bush." Besides illustrating his love of lan-guage, the "Not-I" song delightfully indicates Elesin's sense of play, his humor (e.g., in describing the farmer's flight from the field), his quick and penetrating powers of observation, his dramatic presence, and his love of life. He does not miss a thing; he experiences ev-erything. Thus the "Not-I" song, designed to assure listeners at the market of his sense of responsibility and commitment to self-sacrifice to benefit them, also depicts the Elesin as a man of the world; and it is precisely his sensuality, his appetite for worldly things, that undoes him.

Initially, it appears that because Elesin welcomes Death no one else need face it; he dies an intermediary for others; mediation is his *raison d'être* in the play. Accordingly, the praise songs sung about him both by his Praise-Singer and by the women of the mar-ket speak of his qualities of bravery, honor, and loyalty—all attri-butes of traditional heroes. Yet the threat of offending the ancestor, a theme so important in *A Dance of the Forests* and *The Road*, or the gods in *The Swamp Dwellers*, provides Elesin an excuse for his tragic failure of will.

Iyaloja makes the crucial decisions not to offend the ancestral spirits, among whom the mothers of the market count Elesin, be-cause he plans to die at midnight. According to tradition as it is expressed in the play, one must be careful never to offend another who is dying, for people fear the curses of the departed more than they do those of the living. Evidently a curse from an ancestor can destroy worlds. This fact partially explains all the other characters' continually praising Elesin, especially as his dying is an act of in-tercession for his community, a guarantee of its renewal. Two things Elesin requests involve his being offended, and Iyaloja in-tervenes to prevent this. First, knowing how sensitive the issue is of offending a potential ancestor, Elesin teases the mothers of the market, giving them a good fright. In this case, he abruptly halts their praise songs to him, telling them he is bitterly offended. He prolongs the tease by speaking in riddles, all of this to request of the women that they clothe him in their richest cloth in preparation for his funeral.

Though it is appropriate that Elesin be ceremonially and richly attired for his burial later that night, the fact that he spends his last hours in the company of women—usually symbolic of the prin-ciple of life in Soyinka's plays—, in the liveliest center of the com-munity, and in the richest garb, suggests his materialistic nature. Events which follow confirm this notion. In fact, they reveal him to be most carnal when he should be most spiritual. Then too this episode prepares viewers for another of Elesin's tricks, by means of which he again seduces these women into granting his wishes. In any case, Iyaloja sees to it that he is richly robed.

The second potential source of offense to Elesin involving Iyaloja has to do with a woman he spies in the market place and to whom he is immediately attracted. The offense might have been in the women's refusing him this woman with whom he wants to make love and therefore marries on the eve of his death. Worse, the woman is betrothed to Iyaloja's son. Yet Iyaloja consents to this marriage, which robs her son of his bride, for she hopes by her decision to better enable Elesin to perform his ritual task of benefit to the Yoruba community. Having what he wants would relieve his mind of earth-bound preoccupations and of ill will toward those who deny him his request.

The Praise-Singer and Iyaloja comment on Elesin's restless eyes. It seems he has always been lecherous, and as a powerful elder he has often had his way with women. His being a near ancestor works even more in his favor, but he is also a gifted wooer:

> Enough, enough, you all have cause
> To know me well. But, if you say this earth
> Is still the same as gave birth to those songs,
> Tell me who was that goddess through whose lips
> I saw the ivory pebbles of Oya's river-bed.
> Iyaloja, who is she? I saw her enter
> Your stall; all your daughters I know well.
> No, not even Ogun-of-the-farm toiling
> Dawn till dusk on his tuber patch
> Not even Ogun with the finest hoe he ever
> Forged at the anvil could have shaped
> That rise of buttocks, not though he had
> The richest earth between his fingers.
> Her wrapper was no disguise
> For thighs whose ripples shamed the river's
> Coils around the hills of Ilesi. Her eyes
> Were new-laid eggs glowing in the dark.
> Her skin . . . (19)

Until he has worn down opposers of his desires, he speaks in riddles before speaking plainly. Again, this literary dramatic device of the riddle is reflective of Elesin's royalty, but in this instance, he uses it to draw the market women in. He succeeds, too, in gaining their sympathy:

> Who does not seek to be remembered?
> Memory is Master of Death, the chink
> In his armour of conceit. I shall leave

That which makes my going the sheerest
Dream of an afternoon. Should voyagers
Not travel light? Let the considerate traveller
Shed, of his excessive load, all
That may benefit the living. . . .
Who speaks of pleasure? O women, listen!
Pleasure palls. Our acts should have meaning.
The sap of the plantain never dries.
You have seen the young shoot swelling
Even as the parent stalk begins to wither.
Women, let my going be likened to
the twilight hour of the plantain. . . .
All you who stand before the spirit that dares
The opening of the last door of passage,
Dare to rid my going of regrets! My wish
Transcends the blotting out of thought
In one mere moment's tremor of the senses.
Do me credit. And do me honour.
I am girded for the route beyond
Burdens of waste and longing.
Then let me travel light. Let
Seed that will not serve the stomach
On the way remain behind. Let it take root
In the earth of my choice, in this earth
I leave behind. (20–21)

The women are moved by Elesin's emotional appeal in the first quoted stanza, for he suggests that, as a considerate traveler, he will benefit them if they favorably respond to his request. In the second quoted stanza he appeals to the women's practical sense about the meaningfulness of his act. In the third, he persuades them to honor him. In short, the Elesin is a master rhetorician. Only the Beggar in *The Swamp Dwellers* and, at times, the Professor in *The Road* are so eloquent. Samson in *The Road* is as compelling, but not nearly so exalted as Elesin. Neither are the powerful Mendicants in *Madmen and Specialists*. In his use of language, the Elesin combines the best of all of these characters' traits, particularly their wit and power of persuasion. In any case, this second trick on the women reveals Elesin's considerable seductive powers, his irresistibility, and his zest for life.

The dual message sent out on the drums announcing both his wedding and his funeral in the same night confuses listeners who doubt they are interpreting the drums correctly. These drums add another idiom to the play, and they effectively convey the social drama involving Elesin and his community. More importantly, they

mirror the Elesin's embodiment of the "principle of mediation" between conflicting goals—individual and communal—which he
must somehow resolve for himself and his race. Later, when the
Elesin fails to go through the ritual passage to death, he blames
others, but the point is that Elesin's failure of will results from his
own character.

* * *

ADEBAYO WILLIAMS

Ritual and the Political Unconscious: The Case of *Death and the King's Horseman*†

* * *

Within Soyinka's corpus, *Death and The King's Horseman* has
achieved the status of a classic. Critics with a formalist bias have
hailed its superb characterization, its haunting beauty, and above
all its lyrical grandeur, although an oppositional critic such as
Biodun Jeyifo has objected to the lyrical beauty of the play on the
ideological ground that it seduces us into accepting what he considers to be Soyinka's reactionary worldview in the play. Kyalo Ma-
tivo has even gone so far as to observe that "when great form is not
in service of great content, it is fraud."[1] I have addressed these
objections elsewhere, but whatever the case might be, even the objections reinforce the consensus view that the play is possibly the
most intensely poetic of all Soyinka's dramatic writings.[2]

Written during a period of exile and existential anguish, the play
derives its powerful dynamics from Soyinka's first attempt to grapple
directly on the creative level with the "colonial question"—a question that obsessed his literary peers on the continent for over two
decades. The playwright's contemptuous dismissal of "hidebound
chronologues" notwithstanding, *Death and The King's Horseman* is
the creative equivalent of a return of the repressed. In this play,
Soyinka manages to capture the power and glory of the ancient

---

† From *Research in African Literatures* 24, no. 1 (Spring 1993): 67–79. Copyright © *Research in African Literatures*. Unless otherwise indicated, the notes are adapted from the
author's notes.
 1. Biodun Jeyifo, *The Truthful Lie: Essays in a Sociology of African Drama* (London: New
    Beacon, 1985). [The section referred to here is collected in this Norton Critical Edition];
    Kyalo Mativo, "Ideology in African Philosophy and Literature," *Ufahumu* 7 (1978): 135.
 2. Adebayo Williams, "Marxian Epistemology and the Criticism of African Literature," *Ufa-
    humu* 8, no. 1 (1983): 84–103; Adebayo Williams, "Marxism and the Criticism of African
    Drama," *ODU* 28 (1985): 103–21.

Yoruba state in its dying moment. At the same time, he poses a serious intellectual challenge to those who would deny a conquered people their unique mode of apprehending and making sense of reality.

Death and The King's Horseman represents an attempt to confront on a creative level the arrogance and cultural chauvinism of Western imperialism. Soyinka himself has taken umbrage at the "reductionist tendency" that views the dramatic tension in his play as having arisen from "a clash of cultures." According to him, this "prejudicial label . . . presupposes a potential equality *in every given situation* of the alien culture and the indigenous, on the actual soil of the latter."[3] The bitterly polemical tone of this rebuttal illustrates the extent to which Soyinka's threnodic temperament is affronted by mundane cultural equations. Yet by exploring the sacred terror of ritual suicide within the context of the cynicism and cultural dessications of the colonialists, Soyinka is engaged in nothing less than a sublime cultural battle. By counterposing the notion of honor in the ancient Yoruba kingdom (as seen in the tragic career of its principal custodian of culture) against the cynical presumptions and calculations of the colonial officials, Soyinka exposes the absurdity inherent in all assumptions of cultural superiority.

Death and The King's Horseman opens with a grand panorama of the Yoruba market place. Here, Soyinka deploys all his artistic power to paint a picture of grandeur and vitality. According to an old Yoruba saying, "The world is a market place; heaven is home." Apart from its obvious economic importance, the market occupies a signal cultural, political, and spiritual position in the Yoruba cosmos. First, it is a site of political and cultural ferment. Second, it doubles as that numinous zone in which the distinction between the world of the dead and that of the living is abolished. The ancient Yoruba saying captures this crucial contiguity. In most Yoruba towns, the evening market is regarded as the most important, and before the advent of electricity, it was a most eerie sight indeed. Moreover, the market serves as a barometer for the spiritual and psychic health of the community. The most important communal rites are carried out there. It was therefore a stroke of genius to focus on the market place at the beginning of the play. But even here there is a profound irony, for what is going on between the indigenous culture and the alien culture runs counter to the natural logic of the market—a forum for buying and selling. We are confronted with the bizarre phenomenon of a culture that insists upon

---

3. Wole Soyinka, *Death and the King's Horseman* (London: Methuen, 1975). All further quotations are taken from this edition.

forcing its hardware on another culture without making a commen-
surate purchase in return.

The crisis in the play is thus predicated on what is known in
economics as a trade imbalance or as a trade deficit between the
conqueror's culture and that of the conquered. The praise-singer,
in a moving dialogue with Elesin, captures the angst and spiritual
anguish of his people:

> Our world was never wrenched from
> Its true course. . . . [I]f that world leaves
> its course and smashes on the boulders
> of great void, whose world will
> give us shelter? (17)

Behind the unease and anguish of this intensely poetic lamentation
lie the sympathies of the playwright himself. His very choice of
images, "wrench," "boulders," and "void" betrays a starkly apocalyp-
tic mood.

Against this turbulent background one must situate the vexatious
dynamics that transform Elesin, an otherwise minor cultural functionary of the ruling class, into a world-historic role as the deliverer
of his people. Precisely because his suicide is supposed to compel
respect for the integrity and inviolability of a besieged culture, Elesin's routine function takes on a major historical and political burden. For the people, the success or failure of the ritual therefore
becomes a matter of life and death. Here is the classic example of
a particular ritual that, under historical pressure, transcends its
original cultural signification to assume a greater political and spiritual significance.

Yet, if historical circumstances compel a particular ritual to serve
purposes more complex than its original ones, how can the same
circumstances transform a minor figure into a major historical per-
sonage? Indeed, the reverse is often the case. Karl Marx's brilliant
comparison of the two Bonapartes comes to mind: "[The French]
have not only a caricature of the old Napoleon, they have the old
Napoleon himself, caricatured as he must appear in the middle of
the nineteenth century."[4] In an interesting gloss on this passage,
Terry Eagleton observes: "Bonaparte is not just a parody of Napoleon; he is Napoleon parodying himself. He is the real thing dressed
up as false, not just the false thing tricked out as real. What is in
question now is not a regressive caricature but a caricaturing
regression."[5]

---

4. Karl Marx, *Grundrisse* (London: Basil Blackwell, 1975), p. 98.
5. Terry Eagleton, *Walter Benjamin: Or Towards a Revolutionary Criticism* (London: New
Left Books, 1981), pp. 166–67.

So it is with Elesin. And this is the source of the collective and individual tragedy in *Death and The King's Horseman*. Elesin's consciousness has been shaped by the dialectic of his material and political circumstances. If he appears weak, vacillating, self-pitying, self-dramatizing, and self-indulgent, it is because the old Empire has exhausted itself. If he is cynically preoccupied with pleasure and the spoils of office, if he is skeptical about the credibility of his destiny, his attitude is not unrelated to the fact that the hegemony of the empire had long ago been fissured by internal contradictions as well as by the antagonistic logic supplied by the conquering invaders. As evident in the play, the crumbling empire has already been thoroughly infiltrated by the "other" empire and its various fetishes of political authority and cultural power: batons, bands, balls, cells, gramophones, etc. In a rather resentful categorization of the opulence of the Residency, Soyinka comes close to the truth when he describes it as being "redolent of the tawdry decadence of a far-flung but key imperial frontier" (45).

In its dying moment, the empire can only produce an Elesin, a pathetic but ultimately subversive caricature of his illustrious forebears. In the light of this insight, it is difficult to agree with Jeyifo when he asserts that "the play never really dramatises either the force of Elesin's personality or the inevitability of his action."[6] In actuality, there is no force to dramatize; it is absent from Elesin's personality. It is paradoxical that a Marxist critic should slip into the bourgeois notion that history and literature are no more than the study of the acts of great men. A genuinely materialist aesthetics must not be fixated on great personalities; on the contrary, it must strive to relocate personalities within the social and historical forces which engendered them in the first instance. The character of Elesin is an acute reflection of these forces at play.

In this context, it would be utopian to expect him, a critically misendowed man, to surmount the overwhelming historical and social forces ranged against him. To expect such an act is to expect the impossible. That the playwright fails to recognize this fact demonstrates the extent to which his own imagination has been colored by the lingering efficacy of the ideological apparatus of the old Yoruba state. Indeed, in an attempt to resist the mundane forces of concrete history, Soyinka is compelled to look beyond Elesin to his son, Olunde, who is perhaps the most sensitively drawn character in the play. He is the ideological spokesman for the playwright, who is obviously in profound sympathy with the young man's aspirations. Olunde's material and historical circumstances are quite different from his father's. He is armed with immense personal courage and

6. Jeyifo, p. 32.

conviction; and his considerable intellect has been honed by a sustained contact with the alien culture in all its contradictions and foibles. He is therefore a perfect match and counterfoil to the arrogance and chauvinism of the colonial administrators. As he tells Mrs. Pilkings: "You forget that I have now spent four years among your people. I discovered that you have no respect for what you do not understand" (50); In another cutting riposte, he exclaims with bitter irony, "You believe that every thing which appears to make sense was learnt from you" (53).

Consumed by his contempt and hatred for the hypocrisy and cant of Western civilization, bewildered by his father's lack of honor, Olunde chooses suicide as a means of redeeming the honor of his society and of expiating what must have seemed to him as his father's abominable cowardice and treachery. But rather than alleviating the burden of the people, Olunde's suicide only compounds their misery. The praise-singer again captures this moment of historic stress:

> What the end will be, we are not
> gods to tell. But this young shoot has
> poured its sap into the parent stalk,
> and we know this is not the way
> of life. Our world is tumbling in
> the void of strangers. (75)

Yet despite the enormous integrity of Olunde's self-sacrifice, it is difficult to identify the point at which his role as a cultural hero ends and where his role as the rearguard defender of a backward-looking political order prevails. But Soyinka does not leave us in doubt as to his conviction that, if suicide is the ultimate option available to Africa's revolutionary intelligentsia in the struggle for a cultural revalidation of the continent, it must be embraced without flinching.

This position engenders profound ideological difficulties. To start with, it lays itself open to the charge of promoting a cult of romantic suicide. To leftwing critics, Olunde, by terminating his own life, has succumbed to the whims of a reactionary culture and a flagrantly feudalistic ethos. Indeed, for critics of this persuasion, there might be something paradoxically progressive in Elesin's refusal to honor his oath. Jeyifo is precise and uncompromising on this point. According to him, "The notion of honour (and integrity and dignity) for which Soyinka provides a metaphysical rationalisation rests on the patriarchal, feudalist code of the ancient Oyo kingdom, a code built on class entrenchment and class consolidation."[7]

7. Ibid., p. 34.

It is necessary at this point to probe further, to "problematize" these various antithetical positions. The first step towards accomplishing this goal will be to counterpose Jameson's doctrine of the political unconscious against Jeyifo's instrumentalist Marxist objection to Soyinka's ideological thrust.[8] As it is, the Elesin ritual is a projection of a people's collective consciousness. Elesin's suicide is designed to facilitate the smooth transition of the departing king from the world of the living to the world of the dead. Even for departing royalties, solitude might be a terrifying prospect in what Soyinka himself often somberly refers to as the "the abyss of transition." As the Iyaloja, the unwavering matriarch of culture and tradition, explains:

> He knows the meaning of a king's passage; he was not born yesterday. He knows the peril to the race when our dead father who goes as intermediary, waits and waits and knows he is betrayed. . . . He knows he has condemned our king to wander in the void or evil with beings who are enemies of life. (71)

In Yoruba culture, a king never "dies." A king wandering "in the void" is therefore an abomination, a serious threat to life and communal well-being. Thus, insofar as Elesin's suicide is conceived to usher the departed king into his new kingdom, it is a crucial ritual of continuity, well-being, and hope; hence, the collective anxiety about the dire consequences of its abortion. Yet as Jameson has contended, a political unconscious always coexists uneasily with even the most apparently innocent manifestations of a people's collective consciousness. The question then becomes: What is the political unconscious behind Elesin's ritual and Soyinka's fabulization of it? In other words, what is the historical contradiction for which the Elesin ritual is supposed to be a symbolic resolution?

On one level, the ritual suicide of Elesin is supposed to take the sting out of the trauma of death by enacting the drama of a privileged carrier who willingly undertakes the journey to the unknown. This act in itself might serve to assuage the people's collective anxiety about being forsaken as a result of the departure of the father of the "tribe." On another level, the ritual might well signify a symbolic conquest of death itself. For in the absence of viable oppositional forces in the community, Death becomes the distinguished scourge and ultimate terror of the ruling class: unconquerable, unanswerable, firm, unsmiling.

The Elesin ritual, then, magically transforms death into an ally of the rulers. In death, the power and grandeur of the rulers remain.

8. See Fredric Jameson, *The Political Unconscious: Narrative as a Socially Symbolic Act* (Ithaca: Cornell University Press, 1981).

The transition of individual kings is thus immaterial: the kingdom remains unassailable. Erich Auerbach regards the poetry of Homer as performing analogous functions for the ancient Greek aristocracy. According to him: ". . . rather than an impression of historical change, Homer evokes the illusion of an unchanging society, a basically stable order, in comparison with which the succession of individuals and changes in personal fortunes appear unimportant."[9] Similarly, the Elesin ritual is designed to reconcile the people of the ancient Oyo empire to the supremacy, invincibility, and divine nature of what is essentially a feudal society. It is a socially symbolic act insofar as it negotiates the painful reality of death for the ruling class. Hence, the ritual suicide is one of those insidious strategies of survival and containment that Althusser has characterized as an ideological apparatus of the state.[1] It is the political unconscious behind the Elesin ritual in *Death and The King's Horseman*.

Seen from this perspective, Jeyifo's objection is not without merit. *Death and The King's Horseman* does provide metaphysical rationalization for a patriarchal and feudalist code. The play's complicity with this order is obvious in the sense that the playwright accepts the ritual as a communal necessity. But it is not just the dominant classes that fear death. The terror of death is a common denominator in all societies; it is therefore a supra-class phenomenon. Returning to Althusser's definition of ideology, this particular maneuver of the ruling class is an essential mystification, ultimately beneficial to the entire society.

It is this utopian dimension of the Elesin ritual that Soyinkas leftwing critics have failed to comprehend. While recognizing the power and urgency of negative hermeneutics within the Marxist critical enterprise, Jameson argues that the ultimate task of Marxist criticism is to restore the utopian dimension to the work of art, that is, to view the work of art as an expression of some ultimate collective urge while not overlooking "the narrower limits of class privilege which informs its more immediate ideological vocation."[2] Jameson's conclusion bears quoting at length:

> Such a view dictates an enlarged perspective for any Marxist analysis of culture, which can no longer be content with its demystifying vocation to unmask and to demonstrate the ways in which a cultural artifact fulfils a specific ideological mission, in legitimating a given power structure . . . but [which] must also seek through and beyond this demonstration of the in-

9. Erich Auerbach, *Mimesis: The Representation of Reality in Western Literature* (New York: Doubleday, 1957), p. 42.
1. Louis Althusser, *Lenin and Philosophy and Other Essays* (London: New Left Books, 1971).
2. Jameson, p. 288.

strumental function of a given cultural object, to project its simultaneously utopian power as the symbolic affirmation of a specific historical and class form of collectivity.[3]

Jameson's theory has nothing to do with Durkheim's conservative notion of religious and ritual practice as a symbolic affirmation of unity in all collective entities. The failure of Durkheim's theory stems from its fixation on the utopian impulse, a fixation that overlooks the division of all societies into dominant and dominated groups. The obverse of this inadequate approach is any criticism that simply rewrites or allegorizes a work of art in terms of Marx's insight into history as an arena of conflicts between opposing classes.

In the final analysis, what Soyinka accomplished in *Death and the King's Horseman* was to counterpose the dominant culture of the ancient Oyo kingdom against the equally hegemonic culture of the white invaders. His strategy is a brilliant, decolonizing venture. In an age characterized by new forms of cultural domination that result from the economic marginalization of the third world, such an approach might well represent a more pressing project than analyzing the class content of indigenous cultures. In a perceptive critique of Jeyifo's position on *Death and The King's Horseman*, Gareth Griffiths and David Moody conclude:

> The issue here is less the correctness of Soyinka's choice of subject or of the revolutionary character of the "class" of his protagonists than the project which the choice of subject and protagonist serve. It seems to us that Soyinka's is a profoundly de-colonising project, and that Jeyifo has lost sight of this in his demand that an alternative (although not actually opposed) project be undertaken by African writers. . . . However, the route forward in Nigeria, as in all post-colonial societies, is in part through a preservation of what Soyinka has called "self-apprehension."[4]

In *Death and The King's Horseman*, then, the playwright is an unabashed horseman ("Elesin" in the Yoruba language) of a besieged culture, fighting a desperate battle against the cultural "other." In such turbulent circumstances, he could not direct his gaze at the inequities of the traditional hierarchy, lest his resolve be weakened; neither could he bring himself to recognize that the culture he was defending had already succumbed to the alienating necessity of his-

3. Ibid., p. 291.
4. Gareth Griffiths and David Moody, "Of Marx and Missionaries: Soyinka and the Survival of Universalism in Post-Colonial Literary Theory," in *After Europe: Critical Theory and Post-Colonial Writing*, ed. Stephen Slemon and Helen Tifflin (Sydney: Dangaroo, 1989), p. 81.

tory, lest the rationale for mustering a stiff resistance disappear. This conflict is the political unconscious of the writer himself, and it shows its classic manifestation—Soyinka's prefatory protestations notwithstanding—in this imaginary resolution of a concrete cultural dilemma.

By the same token, his radical critics are also complicit horsemen of the cultural and post-colonial "other." For by insisting on the decadent and oppressive nature of the indigenous culture, they are in ideological collusion with that genetic evolutionism and naively unilinear historicism that seeks to justify the cultural, economic, and political atrocities of colonialism as the inevitable consequence of historical "progress." This is the corollary of the teleological fallacy which regards any capitalist formation as an automatic advancement on all indigenous economic formations. It is the cardinal sin of the founding father of Marxism himself. That Karl Marx, despite his initial unease, eventually made his peace with a flagrantly bourgeois notion of historical development shows the extent to which his own sensibility was steeped in the ideological constellations of the nascent capitalist age.

Eagleton has defined succinctly Marx's epistemological impasse. According to him, "In his effort to theorize historical continuities Marx finds the evolutionist problematic closest to hand, but it is clear that it will not do. For you do not escape a naively unilinear historicism merely by reversing its direction."[5] This lapse of consciousness in all its smug Eurocentric complacency demonstrates how all master narratives, including Marxism, are dogged by a political unconscious which derives from the logic of their own insertion into the historical process. It is the urgent task of all genuinely revolutionary post-colonial discourses to smuggle themselves into this gap in colonial narratives with a view to exploding their internal contradictions. *Death and The King's Horseman* fulfils this historic obligation. Whatever its complicity with the indigenous ruling class might be, the importance of Soyinka's classic for a viable post-colonial cultural and political praxis lies in this achievement.

---

5. Terry Eagleton, "Ideology, Fiction and Narrative," *Social Text* 1 (1979): 73.

DAVID RICHARDS

[*Death and the King's Horseman* and the Masks of Language]†

* * *

Elesin Oba, the central figure of *Death and the King's Horseman,* is the kind of articulate amorist and ritual quester familiar in the plays of Wole Soyinka. His is an eloquence which is charted through successive plays: the Bale of Baroka, Jero, Professor, Kongi, the Madmen.[1] Each character's facility with language is combined with a growing sense of danger as they talk themselves, and others, into the transgression of boundaries and the fracturing of taboo.

Elesin's social position as the King's Horseman defines his role in the rituals which follow the death of the Alafin, the king or *oba* of Oyo. The Horseman will commit suicide in order to follow the dead Alafin into the world of the ancestors. His unique duties and obligations made the best freely available to him: 'The juiciest fruit on every tree was mine.' The rules and protocol of the rites of passage made a refusal of his every whim impossible, yet there is more to Elesin than the grasping appetite of a spoilt aristocrat:

> Split an iroko tree
> In two, hide a woman's beauty in its heartwood
> And seal it up again—Elesin, journeying by,
> Would make his camp beside that tree
> Of all the shades in the forest.[2]

The appeal of Elesin's fast-flowing, humorous imagery transforms acts of ritual piety into lovingly-performed devotions. Elesin may have the dangerous appetite of a decadent, but his language testifies to a zest and vitality which captivates those of whom he demands favours.

Elesin recasts the folktale of the 'Not-I' bird; a spirit bird whose song announces the death of those who hear it. Elesin's poetry moves rapidly through a series of dramatic vignettes of individuals' encounters with the death-bird. As each persona makes their *entrée* into the tale, Elesin builds a vivid description of the traditional

---

† From *Masks of Difference: Cultural Representations in Literature, Anthropology, and Art* (Cambridge: Cambridge University Press, 1994), pp. 267–80. Reprinted with the permission of Cambridge University Press. Unless otherwise indicated, the notes are adapted from the author's notes.
1. See *The Lion and the Jewel* (1963), *The Jero Plays* (1964, 1973), *The Road* (1965), *Kongi's Harvest* (1967), *Madmen and Specialists* (1971), in Wole Soyinka, *Collected Plays,* 2 vols. (London: Oxford University Press, 1973–74).
2. Wole Soyinka, *Death and the King's Horseman* (London: Methuen, 1975), 18–19.

Yoruba *polis*. A world of farmers, priests, courtesans, hunters, gods and animals is created as Elesin's tongue calls into presence a kind of *Alarinjo* masquerade, a Menippean procession of Yoruba social types which, true to its satirical intent, creates an image of social cohesion and completeness while simultaneously subjecting that social text to a withering sarcasm.[3]

> Death came calling
> Who does not know his rasp of reeds?
> A twilight whisper in the leaves before
> The great araba falls?
>
> . . .
>
> He snaps
> His fingers round his head, abandons
> A hard-won harvest and begins
> A rapid dialogue with his legs. (pp. 11–12)

The social, natural and metaphysical world of the Yoruba is contained in Elesin's poem, all controlled by and under the dominion of death.

> There was fear in the forest too.
> Not-I was lately heard even in the lair
> Of beasts. (p. 13)

Even the gods are tied to the world of nature and the society of man by their fear of death:

> Ah, companions of this living world
> What a thing this is, that even those
> We call immortal
> Should fear to die. (p. 13)

In the plenum of his tale, all but Elesin are the subjects of death; his egocentricity soars, putting him beyond the natural world, beyond the world of men, beyond even the gods.

> My rein is loosened.
> I am master of my Fate. When the hour comes
> Watch me dance along the narrow path
> Glazed by the soles of my great precursors.
> My soul is eager. I shall not turn aside. (p. 14)

Elesin is unique in all the world since only he is the sole master of his fate. Elesin is the essential Yoruba man: 'The town, the very land was yours.'

The Horseman's ritual role and the pivotal focus of Soyinka's drama is the transition of Elesin from the world of the living to that

---

3. *Alarinjo*, literally in Yoruba "he who dances while he walks" but referring to the popular dramatic aspect of *egungun* rather than the rituals of the *Ara Orun*.

of the ancestors. This is expressed dramatically in the scene and
dialogue between Elesin and the Praise-singer which is a prelude
to Elesin's dance into the world of the ancestors. Elesin intends to
dance himself into a death-trance in the midst of the market
women. He starts to dance and Elesin and the Praise-singer commence their poetic dialogue:

> PRAISE-SINGER: Elesin Alafin, can you hear my voice?
> ELESIN: Faintly, my friend, faintly.
> PRAISE-SINGER: Elesin Alafin, can you hear my call?
> ELESIN: Faintly my king, faintly. (p. 41)

Elesin is no longer *Oba* but *Alafin*, a promotion in rank, but also
an acknowledgement of the new relationship which exists between
the spirit of the dead Alafin and the spirit of Elesin, as if the two
were now in union. The Praise-singer begins the exchange as himself ('Faintly, my friend, faintly') but is rapidly transformed into the
voice of the departed Alafin ('Faintly, my king, faintly'). For the rest
of the dialogue Elesin talks to the dead king. The dialogue of spirits
detaches the voice from the characters; in the rituals of the dead
the word escapes from human identities as language becomes the
possession of the ancestors. The mask of the *Ara Orun* speaks in
Soyinka's dramatic recreation of the *egungun* rites.

Social persona becomes equally fluid. The hierarchical ranks and
domains of the 'Not-I' *entrée* of the body politic (Alafin, Oba, Praise-
singer) lose their static ordering powers and slip from voice to voice.
The *egungun* is dissolving and reformulating the identification and
fixing of the individual and social selves. The ritual dialogue ends
when Elesin declares that 'strange voices guide my feet'. Elesin
sinks into a deeper trance, the voice of the Praise-singer regains its
body. The Praise-singer returns to prose; he speaks directly at first
as he grapples with the difficulty of relating what he has seen, but
faced with the impossibility of description, his language begins to
flex and grow with proverbial forms.

> No arrow flies back to the string, the child does not return
> through the same passage that gave it birth. Elesin Oba, can
> you hear me at all? (p. 44)

Language and the Praise-singer are both being stretched to the
limits of endurance. The Praise-singer 'appears to break down', so
too does language as the stage directions take over:

> *Elesin dances on, completely in a trance. The dirge wells up*
> *louder and louder. Elesin's dance does not lose its elasticity but*
> *his gestures become if possible even more weighty. Lights fade*
> *slowly on the scene.* (p. 44)

The Praise-singer attempts to express the experience prosaically, then by circumlocution and oblique linguistic strategies, until language is finally lost in music, an illustration of Soyinka's belief that: 'Tragic music is an echo from that void . . . All understand and respond for it is the language of the world.'[4]

*   *   *

The performers of *egungun* are always men, hidden under layers of clothing, sometimes carrying whips, and speaking in disguised voices since they are *Ara Orun*, messengers from heaven. The performers are the spirits of the dead ancestors reincarnated in the form of the masqueraders. In social crises they are called on to carry away ills, execute criminals, and expel dangerous individuals. In less turbulent times they entertain the village. The two traditions of the *egungun* cult, the religious rite and the masquerade entertainment, form a rich context of contemporary practice and cultural history for Soyinka's drama: the 'Not-I' sequence recalls an *alarinjo* masquerade, the drama of transition embodies the ritual of the *Ara Orun*.[5]

The sacred dramas depict the transition of the spirit from the realm of the living to *egbe*, the domain of the dead, and they act as the transitional phase or 'gate' between the two worlds. Similarly, the masquerades have a social function as satire and as the preserver of traditional Yoruba culture. It is this context of African cultural possessions which enables Soyinka to instil a Yoruba presence into the aridity of the anthropological construction of rites of passage. The *egungun* rituals assert social orders but also dissolve them in the drama of transition from one state to another; the liminal rituals both make and unmake the world. For Soyinka, the participant immersed in the ritual is 'enabled to transmit its essence to the choric participants of the rites'.[6] Ritual drama is a communal experience undertaken by the individual on behalf of the community as it reflects 'powerful natural' or 'cosmic influences' which are 'internalized' and the 'titanic scale of their passions' transforms the stage into the 'affective, rational and intuitive milieu of the total communal experience, historic, race formative, cosmogonic'.[7]

*   *   *

Soyinka's Elesin is informed by Soyinka's particular borrowings from and reconstructions of Yoruba belief. As a participant in the

---

4. Wole Soyinka, *Myth, Literature, and the African World* (Cambridge: Cambridge University Press, 1978), p. 145.
5. There are many forms of Yoruba masked rituals which inform Soyinka's dramaturgy, the most significant being *egungun* in all its forms. It is so popular and widespread that it has developed its own poetic convention. * * *
6. Soyinka, *Myth, Literature, and the African World*, p. 33.
7. Soyinka, *Myth, Literature, and the African World*, p. 43.

rituals of the *ogboni* cult, and as an Ogun-type and culture hero, his ritual persona stands precisely poised in the transitional spaces between worlds: the human and the divine, the living and the ancestors, the past and the future. Yet true to the narrative of the myth of Ogun, his creative role as a figure of transition also involves acts of destruction.

Ruin begins with the very gift of eloquence which enabled Elesin to triumph as the essential Yoruba man. Elesin's smooth-tongued conquest of the market-women procures the acquiescence necessary for him to marry a young woman on the eve of his ritual suicide. Elesin artificially embroils sexual desire in the wider metaphysical and social processes of transition from the world of the living to the world of the ancestors. To procure his young bride he argues that his spirit should not be burdened by the weight of unused and henceforth unuseful seed which would be better 'planted in the earth of his own choice', and that the ensuing offspring, conceived at a critical time, would be a special gift to the living he leaves behind because it would be a child of transition, neither of this world nor of the next. Yet what he proposes is a dubious gift since it is an *abiku*, a half-child, a miraculous monstrosity, a destroyer of mothers and a symbol of cultural and political deformity in the nation.

The *abiku* is a lesser chthonic power in the Yoruba pantheon, a child born with a desire for death. It returns again and again to its mother always dying in infancy until its mother also dies from the exhaustion of childbirth. Ulli Beier explains Soyinka's fascination with *abiku* as a symbol of man's obsession with 'causing extinction in his own image', and Soyinka's poem, 'Abiku' expresses this theme:

> Night, and Abiku sucks the oil
> From lamps. Mothers! I'll be the
> Suppliant snake coiled on the doorstep
> Yours the killing cry.
>
> The ripest fruit was saddest
> Where I crept, the warmth was cloying.
> In the silence of webs, Abiku moans, shaping
> Mounds from the yolk.[8]

Iyaloja, disturbed by Elesin's proposed marriage, accuses him of purely lustful intent. Elesin protests:

> Who speaks of pleasure? O women, listen!
> Pleasure palls. Our acts should have meaning.[9]

---

8. Ulli Beier, "A Dance of the Forests", *Black Orpheus* 8 (1960): 57; Wole Soyinka, *Idanre and Other Poems* (London: Rex Collings, 1967), p. 30.
9. Soyinka, *Death and the King's Horseman*, p. 20.

It is delightfully disingenuous in its truth-twisting, but Elesin's powerful gift augurs the potential for dangerous corruption. Iyaloja, and the market-women, captivated but also alarmed by the manipulative power of Elesin's rhetoric, express a growing sense of tension: 'This language is the language of our elders, we do not fully grasp it'. 'The voice I hear is already touched by the waiting fingers of our departed. I dare not refuse.'[1]

The dominant poetic form of Elesin Oba's and the Praise-singer's language is the aphoristic wisdom of the proverb. Yoruba idiom is itself highly elaborated with proverbial speech involving puns and metaphors which can only be elucidated by reference to the common currency of proverbs. Soyinka's adoption and transliteration of proverbial form mirrors naturalistic Yoruba speech. Soyinka's borrowings from traditional Yoruba proverbs are extensive; there is hardly a dramatic moment in the dialogue between Yoruba characters which is not expressed by a proverb taken from Yoruba idiom. The Praise-singer scolds Elesin:

> Because the man approaches a brand-new bride he forgets the long faithful mother of his children.
> (*Aríyàwó-ko-ìyálé.*)[2]

Elesin uses proverbs to bolster his authority and for self-aggrandisement:

> Where the storm pleases, and when, it directs
> The giants of the forest.
> (*Ibi ti o wu èfúfù lèlè ní í darí ìgbé sí, ibi ti o wu olówó eni ni ran ni lo.*)
>
> What elder takes his tongue to his plate,
> Licks it clean of every crumb? He will encounter
> Silence when he calls on children to fulfil
> The smallest errand!
> (*Àgbà t'ó je àje-ì-wèhìn ni y io ru igbá rè dé' lé.*)[3]

Iyaloja uses proverbs as a warning to Elesin to curb his appetites:

> Eating the awusa nut is not so difficult as drinking water afterwards.
> (*Ati je àsálá (Awusa) kò tó ati mu omi sí i.*)[4]

1. Soyinka, *Death and the King's Horseman,* pp. 20–21.
2. Soyinka, *Death and the King's Horseman,* p. 9; the proverb in Yoruba is from Oloye J. O. Ajibola, *Owe Yoruba* (Ibadan: Ibadan University Press, 1971), p. 54.
3. Soyinka, *Death and the King's Horseman,* p. 14; the proverbs in Yoruba are from Ajibola, p. 78, and Isaac O. Delano, *Owe L'Esin Oro* (Ibadan: Ibadan University Press, 1966), p. 74.
4. Soyinka, *Death and the King's Horseman,* p. 22 (Ajibola, p. 56; Delano, p. 54).

Elesin expresses his readiness to join the ancestors through proverbs:

> The kite makes for wide spaces and the wind creeps up behind its tail; can the kite say less than—thank you, the quicker the better?
> (*Àwòdì to'o nre Ìbarà, èfùfù ta á n'ídi pá o ni' Isé kúku yá.*)

> The elephant
> Trails no tethering-rope; that king
> Is not yet crowned who will peg an elephant.
> (*Ajanaku ko l'ēkàn, oba ti yio mu erin so koi je.*)

> The elephant deserves
> Better than that we say 'I have caught
> A glimpse of something'. If we see the tamer
> Of the forest let us say plainly, we have seen an elephant.
> (*Àjànàkú kuro ninn 'mo ri nkan fìrí', bi a ba ri erin ki a ni a ri erin.*)

> The river is never so high that the eyes
> Of a fish are covered.
> (*Odo ki ikun bo eja l'oju.*)[5]

When Elesin fails in his suicide and he is imprisoned by the colonial authorities, Iyaloja and the Praise-singer condemn him with the cruel irony of proverbs.

> We said you were the hunter returning home in triumph, a slain buffalo pressing down on his neck; you said wait, I first must turn up this cricket hole with my toes.
> (*A kì í ru eran erin l'órì ki a máa f'ese wa ìrè n'ile.*)

> What we have no intention of eating should not be held to the nose.
> (*Ohun ti a kì í je a kì ífí run imú.*)

> The river which fills up before our eyes does not sweep us away in its flood.
> (*Odo ti o t'oju eni kun ki igbe 'ni lo.*)

> The bush-rat fled his rightful cause, reached the market and set up a lamentation. 'Please save me!'—are these fitting words to hear from an ancestral mask? 'There's a wild beast at my heels' is not becoming language from a hunter.
> (*Okete fi ija sehin o de oja o wa kawo l'eri, and E jowo, e gba mi o, ko ye egungun; eran ni o nle mi bo, ko ye ode.*)

---

5. Soyinka, *Death and the King's Horseman*, p. 41 (Ajibola, p. 57; Delano, p. 55); Soyinka, *Death and the King's Horseman*, p. 42 (Delano, p. 44); Soyinka, *Death and the King's Horseman*, p. 43 (Ajibola, p. 45; Delano, p. 45); Soyinka, *Death and the King's Horseman*, p. 43 (Delano, p. 119).

If there is a dearth of bats, the pigeon must serve us for the offering.
(*Bi a kò bá rí àdán à fi òòdè sebo.*)[6]

The English-language medium of the play is greatly enlarged in its range of metaphorical references by the constant insertion of a Yoruba idiom. In all but one instance it is the Yoruba characters who speak in proverbs. The single example of the District Officer's proverb is delivered as a justification for his action in 'saving' Elesin from death:

I thought, are these not the same people who say: the elder grimly approaches heaven and you ask him to bear your greetings yonder; do you really think he makes the journey willingly? (*Àgbàlagbà nfi ìrójú lo sòrun a ni ki o kílé kí ó k'ónà; ojú rere l'o finlo?*)[7]

Pilkings' misapplication of the proverb in this case only displays his lack of comprehension of the culture he pretends to rule; just as his wearing of a masquerader's costume to the viceroy's ball commits a blasphemy against the *egungun*. His incomprehension of the significance of Elesin's ritual role in his culture further emphasises the richness of the Yoruba language compared to that of its oppressors. The proverb in the mouth of the District Officer exposes an ostentatious misrepresentation and incomprehension of Yoruba culture; elsewhere the confrontation with the historical situation of colonialism is achieved by a manipulation of the traditional idiom. The proverb '*Orule bo àjá mole, aso bo ese idi, awo fẹre bo inu ko je ki a ri iku aseni*' is rendered into English by Delano as, 'the roof covers the ceiling, the clothes cover the bad parts of the body, the thin skin which conceals the heart prevents us seeing the death planned by the secret plotter', which Soyinka transforms into:

We know the roof covers the rafters, the cloth covers the blemishes; who would have known that *the white skin covered our future,* preventing us from seeing the death our enemies had prepared for us.[8]

However, there is more to Soyinka's use of the proverb than either a desire for authentic linguistic colour or anti-imperialist sentiment; the syntax of the proverb form enables Soyinka to enunciate

---

6. Soyinka, *Death and the King's Horseman*, pp. 68, 75 (Ajibola, p. 49; Delano, p. 2); Soyinka, *Death and the King's Horseman*, p. 68 (Ajibola, p. 89; Delano, p. 146); Soyinka, *Death and the King's Horseman*, p. 69 (Delano, p. 145); Soyinka, *Death and the King's Horseman*, p. 69 (Delano, p. 116); Soyinka, *Death and the King's Horseman*, p. 75 (Ajibola, p. 59).
7. Soyinka, *Death and the King's Horseman*, p. 64 (Ajibola, p. 80; Delano, p. 141).
8. Soyinka, *Death and the King's Horseman*, p. 63 (Ajibola, p. 57; Delano, p. 149).

his wider philosophical and social theories. Iyaloja's intricately proverbial speech in praise of Elesin is again a translation and transformation of the Yoruba:

> It is the death of war that kills the valiant,
> Death of water is how the swimmer goes
> It is the death of markets that kills the trader,
> And death of indecision takes the idle away
> The trade of the cutlass blunts its edge
> And the beautiful die the death of beauty.
> It takes an Elesin to die the death of death . . .
> (*Ikú ogun ní i pa akíkanjú, iku odò ní ípa òmùwè, ikú ara
> rire ni ipa arewa, màjàmàsá ni ipa onitiju; òwò ti ada ba
> mo ni ika ada l'ehin.*)[9]

Soyinka's translation of the Yoruba proverbs also recalls a biblical
parallel in its use of the Hebrew superlative. But these gnomic pronouncements are profoundly ambiguous. The first implied sense is
that social roles determine identity and that 'specialists' die sympathetic deaths according to the inclinations of their natures and
skills. Yet it also implies that it is the end of the medium of their
lives which destroys people; thus the end of war marks the end of
valour, and so on. The Yoruba syllogisms twist their way through
paradox and contradiction to attain the conclusion that 'the death
of death' envisages the possibility of eternal life and the social
continuity which Elesin's death ensures. But the key to Iyaloja's
proverbial speech is not only to be found in her transcendent conclusion, but also in the 'torsions' the language undergoes in the
process of utterance. The speech focuses on the shifting of meanings within words in different contexts, as in 'It takes an Elesin *to
die the death of death.*' An internal tension is evoked as the semantic
field of the word is subjected to the proverb's paradoxical convulsions. Her speech spirals through opposing conditions from consolation, to the beneficent refinement of spiritual expertise within
a sympathetic universe which acknowledges individual predilec-
tions, to a nihilistic finality and closure, to the collapse of a social
order and the loss of the transcendent capacity of ritual.

Proverbs have formal and cognitive similarities to Soyinka's philosophical and metaphysical notions of the transition from the world
of the living to the world of the dead, making them especially suited
to his ritual drama. The ritual state is a state of paradox and the
proverb is the vehicle for the expression of paradox. A transposition
or commutation occurs between the ritual of transition and the
proverb which enables the ritual to be present in the rich verbal
texture of the play. Proverbs approach most closely the poetic ex-

9. Soyinka, *Death and the King's Horseman*, p. 43 (Ajibola, p. 80; Delano, p. 141).

pression of creative paradox which is the dominant metaphysic of Soyinka's construction of the Yoruba social order.

Yet these proverbs have a perfectly clear meaning because they are used rhetorically and dramatically and not just figuratively and metaphorically. As Albert Cook has written:

> The metaphoric framing of the proverb draws on the subsidiary differences between the items compared . . . only for rhetorical force: the hearer's effort to spell out the analogy and the likeness exhausts this force, whereas in poetic metaphors the differences between the items of likeness induce the hearer to dwell on the myth-suggestive, changed ground that the differences and the likeness taken together activate.[1]

The rhetorical force of the proverbs in Soyinka's play, while evoking the metaphysical paradox, directs the reader back again to the social matrix from which the proverb originated. The 'trajectory', as it were, of Soyinka's play is always towards the social, and not out from the social towards the misty paradoxes of eternity, although he uses these areas to charge his poetry with a sense of the numinous. The proverb has a practical application in the society of the play, for Soyinka maintains, at the local syntactical level as at the grand and metaphysical, a dialectical dialogue between the numinous ideal and the social.

In his introduction to *Death and the King's Horseman*, Soyinka writes:

> The confrontation in the play is largely metaphysical, contained in the human vehicle which is Elesin and the universe of the Yoruba mind—the world of the living, the dead and the unborn, and the numinous passage which links all three: transition. *Death and the King's Horseman* can be fully realised only through an evocation of music from the abyss of transition.[2]

He points to the play's 'threnodic essence', a song of lamentation which is the play's quintessential expression of a sense of loss. Plangency is evoked in Elesin's failure and his transformation from a role of sacred honour to impious dishonour which is paralleled by an equal shift in the type and quality of his language.

> My powers deserted me. My charms, my spells, even my voice lacked strength when I made to summon the powers that would lead me over the last measure of earth into the land of the fleshless.
>
> . . .

1. A. S. Cook, *Language and Myth* (Bloomington: Indiana University Press, 1980), p. 219.
2. Soyinka, *Death and the King's Horseman*, "Author's Note."

It is when the alien hand pollutes the source of will, when a stranger force of violence shatters the mind's calm resolution, this is when man is made to commit the awful treachery of relief, commit in his thought the unspeakable blasphemy of seeing the hand of the gods in this alien rupture of his world.[3]

This is articulate enough, but wholly different from his earlier eloquence: poetic metaphor, quick-tongued allusiveness, dramatic and linguistic tensions have all dissipated; he has lost the world he once held in his linguistic grasp in the 'Not-I' *entrée* to the world of the play. Instead of proverbs he now speaks in abstractions: 'the source of will', 'the force of violence', 'mind's calm resolution', 'awful treachery of relief', 'alien rupture'. Elesin no longer controls his world through proverbial language, since he has lost the capacity to give a voice to 'the Yoruba mind' which proverbs express. Instead he grapples desperately with a devalued language where there was once a profound and confident image of a world held in equilibrium by the creative ego of Elesin. The play replicates the binary structure of the myth of Ogun; having made the world by his creative ritual acts, Elesin, like Ogun at Ire, unmakes it in an act of destructive failure.

It is at this point that the orality of the play becomes evident by its absence. A disjuncture is felt between this speech and Elesin's earlier proverbial extravagance because, when heard, this speech is virtually unintelligible, dramatically it is 'inaudible'. The play has already dramatised several kinds of language, proverbial, numinous and colonial dialogues, which have established the antithesis of poetic and anti-poetic speech. Elesin in his disgrace introduces a further dimension—a language which is an imitation of philosophical discourse lacking both the numinous rhapsody and the social expressiveness of the proverb. Elesin's new speech jars on the ear and wrenches the carefully established rhythm of proverbial speech out of its metre into language without Yoruba decorum. By cruel contrast, Iyaloja answers this speech with apt proverbs, revealing the world and the language which Elesin has lost.

The use of discordant speech as an indication of wider social disorder is familiar in Soyinka's works, but it is particularly the case in *Death and the King's Horseman* where the proverbial commonplace, heightened to the level of enunciating a social and religious cohesiveness and harmony, is counterpointed with cacophony. Soyinka's play documents the loss of a distinctive 'Yoruba world', with its powerful religious nucleus and rules formulated by a rich and productive proverbial speech, but Soyinka warns producers of his play not to transform his metaphysical drama into a 'facile' clash of

3. Soyinka, *Death and the King's Horseman*, pp. 68, 69.

cultures. His evocation of 'the universe of the Yoruba mind' shows that world 'alongside' other worlds, notably the British imperialists'; a vision of cultures resonant in each other.

The play documents the historical process of 'closure' and 'enclosure' of traditional Yoruba culture which is caused by the failure of its language and its ritual to perpetuate and regenerate its social forms. The play represents Yoruba culture within a tragic view of history. Indeed, that tragic process is begun by Elesin himself in the 'Not-I' sequence with his procession of Yoruba social types. The Yoruba world of natural, social and metaphysical orders is made to cohere into a unity, but a unity which is also an enigmatic paradox: a social life made coherent by ritualised death. *Death and the King's Horseman* reconstructs a society as a myth. Elesin is the 'I' which resolves the enigma of 'Not-I', the perfectly expressive mythical voice of the Yoruba world of the play and which, when he fails, sends 'Our World . . . tumbling in the void of strangers.'

* * *

OLAKUNLE GEORGE

[Tragedy, Mimicry, and "The African World"]†

* * *

In the twenty-odd years since its first publication, *Death and the King's Horseman* has come to occupy a stable place of prestige in modern African drama. According to the playwright's prefatory note, the play's primary plot is based on events that actually happened in Oyo, "ancient Yoruba city of Nigeria, in 1946." It is set in the colonial era, when Oyo was still part of the British Western Nigerian Protectorate. The plot revolves around a Yoruba traditional practice whereby, on the death of the king of Oyo (the *Alaafin*), the commander of the king's stables—in the play, the Olori Elesin— has to commit suicide in order to accompany the dead king to the world of the dead.

In the play, the colonial district officer, Simon Pilkings, intervenes in an effort to put a stop to what he sees as a barbaric custom. He arrests Elesin, preventing him from commiting the act. Olunde, Elesin's heir (a medical student in England who has hurriedly returned home to perform the necessary burial ceremony) feels anger

† From "Cultural Criticism in Wole Soyinka's *Death and the King's Horseman*," *Representations* 67 (Summer 1999): 67–91. Copyright © 1999 by The Regents of the University of California. Reprinted by permission. Unless otherwise indicated, the notes are adapted from the author's notes.

at Pilkings's colonialist arrogance and shame at his father's evasion of the one duty for which his entire life had been a preparation. Fearing the catastrophe that could befall the community on account of this disruption of the cosmic balance of his people, and in order to restore the family honor dreadfully tarnished by his father's failure, the son commits suicide: "better late than never" seems to be the logic. On learning of his son's superior will, Elesin kills himself in shame, in full view of Pilkings and his guards.

Although based on a true historical event, Soyinka's play changes some of the precise historical details. As his prefatory note informs us: "The changes I have made are in matters of detail, sequence and of course characterisation. The action has also been set back two or three years to while the war [World War II] was still on, for minor reasons of dramaturgy."[1] In seeking to understand the play, we have the playwright's own interpretation as an originary lead, but it is a lead that will show itself to be part of the cultural drama being played out. According to Soyinka's account of Yoruba metaphysics, what Pilkings sees as feudalistic barbarism is a very important mechanism of communal regeneration. The Elesin, at the moment of self-sacrifice, embodies the collective social and psychic aspirations of the Oyo community; he is a ritual scapegoat who mediates the world of the living, the dead, and the unborn. By his willful death at the summons of the community, he accedes to the world of the dead on behalf of the living and the unborn. His death thus ensures renewed harmony between the three levels of existence constitutive of traditional Yoruba cosmic order. Indeed, on Soyinka's terms, "suicide" is a misnomer. That is, Elesin's death does not turn on a brutalization of the corporeal body; rather, it operates via an "act of will" through which his total being submits to a monitored dissolution almost anaesthetic in essence. Elesin's calling is hereditary, tied to lineage: his father occupied the social position he currently occupies, and, all things being equal, his heir will do likewise, thereby ensuring the continuity of Oyo tradition and social-spiritual harmony.

The crucial role he plays in his society's well-being makes Elesin a highly revered citizen, pampered with collective awe, praise, and whatever else his worldly self desires:

> . . . . In all my life
> As Horseman of the King, the juiciest
> Fruit on every tree was mine. . . .
> . . . .

---

1. Wole Soyinka, *Death and the King's Horseman* (New York: Hill and Wang, 1987). All further quotations from the text are taken from this edition and cited parenthetically in the text.

> The honour of my place, the veneration I
> Received in the eye of man or woman
> Prospered my suit and
> Played havoc with my sleeping hours. (18)

These lines are from act 1 of the play; against it as background, we can see the sense in which Simon Pilkings's intervention affronts the entire Oyo community—and Elesin himself even more severely. However, Soyinka complicates the drama by rendering his Elesin as an eminently worldly figure—a lover of food and wine, dance and women. Immediately following the lines above, Elesin adds:

> And they tell me my eyes were a hawk
> In perpetual hunger. Split an iroko tree
> In two, hide a woman's beauty in its heartwood
> And seal it up again—Elesin, journeying by
> Would make his camp beside that tree
> Of all the shades in the forest. (18–19)

It is this love of the flesh that makes Elesin coerce the market women into allowing his marriage to a virgin (already betrothed to another man) on the very night he is supposed to die. In a poignant moment of self-analysis after his failure, Elesin, shackled and confined to a cell, confides to his bride:

> You were the final gift of the living to their emissary to the land of the ancestors, and perhaps your warmth and youth brought new insights of this world to me and turned my feet leaden on this side of the abyss. For I confess to you, daughter, my weakness came not merely from the abomination of the white man who came violently into my fading presence, there was also a weight of longing on my earth-held limbs. (65)

The possibility this claim opens up is that Elesin's failure to die at the appointed time is due more to his own *human* weakness than to the agency of British colonialism: "I would have shaken [the 'weight of longing on my earth-held limbs'] off, already my foot had begun to lift but then, the white ghost entered and all was defiled" (65).

This is the reading the playwright solicits—indeed, demands. "The bane of themes of this genre," writes Soyinka, "is that they are no sooner employed creatively than they acquire the facile tag of 'clash of cultures,' a prejudicial label which, quite apart from its frequent misapplication, presupposes a potential equality *in every given situation* of the alien culture and the indigenous, on the actual soil of the latter."[2] Against such a "sadly familiar reductionist ten-

---

2. Soyinka, *Death and the King's Horseman*, "Author's Note"; emphasis in the original.

dency," Soyinka insists that the district officer should not be cast as a major player in the tragic event. "No attempt," says he,

> should be made in production to suggest it. The Colonial Factor is an incident, a catalytic incident merely. The confrontation in the play is largely metaphysical, contained in the human vehicle which is Elesin and the universe of the Yoruba mind —the world of the living, the dead, and the unborn, and the numinous passage which links all: transition. *Death and the King's Horseman* can be fully realized only through an evocation of music from the abyss of transition.[3]

On Soyinka's intentionalist testimony, then, the conflict in the play is principally an interior one: the "Yoruba mind" in confrontation with itself, "man" called to account by his own universe of values. In the contrast between the Elesin of act 1 and act 5 (before his failure and after it) Soyinka wants us to see a figure who is defeated primarily within the matrix of his own culture and self-understanding. Viewed this way, Simon Pilkings merely wanders into a struggle that is both too timeless and too interior to Elesin-as-subject for his narrow colonialist confidence to grasp or single-handedly influence.

The Aristotelian tenor of such a reading is rather obvious, Elesin being the doomed protagonist whose human flaw facilitates an intersection of events toward catastrophe.[4] And yet, Soyinka insists that the play's *tragedy*—by which I mean its universal meaningfulness, or what he calls its "threnodic essence"—is firmly rooted in traditional Yoruba cosmology and its ritual enactment in festival and music. Further, Soyinka's reading demands that the colonial factor be subordinated to the specificity of the Yoruba worldview. A crucial dimension of the play's theoretical value for postcolonial cultural studies is to be found here; that is, in the playwright's dual insistence (1) that the play's philosophical pedigree lies in the resources of Yoruba metaphysics even as it reminds us of classical Western tragic drama and (2) that the colonial intervention is peripheral to the action—"catalytic merely," to the interior dynamic the play claims as its province. As many commentators have observed, the playwright's emphasis on Elesin as the locus of conflict is consistent with his interpretation of the Yoruba myth of origins

---

3. Soyinka, *Death and the King's Horseman*, "Author's Note."
4. Henry Louis Gates, Jr. provides a formalist/Aristotelean reading of the play and of Soyinka's art in general in "Being, the Will, and the Semantics of Death," *Harvard Educational Review* 51, no. 1 (1981): 163–73; see also D. S. Izevbaye, "Mediation in Soyinka: The Case of the King's Horseman," in James Gibbs, ed., *Critical Perspectives on Wole Soyinka* (Washington, D.C.: Three Continents Press, 1980), 116–25. [Both essays are reprinted in this Norton Critical Edition in whole or in part.]

and theory of tragic art, developed most famously in "The Fourth Stage: Through the Mysteries of Ogun to the Origin of Yoruba Tragedy."[5] A number of critics have also argued that Soyinka's reading of his own play is not persuasive. I shall have occasion to return to these issues in the final section of this paper. For now, let me draw attention to two characters who might at first be taken for mere minor figures in the movement of the tragic action proper: Joseph and Amusa.

Contemplating Mimicry

Joseph is house-help to Simon Pilkings and his wife, Jane; Amusa is a sergeant in the colonial police. They come across as inarticulate, obsequious fools who provide comic relief, and their structural purpose lies in being the dramatist's vehicle for pointing up certain "natives'" subservience to the colonial machine. At one level, one can say that they embody the consequences of such a submission, namely, docility and intellectual confusion. In being so unimpressive, they are set up as a mirror against which the lyricism of, say, Iyaloja (literally, mother at the market—the leader of the women traders) or Elesin, acquires full visibility. It would be reductive to understand both characters in this way, however. Joseph appears only once—in act 2—while Amusa appears thrice, but very briefly on each of these occasions. Despite their limited time onstage, however, both characters call attention to the blindspots that underlie the cultural or metaphysical conflict that is enacted on the surface of the play. Being "eunuchs" of the white man, as the market women see Amusa, and at times frustrating "natives" to the Pilkingses, Amusa and Joseph belong to both camps and to none. This liminality emerges in the text as an immanent cultural critique, so to speak. In their ineptitude, they silently reconfigure the very terms of the conflict as the major characters articulate it, and as the play's rhetorical mood might otherwise lure us to understand it.

In act 2, the Pilkingses call in Joseph to inquire about the meaning of the native drums throbbing in the background, and this exchange ensues:

> PILKINGS: Let's ask our native guide. Joseph! . . . (JOSEPH re-
> enters) What's the drumming about?
> JOSEPH: I don't know master.
> PILKINGS: What do you mean you don't know? It's only two

5. See Wole Soyinka, "The Fourth Stage: Through the Mysteries of Ogun to the Origin of Yoruba Tragedy," in *Myth, Literature, and the African World* (Cambridge: Cambridge University Press, 1976), pp. 140–60. The essay also appears in Soyinka's *Art, Dialogue, and Outrage* (Ibadan: New Horn Press, 1988), pp. 21–34.

years since your conversion. Don't tell me all that holy water
nonsense has wiped out all your tribal memory.
JOSEPH (visibly shocked): Master! (30)

Simon's frustrated explosion and Joseph's shocked reaction prompt
Jane to remark: "It isn't my preaching you have to worry about, it's
the preaching of the missionaries who preceded you here. When
they make converts they really convert them. Calling holy water
nonsense to our Joseph is really like insulting the Virgin Mary before a Roman Catholic. He's going to hand in his resignation tomorrow you mark my word" (30–31).

Joseph's uncritical acceptance of Christianity witnesses here to
something more interesting than the threadbare observation that he
has "sold out." By his acquiescence Joseph stirs up a contradiction
built into the colonial enterprise and its discursive explanation of
that enterprise. The exchange dramatizes a fissure between church
and state, one originating in the metropolitan center and reenacted
here at the colonial frontier. In this reading, Simon represents the
colonial bureaucratic apparatus that is intermittently dogged by the
"holy water nonsense" of Christian missionaries in the colonies.
Joseph's naïveté thus reveals Simon's secular estrangement from the
religion that, by an influential strand of his own culture's self-
understanding, marks him as European.[6] In the spectacle of a "native" internalizing Christian doctrine so thoroughly that he irritates
the "white man," *Horseman* distances the European self at play in
the real world from the self spelled out in its discourse of self-
apprehension.

It might be argued that this self is in fact not Christian but
secular-scientific, in which case the scene becomes a figuration of
the secular self (Pilkings) showing disdain for religious mythmak-
ing. But even here, Joseph's immanent critique retains its edge, for
in the discourse of colonialism in Africa, what defines European-
ness is *both* Christianity and secular-scientific sophistication. Where
colonial discourse rests precariously on a rhetorical suturing of
these two identities, Pilkings's exasperation introduces a disjunc-
tion. In the brevity of his time on stage, Joseph prompts a fissure

6. The following historical studies give a good sense of the details of European colonialism
from the late nineteenth century to the first half of the twentieth in various parts of
black Africa: A. Adu Boahen, *African Perspectives on Colonialism* (Baltimore: Johns Hop-
kins University Press, 1987); Andrew Roberts, ed., *The Colonial Moment in Africa* (Cambridge: Cambridge University Press, 1990). See also A. Adu Boahen, ed., *Africa under
Colonial Domination, 1880–1935*, UNESCO General History of Africa Series, vol. 7
(London: Heinemann; Paris: UNESCO; Berkeley: University of California Press, 1990),
esp. pp. 132–228. Expectedly, Christianity as ideology and institution emerges in these
studies as a complex but organic "instance" in the colonial social whole. For an inform-
ative study of the political economy of British colonialism in west Africa, see Anne Phil-
lips, *The Enigma of Colonialism: British Policy in West Africa* (London: James Currey,
1989).

between the European self instanced by missionaries and the self instanced by the colonial, "rationalist" administrator.

The lesson Joseph offers is further elaborated in Amusa's career. He is a dutiful police officer and a devout Muslim, but our first glimpse of his predicament occurs when he arrives at the Pilkingses' to report the ritual suicide that is to take place later that night. Here are the stage directions:

> The verandah of the District Officer's bungalow. A tango is playing from an old hand-cranked gramophone and, glimpsed through the wide windows and doors which open onto the fore-stage verandah are the shapes of SIMON PILKINGS and his wife, JANE, tangoing in and out of shadows in the living room. They are wearing what is immediately apparent as some form of fancy-dress. The dance goes on for some moments and then the figure of a 'Native Administration' policeman emerges and climbs up the steps leading onto the verandah. He peeps through and observes the dancing couple, reacting with what is obviously a long-standing bewilderment. He stiffens suddenly, his expression changes to one of disbelief and horror. In his excitement he upsets a flowerpot and attracts the attention of the couple. They stop dancing. (23–24)

The "fancy-dress" referred to is the *egungun* mask worn by Simon and Jane Pilkings. These are masks that have been confiscated from the natives, masks that represent, in the traditional scheme of things, the spirit of dead ancestors incarnated.[7] Confronted with his boss and the boss's wife dancing in a costume that signifies the spirit of the dead, Amusa runs into an epistemological conflict: He has come to report an unlawful tribal custom having to do with death (that is, ritual suicide), and now his boss presents himself costumed as the embodiment of death. Amusa thus refuses to make the report so long as Simon remains in the *egungun* costume. As he puts it in his pidgin English, "Sir, it is a matter of death. How can man talk against death to person in uniform of death? Is like talking against government to person in uniform of police. Please sir, I go and come back" (25).

What Amusa reveals here is that his conceptual universe remains deeply tied to traditional Yoruba culture even though the secular demand of his job requires him not only to repudiate that culture but also to subject it to the discipline of colonial modernity:

> JANE: Oh Amusa, what is there to be scared of in the costume?
> You saw it confiscated last month from those *egungun* men

---

7. Chinua Achebe's *Things Fall Apart* (New York: Astor-Honor, 1959) provides what is perhaps the most well-known literary use of the mask motif in the figure of "Evil Forest"; see chaps. 10 and 22 of the novel.

who were creating trouble in town. You helped arrest the cult
leaders yourself—if the juju didn't harm you at the time how
could it possibly harm you now? And merely by looking at it?
AMUSA (without looking down): Madam, I arrest the ringleaders
who make trouble but me I no touch *egungun*. That *egungun*
itself, I no touch. And I no abuse am. I arrest ringleaders
but I treat *egungun* with respect. (25)

We might say that the demands of economic subsistence compel
Amusa to arrest the *egungun* on the authority of the colonial admin-
istrative apparatus, but the superstructural overlay—the material
culture and its constitutive institutions—metonymically represented
by the *egungun* stands in conflict with the enforced economic dis-
pensation.

Act 3 gives us a representation of the new superstructural ensemble forcibly getting entangled with the one that remains formative
and resilient in Amusa's "big pagan heart" (24). The scene is the
marketplace, and Amusa has come to arrest Elesin, who is at that
moment consummating his marriage to the virgin. The trance sequence that closes act 3 is one of the most powerfully realized
moments in all of Soyinka. The evocation of Elesin's movement
toward the final assertion of will that will ease him into the world
of the dead is achieved by means of poetry. Thus in the following
excerpt, the thorough interiority of Elesin's undertaking is given the
status of unquestionable social value, and the dramatist's tool is
the Praise-Singer's lament:

PRAISE-SINGER: How shall I tell what my eyes have seen? The
Horseman gallops on before the courier, how shall I tell what
my eyes have seen? He says a dog may be confused by new
scents of beings he never dreamt of, so he must precede the
dog to heaven. He says a horse may stumble on strange boulders and be lamed, so he races on before the horse to
heaven. It is best, he says, to trust no messenger who may
falter at the outer gate; oh how shall I tell what my ears have
heard? But do you hear me still Elesin, do you hear your
faithful one? (ELESIN in his motions appears to feel for a
direction of sound, subtly, but only sinks deeper into his
trance-dance.) (44)

In this we see the playwright relying on the sheer capacity of
poetry to persuade. By putting before us the spectacle of Elesin's
ritual dance, the tender encouragement of the choral retinue (Iyaloja and the market women) singing a dirge in the background, and
the incantatory exhortation of the Praise-Singer, Soyinka poses the
self-assurance of the native culture against the colonial apparatus,
which sees the entire ritual as heathen savagery. And by finessing

that moment with some of the most lyrically elegant lines in his dramatic works, Soyinka invites us to take on a worldview by partaking of it as an aesthetic experience. However, although this moment is designed as the play's pivotal moment (and the dramatist, as I suggested, put a lot of his talent into rendering it memorably), there is yet an ostensibly comical moment that has considerable significance for the kind of reading I am pursuing here. The scene involves Amusa, the market women, and the schoolgirls. As Amusa tries to bully his way into the bridal chamber to arrest Elesin, the schoolgirls (daughters of the market women) lose their patience. In a swift change of code, they take on the personae of European colonialists at a party. Over the next fifty-two lines, the playacting mounts and approaches such verisimilitude that Amusa is drawn in. By the end of the girls' performance he is so enchanted that, in a reflex action typical of his duties for the colonial regime, he comes to attention at the command of the girls:

> GIRLS . . .
>
> . . . .
> —Is there racing by golly?
> —Splendid golf course, you'll like it.
> —I'm beginning to like it already.
> —And a European club, exclusive.
> —You've kept the flag flying.
> —We do our best for the old country.
> —It's a pleasure to serve.
> —Another whisky old chap?
> —You are indeed too too kind.
> —Not at all sir. Where is that boy? (With a sudden bellow.)
>   Sergeant!
> AMUSA (snaps to attention): Yessir!
> (The women collapse with laughter.) (38–39)

In my reading of Amusa's earlier altercation with Simon, I suggested that it dramatizes his predicament in a social nexus where a new (colonial) infrastructure collides with the old (native) superstructure. In the altercation with the schoolgirls, the new superstructural ensemble ushered in by colonialism is embodied—albeit in jest and derision—in the new generation of natives. What the schoolgirls enact is the subterranean formation of a resentful but slowly acculturating elite—the educated, "Westernized" native. This new native can convincingly mimic the white man even to Amusa—who, we should remember, knows his white men, working as he does at close quarters with them.

Implicit in the schoolgirls' performance is an enactment of class formations and realignments amid radical social change. The new native, as embodied in the schoolgirls, constitutes the white man's future adversary. Paradoxically, he is a more formidable adversary because he resembles the white man and speaks his language more securely than Amusa. In the presence of this new native, Amusa can be made to cower exactly as he does in the presence of white men. The mothers put the children's destiny most concisely while expressing wonder at their performance:

> WOMEN: Do they teach you all that at school?
> WOMAN: And to think I nearly kept Apinke away from the place.
> WOMAN: Did you hear them? Did you see how they mimicked the white man?
> WOMAN: *The voices exactly.* Hey, there are wonders in this world!
> IYALOJA: Well, our elders have said it: Dada may be weak, but he has a younger sibling who is truly fearless.
> WOMAN: *The next time the white man shows his face in this market I will set Wuraola on his tail.* (39–40, emphasis added)

The schoolgirls, then, can be read as a budding avant-garde of sorts, defending the dignity of the community against an alien colonial structure. They are able to do so, as we have seen, because they can readily access the cultural patterns of that structure, can on a whim imitate its form. If there is an irony here, it is the irony of mimicry, one that complements and reinforces the versions I have already indicated in the trio of Simon, Joseph, and Amusa.

The historicity and import of these spectacles of mimicry have been theorized by Homi Bhabha, one of the most visible figures in contemporary theorizations of colonialism and its discursive conditions. * * * Bhabha's work is powered by a poststructuralist perspective on language and social organization. The aspect of his work that I find pertinent to my present purposes is his account of what amounts to the deconstructive implications of the native's collusion in the colonial enterprise. In "Of Mimicry and Man: The Ambivalence of Colonial Discourse," Bhabha considers the paradoxical process whereby colonial discourse figures the colonized subject as a "mimic man"—a subject who is normalized toward a standard that, by definition, must not be attained.[8] In this reading, English-

---

8. Homi K. Bhabha, *The Location of Culture* (London: Routledge, 1994), pp. 85–92. In my account and deployment of Bhabha's theory of the paradoxes of colonial representation and administration I use mimicry and/or hybridity as basically synonymous concepts. The latter is elaborated in Homi Bhabha, "Signs Taken for Wonders: Questions of Ambivalence and Authority under a Tree Outside Delhi, May 1817," in Henry Louis Gates, Jr., ed., *"Race," Writing, and Difference* (Chicago: University of Chicago Press, 1986), pp. 163–84; reprinted in Bhabha, *Location,* pp. 102–22. I have benefited from Robert Young's account of Bhabha's work in *White Mythologies: Writing History and the West* (London: Routledge, 1990).* * *

ness is English because the native—who is colonized so as to attain it—can only be by nature anglicized, and thus is always not-quite English. The mimic man is thus "the effect of a flawed colonial mimesis, in which to be Anglicised is *emphatically* not to be English."[9] This enabling contradiction (enabling because it serves the practice of colonial subjugation concretely as well as at the level of representation) becomes the locus of a counterinsurgency; the more effectively colonialism produces a "mimic man," the more severely that product implicitly deconstructs its claims and authority: "It is as if the very emergence of the 'colonial' is dependent for its representation upon some strategic limitation or prohibition *within* the authoritative discourse itself. The success of colonial appropriation depends on a proliferation of inappropriate objects that ensure its strategic failure, so that mimicry is at once resemblance and menace."[1]

Bhabha's account is useful because it implicates both colonizer and colonized in the dynamic of mimicry. By extension, the texts addressed to or resulting from the drama of a colonial encounter can be read by way of the logic of mimicry. Following Bhabha's account, we may legitimately recover in *Horseman* a drama of identity proper to the site of a colonial encounter such as is figured in the play. On these terms, Joseph and Amusa can be read as "mimic men": their discursive and institutional "partial fixation" as obliging colonial subjects, to use Bhabha's term, emerges as a demystification of the authoritative fantasy at the core of the colonizer's claim to mastery. We have seen how Joseph serves to reveal the contradiction in Simon's understanding of himself and his position as law enforcer on behalf of imperial Europe. We have also seen how Amusa's comic blundering actually points to an epistemological and social disorientation and reorganization in the midst of which he is a structural pawn and whipping boy, as well as a liminal figure of unmeditated critique. By means of these three characters, *Horseman* enacts the paradox of social identity—colonizer and colonized—amid the ferment of a structural transition predicated by the colonial event. The schoolgirls are as much part of that upheaval and reordering as the white colonialist. In them the play instances the "new natives," the educated Africans who necessarily participate in the structure of colonial modernity by being its product. In the colonial encounter between Africa and the West, *Horseman* seems to say, every social location is touched by contradiction.

Having said this, I should add that in order to arrive at the real intricacy of *Horseman* as cultural criticism, Bhabha's theory needs

9. Bhabha, *Location*, p. 87.
1. Bhabha, *Location*, p. 86.

to be surpassed. As Robert Young has noted, although the dynamic of mimicry as menace to the colonialist psyche is formulated in psychoanalytical terms, Bhabha tends to elevate its purchase to the level of a specifically "revolutionary" insurgency.[2] He often tends to celebrate the subversive indeterminacies of psychic processes as if these translate into politico-historical upheavals. To be sure, his critical vocabulary suggests a primarily psychoanalytical concern, and he sometimes appears to circumscribe his claims and their theoretical purchase within the level of the psyche. Too often, however, his peculiar fondness for the rhythm of words pushes him squarely onto the level of the sociopolitical. Consequently, there is in Bhabha's theory a conflation of the psychic terrain with the sociopolitical, even as his own premises would seem to suggest that such a conflation is conceptually problematic.

It is not my intention to open the debate as to whether or not psychoanalysis can lay claim to being a theory of society in the specifically political sphere. I broach the question here because it emerges in Bhabha's theory as the index of an unthematized tension, and hence a limitation. At too many enthusiastic moments, Bhabha substitutes lyricism for persuasion, rather the way Soyinka seeks to persuade by plain affective eloquence. But if Soyinka's medium—that is, drama and the textual dynamic of make-believe —always already demands a set of expectations other than reasoned persuasion, Bhabha's theory cannot invite a similar treatment, a suspension of hard questions of logic and systematicity. Thus, one crucial limitation in Bhabha's theory is that the category of the psyche cannot in itself pose the issue of *differential* social locations. After sorting out the drama of hybridity enacted in the interactions between Joseph and Amusa and Simon and Jane Pilkings on the one hand, and Amusa and the schoolgirls on the other, our analysis can yet profit from further specifications that the notion of mimicry cannot yield with any depth.

One such specification, the one that is relevant to the argument of this paper, is that a substantive distinction needs to be made between the sociopolitical valence of, say, Amusa's and Joseph's acquiescence, and the schoolgirls' ambivalent acculturation. If it is true that all the characters I have considered enact the paradoxes of identity inherent to a colonial order, it is also true that the differences in their social location can be specified only on the terrain of a materialist consideration. Simon wields an institutional power that his "boys" are concretely subject to, and, by the fact of their Western education, the schoolgirls are bound for a greater institu-

2. Young, *White Mythologies*, p. 149.

tional authority than Joseph and Amusa, barely literate, can ever hope for. This appropriately leads us to Olunde, the only African character who is already poised on the cultural terrain mimicked by the girls. His is the voice of the educated African, and it is to him that I should now like to turn.

Sober Western Suits

A medical student in England, Olunde is presented as having seen the West on its own grounds, complete in its wartime vulnerabilities. He attends to English soldiers wounded in World War II and has therefore seen England in the throes of a universal human predicament. But he has also mastered the language, so much so that he can argue Jane to a stalemate. As Simon says, "He's picked up the idiom alright. Wouldn't surprise me if he's been mixing with commies or anarchists over there" (66). On one level, Olunde is Soyinka's vehicle for explicitly criticizing European cultural arrogance. The playwright goes so far as to put direct articulation of Olunde's location in his father's mouth, just as, as we saw earlier, he puts the articulation of the girls' promise (as anticolonial nationalists) in their mothers'. In a cell, and having been denounced by Olunde as an "eater of left-overs" (61), Elesin takes consolation in the fact of his son's rejection. Addressing Simon, Elesin warns: "You may have stopped me in my duty but I know now that I did give birth to a son. Once I mistrusted him for seeking the companionship of those my spirit knew as enemies of our race. Now I understand. One should seek to obtain the secrets of his enemies. He will avenge my shame, white one. His spirit will destroy you and yours" (63).

On another level, however, Olunde's character presents a profound paradox that, at the level of authorial intention, the play as an intentional structure can neither thematize nor successfully repress. If we pose Olunde's cool and "enlightened" confrontation with Europe against Amusa's jittery confoundment within it, we stand to approach this dimension of the play. Two lines after Amusa makes his final exit in act 4, Olunde comes on stage for the first and only time we see him alive. From Jane we have already been warned that this young man may be "much too sensitive . . . the kind you feel should be a poet munching rose petals in Bloomsbury" (28). We know from Simon, too, that he is a "most intelligent boy," a go-getter who has the courage to defy his father and escape in a boat bound for medical school in the "land of the nameless" (60). And we know from the market women that there runs in his very blood an aristocratic destiny: "It is not he who calls himself Elesin

Oba, it is his blood that says it. As it called out to his father before him and will to his son after him. And that is in spite of anything [the] white man can do" (35).

When we finally meet him, he has come in looking for Simon Pilkings at the ball where the colonial functionaries have congregated to welcome the visiting English royal party. The stage directions present him in the following way: "A figure emerges from the shadows, a young black man dressed in a sober western suit. He peeps into the hall, trying to make out the figures of the dancers" (49). Soon after, his first line comes with the playwright's strategic illumination:

> OLUNDE (*emerging into the light*): I didn't mean to startle you madam. I am looking for the District Officer.
> JANE: Wait a minute . . . don't I know you? Yes you are Olunde, the young man who . . . (50, emphasis mine)

Where all along we have only heard others on both sides of the cultural divide talk about him with a sense of readable ontology (the natives) or enigmatic promise (the Pilkingses), his entrance here measures up to his reputation. With the stage cue and pacing of his entrance, with the symbolism of a "young black man dressed in a sober western suit" (49) observing a group of white people dancing in strange—"fancy"—costumes, Soyinka gives Olunde an aura only further nourished by the quiet authority with which he moves and speaks. His subsequent argument with Jane, coupled with his suicide, simply completes the picture.

Critics have said a good deal about the argument between Olunde and Jane in this scene. Cleverly showing Jane that self-sacrifice is an impressive human value—"an affirmative commentary on life" (51)—rather than an aberration peculiar to primitives, Olunde compels Jane's respect, if not agreement. By means of this exercise in cultural comparison, Soyinka positions the native and the European in dialogue. What interests me is not the argument as such, but the mere fact that Olunde discourses with Jane at all. Amusa, we recall, refuses until the very end to address Jane and Simon in the *egungun* costume. Indeed, he is ultimately punished for his intransigence: Simon relieves him of his duties (49). By contrast, to Jane's query about whether or not he is shocked, Olunde's response is a defensive-aggressive "Why should I be?" (50). And yet, he almost immediately goes on the offensive: "No I am not shocked Mrs Pilkings. You forget that I have now spent four years among your people. I discovered that you have no respect for what you do not understand" (50).

For dramaturgical reasons, of course, it is important that Olunde be sufficiently free of "tribal superstition" to be able to address Jane:

The argument prepares us for his subsequent philosophical objection to his father's failure. It is also consistent with his overall characterization, since he is a Westernized African. But we may begin to understand Olunde and the historical juncture he typifies by remarking the simultaneous defensive-aggressive posture just indicated. It is instructive that Olunde defensively asserts his secularization only to confront Jane Pilkings with its roots and consequence. Rhetorically, it is as if he needs to be secularized on the terms of his Western education, and yet not fully within those terms. What Jane might otherwise grasp as his liberation from the mumbo jumbo of natives thus becomes in Olunde's retort the condition of his exasperation at her presumptiveness: "No I am not shocked Mrs Pilkings. You forget that I have now spent four years among your people. I discovered that you have no respect for what you do not understand." His altercation with Jane Pilkings becomes even more interesting when we realize that the *egungun* mask that she is wearing at that moment operates via a logic of immediate transparency. As Amusa insists, the mask signifies the spirit of the dead, regardless of who is wearing it. Where Amusa is locked into the total transparency of the mask as signifier of the world of the dead, Olunde pays attention to *who* is wearing the mask. For Olunde, intentionality mediates his reaction to Jane dressed as *egungun*, and since a white colonial functionary cannot wear the mask for the same reason that a native wears it, he is able to see Jane as Jane. He thus disregards her status at that moment as "mask in motion"—which is to say, a spirit of the dead in material incarnation.[3]

We can delineate here another instance of immanent critique: Marked by his culture as a deserter and a white man's stooge, Amusa remains closer to the letter, as it were, of Yoruba worldview. By taking the masked figure on its pure physicality and the metaphysical status traditional culture confers on such physicality, Amusa is being more faithful to the logic of ancestor worship as it is encoded in masquerade traditions. Although Olunde is a more formidable defender of local traditions, his Westernization comes across here as an effortless secularization. This secularization allows him to negate, in the process of mediating, the unadorned logic of Yoruba tradition; but as we have just seen, such mediation is ena-

3. I borrow the phrase "mask-in-motion" from Henry Louis Gates, Jr.; see his *Figures in Black: Words, Signs, and the "Racial" Self* (Oxford: Oxford University Press, 1987). Here is the relevant passage: "The Western concept of mask is meaningless to, say, the Yoruba, precisely because the doll in wood cannot of itself signify. Once in motion . . . the misnomer 'mask' becomes 'mask-in-motion,' or what 'mask' itself implies to the Yoruba. Mask becomes functional—indeed, becomes—only in motion" (168). For basic ethnographic information on the masking tradition, see S. O. Babayemi, *Egungun among the Oyo Yoruba* (Ibadan: Ibadan University Press, 1980).

bling insofar as Olunde needs it in order to point to Jane's misrec-
ognition. Olunde's Westernization, then, emerges in the play as a
constitutive paradox: it is at once a condition of political and institutional enablement as well as what Homi Bhabha calls hybridity;
indeed, the hybridity is the enablement. By hybridity, I do not mean
a condition where two discrete entities coexist or intersect in the
same agent while at the same time retaining their distinct shapes
and self-sufficiency. Rather, I mean a situation where the two entities or identities are incommensurable and can therefore be entangled in the same subject only in a context of mutual deformation.
The paradox lies in the fact that the subject of such hybridity functions ultimately as a result of deformation. Consequently, Olunde
is alienated from—or can effortlessly alienate—the traditional logic
of masking, but that very capability is the condition of possibility
of his confrontation with Jane and Simon.

* * *

Wole Soyinka: A Chronology

1934   Born in Abeokuta, western Nigeria, son of Samuel Ayodele and Grace Eniola Soyinka.

1944–54   Attends Abeokuta Grammar School.

1946–50   Student at Government College, Ibadan, an elite high school in western Nigeria; starts writing poems.

1950–52   Employed as a clerk in a pharmaceutical store. Short stories are broadcast on national radio.

1952–54   Student at University College, Ibadan. Excels in literature and languages, including French and Greek.

1954–57   Attends the University of Leeds in northern England, where he works with distinguished Shakespearean scholar Wilson Knight. Obtains a B.A. English Honors degree in 1957. Begins writing two plays, *The Swamp Dwellers* and *The Lion and the Jewel*.

1958   Works as a play reader at the Royal Court Theatre in London. Directs *The Swamp Dwellers*.

1960   Nigerian independence from Britain. Returns to Nigeria and starts research on African drama as a Rockefeller Research Fellow. Writes *Camwood on the Leaves* and *The Trials of Brother Jero*. Forms the 1960 Masks, a theater group, which produces *A Dance of the Forests*, written to "celebrate" Nigerian independence.

1962   Appointed a lecturer in English at the University of Ife. Resigns in protest at the policies of the western Nigerian regional government.

1964   Active in western Nigerian politics. Forms The Orisun Theatre Company. Produces *The Lion and the Jewel*.

1965   Senior lecturer at the University of Lagos. Production of *Kongi's Harvest* in Lagos and *The Road* at the Commonwealth Arts Festival in London. Publication of *The Interpreters*, his first novel. Arrested for holding up a radio station in Ibadan, but acquitted for lack of evidence.

1966   Two military coups in Nigeria put the country on the brink of civil war.

1967   The eastern region of Nigeria cedes from the Nigerian Federation and renames itself Biafra; the ensuing civil war lasts for three years. Publishes *Kongi's Harvest and Idanre and Other Poems*. Productions of *The Trials of Brother Jero* and *The Strong Breed* at Greenwich Mews Theater, New York. Awarded the John Whiting Drama Award (with Tom Stoppard). Arrested and incarcerated without changes because of his efforts to end the civil war. He is not released from prison until 1969.

1968   Awarded Jock Campbell–New Statesman Literary Award for *The Interpreters*. *Kongi's Harvest* produced by Negro Ensemble Company in New York.

1969   Released from prison. Becomes head of the Department of Theatre Arts at the University of Ibadan.

1970   Directs *Madmen and Specialists* at the Eugene O'Neill Theater Center, Waterford, Connecticut.

1971   Directs *Madmen and Specialists* at Ibadan. Begins self-imposed exile from Nigeria and settles in Accra, Ghana.

1972   Publication of *The Man Died,* his prison memoirs.

1973   Visiting Professor at the University of Sheffield and Fellow of Churchill College, Cambridge. Production of *The Bacchae of Euripides* in London.

1974   Co-founds the Union of Writers of the African Peoples and is elected Secretary General.

1975   Returns to Nigeria and is appointed Professor of Comparative Literature at the University of Ife. Publication of *Death and the King's Horseman*.

1976   Publishes *Myth, Literature and the African World* and *Ogun Abibiman*.

1977   Administrator of the International Festival of African and Negro Arts and Culture (FESTAC) in Lagos. Directs *Opera Wonyosi*.

1979   Directs *Death and the King's Horseman* at the Goodman Theater, Chicago, and later at the Kennedy Center in Washington, D.C.

1981   Visiting Professor at Yale University. Publication of *Aké*, an autobiography covering his childhood years.

1983   Production of *Requiem for a Futurologist*.

1984   Releases *Blues for a Prodigal,* a film on the disputed Nigerian elections of 1983. Production of *The Road* at the Goodman Theater in Chicago and of *A Play of Giants* at the Yale Repertory Theater.

1986   Awarded the Nobel Prize for Literature.

1987   Production of *Death and the King's Horseman* at Lincoln Center in New York.

1988   Publication of *Mandela's Earth.*
1989   Publication of *Isara: A Voyage around "Essay,"* a semi-autobiographical account of his father and his associates.
1991   *A Scourge of Hyacinths* is broadcast on BBC Radio 4.
1992   *From Zia, with Love* is produced in Siena, Italy.
1994   Publication of *Ibadan: The "Penklemes" Years—a Memoir,* the third part of an autobiographical trilogy covering the years 1946–1965.
1995   Involved in the organization of massive protests following the cancellation by the military regime of the federal elections won by Moshood Abiola. Production of *The Beatification of Area Boy* at the West Yorkshire Playhouse, Leeds.
1996   Forced into exile after his life is threatened by the military regime. Launches an international campaign against the Nigerian dictatorship. Publication of *Open Sore of a Continent: A Personal Narrative of the Nigeria Crisis.*
1997   Charged with treason by the Nigerian military regime and tried *in absentia.*
1998   Returns to Nigeria.
1999   Publication of *The Burden of Memory, the Muse of Forgiveness.*

Selected Bibliography

• indicates works included or excerpted in this Norton Critical Edition

Aboyade, B. Olabimpe. *Wole Soyinka and Yoruba Oral Tradition in "Death and the King's Horseman."* Ibadan, Nigeria: Fountain Publications, 1994.

Adedeji, Joel. "Wole Soyinka and the Growth of Drama." In *A Comparative History of Literature in European Languages.* Budapest: Akad'emiai Kiad'o, 1986.

Alston, Anthony. "Death and the King's Horseman." In *Yoruba Drama in English: Clarifications for Productions.* Ph.D. diss., University of Iowa, 1985.

Appiah, Anthony. "An Evening with Wole Soyinka." *Black American Literature Forum* 22, no. 4, Wole Soyinka issue, pt. 2 (Winter 1988): 777–85.

• ———. *In My Father's House: Africa in the Philosophy of Culture.* New York: Oxford University Press, 1992.

Booth, James. "Self-Sacrifice and Human Sacrifice in Soyinka's *Death and the King's Horseman.*" *Research in African Literatures* 19, no. 4 (Winter 1988): 529–50.

Brooks, Marty. "The "Failed Messenger." *Black American Literature Forum* 22, no. 4, Wole Soyinka issue, pt. 2 (Winter 1988): 723–33.

Crow, Brian. "Soyinka and His Radical Critics: A Review." *Theatre Research International* 12, no. 1 (Spring 1987): 61–73.

Dubost, Thierry. "La Mort et l'écuyer du roi: La Renaissance d'un monde." *Commonwealth* 15, no. 2 (Spring 1993): 43–49.

• Gates, Henry Louis, Jr. "Being, the Will, and the Semantics of Death." *Harvard Educational Review* 51, no. 1 (1981): 163–73.

• George, Olakunle. "Cultural Criticism in Wole Soyinka's *Death and the King's Horseman.*" *Representations* 67 (Summer 1999): 67–91.

• Gibbs, James, ed. *Critical Perspectives on Wole Soyinka.* London: Heinemann, 1980.

———. *Wole Soyinka.* London: Macmillan, 1986.

Gotrick, Kacke. "Soyinka and Death and the King's Horseman or How Does Our Knowledge—or Lack of Knowledge—of Yoruba Culture Affect Our Interpretation." In *Signs & Signals: Popular Culture in Africa.* Umeêa Studies in the Humanities. Umeêa: Acta Universitatis Umensis 1990, 137–48.

Gurr, Andrew. "Third-World Drama: Soyinka and Tragedy." *Journal of Commonwealth Literature* 10, no. 3 (1976): 45–52.

• Hepburn, Joan. "Mediators of Ritual Closure." *Black American Literature Forum* 22, no. 3, Wole Soyinka issue, pt. 2 (Autumn 1988): 577–614.

• Izevbaye, Dan. "Mediation in Soyinka: The Case of the King's Horseman." In *Critical Perspectives on Wole Soyinka,* edited by James Gibbs. Washington, D.C., 1980, 116–25.

———. "Elesin's Homecoming: The Translation of the King's Horseman." *Research in African Literatures* 28, no. 2 (Summer 1997): 154–70.

Jain, Jasbir. "The Unfolding of a Text: Soyinka's *Death and the King's Horseman.*" *Research in African Literatures* 17, no. 2 (Summer 1986): 252–60.

• Jeyifo, Biodun. *The Truthful Lie: Essays in the Sociology of African Literature.* New Beacon, 1985, 11–45.

• Jones, Eldred. *The Writings of Wole Soyinka.* London: James Currey, 1988.

Jones, Laura, and Henry Louis Gates, Jr. "Postmortem for a Death . . ." *Black American Literature Forum* 22, no. 4, Wole Soyinka issue, pt. 2 (Winter 1988): 787–803.

Katrak, Ketu. *Wole Soyinka and Modern Tragedy: A Study of Dramatic Theory and Practice.* New York: Greenwood Press, 1986.

Maduakor, Obí. *Wole Soyinka: An Introduction to His Writing.* New York: Garland, 1986.

Morell, Karen L., ed. *In Person—Achebe, Awoonor, and Soyinka at the University of Washington.* African Studies Program, Institute for Comparative and Foreign Area Studies. Seattle: University of Washington, 1975.

Ogundele, Wole. " 'Death and the King's Horseman': A Poet's Quarrel with His Culture." *Research in African Literatures* 25, no. 1 (Spring 1994): 47–60.

• Ojaide, Tanure. "Teaching Wole Soyinka's *Death and the King's Horseman* to American College Students." *College Literature* 19/20, nos. 3–1 (October 1992): 210–14.

Olaniyan, Tejumola. *Scars of Conquest/Masks of Resistance: The Invention of Cultural Identities in African, African-American, and Caribbean Drama.* New York: Oxford University Press, 1995.

Osofisan, Femi. "Tiger on Stage: Wole Soyinka and Nigerian Theatre." In *Theatre in Africa,* edited by Oyin Ogunba and Abiola Irele. Ibadan: Ibadan University Press, 1978, 151–75.

Pearse, Adetokunbo. "Myth and Meaning in 'Death and the King's Horseman.' " *Lore and Language* 3, no. 8 (January 1983): 20–30.

Quayson, Ato. *Strategic Transformations in Nigerian Writing: Orality and History in the Work of Rev. Samuel Johnson, Amos Tutuola, Wole Soyinka, and Ben Okri.* Bloomington: Indiana University Press, 1997.

Reed, Ishmael. "Soyinka among the Monoculturalists." *Black American Literature Forum* 22, no. 4, Wole Soyinka issue, pt. 2 (Winter 1988): 705–9.

• Richards, David. *Masks of Difference: Cultural Representations in Literature, Anthropology and Art.* Cambridge: Cambridge University Press, 1994.

• Rohmer, Martin. "Wole Soyinka's 'Death and the King's Horseman,' Royal Exchange Theatre, Manchester." *New Theatre Quarterly* 10, no. 37 (February 1994): 57–69.

Soyinka, Wole. *Myth, Literature and the African World.* Cambridge: Cambridge University Press, 1978.

• ———. *Art, Dialogue and Outrage: Essays on Literature and Culture,* edited by Biodun Jeyifo. Ibadan: New Horn Press, 1988.

• Williams, Adebayo. "Ritual and the Political Unconscious: The Case of *Death and the King's Horseman.*" *Research in African Literatures* 24, no. 1 (Spring 1993): 67–79.

Wright, Derek. *Wole Soyinka Revisited.* New York: Twayne, 1993.